AF259085

LESSONS OF HISTORY II
FOR THE
NIGERIA REPUBLIC
AND OTHER WORLD ESSAYS

DR. OTOLORIN B. ADENIJI-BELLO NMD, PH.D, MS, MB

Contents

Dedication

This book is dedicated to the memories of my late grandfather and my late father whose patriotism and foretell of political imbroglio were right on target.

It is also dedicated to my mother for her discerning clarity of the Nigerian scene.

All my country men and women whose aspirations have been blunted but had to settle for what they are left with.

To my wife, Yeside, and our children for their encouragement and steadfast support to put these imprints on the Nigerian history.

And to all Nigerian youths whose hope hang in the balanceand dwindle.

Acknowlegdement

I sincerely appreciate the Almighty God who in His infinate mercy and divine guidance made the completion of this book a reality since I conceived the implementation.

My acknowledgement goes to Mr. Toluwanimi Cyril Olajide who oversaw, designed and arranged this book as assisted by his efficient Personal Assistant, Esther Olufunmi Makanjuola.

My gratitute also goes to DFI press for the print production of the book.

A big thank to Mrs. Kikelomo Oladele of Spectrum Books, for editing this book thoroughly.

Finally I appreicate my friends and family, especially my wife for her concern and care ever since I've started writing this book. May the Lord bless and show up for you when needed . I thank you all.

"Lessons of History II for the Nigeria Republic"

Outline

The settling of the question of Nigerian nationhood viz the commonality of the Nigerian character.

a. Ambition galore of the people with less intent on fulfilling the purpose sworn to carryout

b. Money being the only desire and not the purpose of the contract for which the money is paid.

c. Duplicity of character, common to the world over in business but new height, here, in Nigeria, by hook or crook!

2a. Historical connection between the Hausa-Fulani-ethnics with the Yorubas – to Itsekiri as well as Ijaws extension.

The connection of Benin – Edo – to the riverine areas of the South- South to Yorubaland.

2b. The question of who are the yoruba - Ijebu(s)

3. The landlocked Igbos unrelated to anyone except for the likeness of character make-up. The same dismal behavior and wanton brutality against kinsmen is prevalent among a few members of the same society, sometimes dastardly. That may be the real connection to the rest of the country not to talk of love of money, sometimes on a high scale and dominant in the character.

4. Personal ambition and individual self actualization with no regards to the well-being of the community, seems to be the rule of the emancipation of the average Nigerian. These borders on the personal frame of reference ethos.

Preface

Introduction and explanation of the style and arrangement of the book is necessary for the reader's understanding. The significance of the sections of the book need to be understood too.

The first segments deals with the debacle of the present Nigeria state or nation, if you will. What is the present picture intrinsic or physical and the historical fabric of connection of the people before the colonial imperial power intrusion?

The second segment, while tied to the first, deals with the agitation for independence from the colonial rulers by the elite Nigeria societies starting with the Egba self government in Abeokuta in the present Ogun state in 1800s. The section also highlights the misconception of the players and absence of deep thought connection of the indigenous people and their plights. There is need to settle the ethnicity question.

I believe that, there is a need to reign in, any ill-concepts which may give thoughts to ill-conceived idea for secession or separation of any ethnic group from the country either because of a sense of disenfranchisement or slight outlook of self from the general population. This section also touches on the actors who led the independent fight and the chaos precipitated from their impatience and misunderstanding of their services - to the people they thought they were serving.

This book is also an attempt to set the record straight and is devoid of tribal polemics of past writers. It will be hard to put down by students of Nigeria history and patriotic Nigerians who want to know the missing truths of Nigerian history. This is not praise-singing of any of the personalities in the Nigerian theater of politics or governments. It is a serious attempt to focus the attention of the reader on Nigeria and the personalities which have affected its development or demise or apparent slowdown with the instrument of government power. Viewpoints and personalities are narrowed considerably to their relevance to the events which affect the country and her destiny.

There are no apologies offered here to the die-hard followers of whichever of the personalities touched by this expose. Let the chips fall wherever they may. There would be no praise of any cult of personality.

The third segment is the collection of the author's view of some events in some of the third world nations and the role played by the imperialist nations of the west.

The essays are a convolution of reactions to the events happening around the world and the frustration of the serious Third World observer at the arrogance of the Western democracies championed by the United States of America. What this book is not about is the advocating of a return to socialism as known in the West. Rather, the book appeals to the sensibilities of the Western governments of Europe and the United States to come to the aid of serious, democratically-minded leaders of the Third World in building their shattered or non-existing economies. In doing so, such individuals must be able to present methods which would not be too draconian to the plight of the people they intend to govern to the point of exploitation of their resources to the advantage of the people of the West. This would not be an acceptable quid-pro-quo of democracy.

1

NIGERIA AT A GLANCE

Here is the catalogue of the Nigeria Republic before and after amalgation of 1914 with the attendant character of the citizenry.

There is no shortage of ambition in this country as far as amassing of personal material wealth is concerned. Nigerians would study the stipulated letters of the goal to be attained to lay their hand on the riches, not for the deep knowledge or the sustenance of their communities. Note that I am not limiting the desire for money to Nigerians. It is a result of the abject poverty of the greater majority of the world's population. Some would argue for equidistribution of the wealth while others would affirm that, it is a natural phenomenon and it must continue the way it is for the people to appreciate the mystery of existence; and consequently the power of the universe and the order of existence.

I am of the opinion that the individuals with the wealth of money and materials do not desire to share too much with the general population considering whatever sacrifices they made to acquire the wealth and gain relevance in the society. But share we must for the total health and progress of the society at large.

Let me first of all state here that I am not an academic historian in the western educational sense, but I can confidently state that I was a witness to the formation of the modern Nigeria country. And I know the faces of the players though a small boy, curious and attentive to the various parts played by the actors of the period.

These actors included my grandfather Abdullahi, Muhammadu Popoola Raji, Mobolaji Herbert Macaulay, Lawyer Imam Augusto, Chief Bode Thomas, Chief Obafemi Awolowo, Chief Adeyemo Alakija, Nnamdi Azikiwe, Akerele Doherty, Dr. Akinola Maja, Dr. (Sir) Kofo Abayomi, Alhaji Ahamadu Bello-the Sardauna of Sokoto, Dr. Salawu, Arthur Preston, Williamses, Coker etc.

I learned my ABC early, despite the insistence of our dad to delve into the Quaranic Studies more than others. This was courtesy of my immediate older brother who passed on to life beyond in his teenage years. My brother, Abudul Rahman Segun Akanni was a brilliant, thoughtful, selfless, kind, encouraging and gentle being.

He was my parents' confidant, always helpful and attentive to their desires through services to their needs. These are the examples and legacy he left for me.

Unfortunately, he died of malaria-plasmodium falciparum – the most lethal of the species, which later became the focus of my doctoral studies at Uppsala's Biomedical Institute in Sweden.

I will not bore you with too much details at this time! But let me quickly point to my early education in the Western European mode-viz British education. The colonialist would not allow a child carrying blatant muslim names to be registered in any elementary school in Lagos. Those of us with prominent muslim parents had to take indigenuous Yoruba names, to be registered. Some parents refused and their children where left behind without the necessary western education. I became a catholic and protesant christian in order to be educated. The establishment of Muslim schools was not permitted until quite some time.

2

PRESENT STATE OF NIGERIA

There is the need to attend to the amalgamation of the various ethnic entities which comprise the country, Nigeria. There is also the need to talk about the character make-up of the various ethnic groups within the country today. These character make-up has fused so much that it seems to have evolved into character-identity of the individual personality with few exceptions. As these ethnic groups are African, there is so much similarity in the inherited cultures, the admixture of the Islamic religion and the colonial Christianity notwithstanding. The African way of life still hold sway, no matter how much admiration some not-so-established colonial groups exhibit for the European colonial culture. The admiration may be a result of non-establishment of profound cultural governing process, before the Europeans came in and found one for them via Christianity or what have you.

Now, because of the multiplicity of ethnics, every ethnic group would find fault with every other one except its own within the country, sometimes with merit. This kind of behavior breeds hegemonous ethnocentric nepotism. Some ethnic clan exhibit this more than the others. This is very common with the Igbo Clan, always feeling that it knows better how to do anything, in fact everything, better than the others. This is a reflection of deep colonial mentality and basic ignorance of harmonious social co- existence with other ethnic groups.

3

THE COLONIAL BEACH HEAD

Meanwhile, the British colonial rulers established an indirect rule in northern part of the Nigeria country. With the Northern Caliphate rulers, a traditional oligarchy which could not be altered by force, the average northerner felt a sense of superiority to his southern counterpart that his culture was not tampered with, by the colonial rulers through direct assault. This behaviour is more or less carried forward in their relationship with the other ethnic entities.

The Yorubas, having established kingdoms similar to the Caliphate but different in centralization than the north, felt victimized by the colonial interventions on one side or the other during their inter-ethnic wars. These wars or battles were numerous as each side wished to establish supremacy over the others while leadership resided in Oyo. To complicate this situation, was the role of the newly freed slaves from America, Brazil, Portugal and the British enclaves. These newly freed slaves were mostly of Yoruba origins extending to the delta and the riverine areas of the South- South Nigeria. They are easily recognized by the retention of their slave masters last names which gave them some priviledges with colonial rulers, and clothings of identity(s).

These names are usually English, Portuguese, German and in some instance Spanish names such as Williams, Jones, Johnson, Thomas, Pratt, Coker, Dickens, Preston Pinheiro, Pellegrino, Pedro, Macgregor, George, Davies, Haastrup, Macaulay, Augusto, Randle, Braithwaite. They constitute a bulwark of early educated Nigerians in the Western mode. Hence, they were in the front for the demand for independence. They also regarded themselves as the elite of the Yoruba society setting the roles of acceptable norms of the society. Such was the case with Bank-Anthony, Grillo, Ransome, Leigh, Allen, Davies, Lawson, Da-Rocha, Willoughby, Wright and so on.

They were quickly assimilated by the indegenous people as their African cultures were reflected in their relationship with the people. Some others retained their foreign last names to benefit from the largess of the colonial rulers.

Some of them refused to continue with their slave masters' names. The Nigerians who returned to their African ancestrial names include Kofoworola Abayomi, Adeyemo Alakija, Dr Akinola Maja, Dr Salawu, Mayor Olorunnimbe.

Depending on the concentration of the foreign name population, agitation and hegemony and nepotism among their namesakes with unnecessary, baseless, feeling of importance and superiority over the indigenous Yoruba reigned! Their common attitudes spurred the rapid embrace of western education by the indigenes, while the Igbos stayed in the landlocked areas of the eastern part of the country. This also explained the restive existence of the Igbos to the Western education. And the Hausa-Fulani also of the north for that matter. But the resistance was broken by force in Igbo land by the colonial rulers.

The scenario of the rush for the English, nay the Western education which had been set in place before and with independence's demand, now reached a climax. The growth from the independence movement resulted in the trading of blames from one political party to another and from one ethnic group to another. Sometimes, such virulent anger was capable of consuming the perpetrator. All this point to the failure of those who went into the political landscape and pretended to lead the people of Nigeria since the attainment of independence for the amalgamated country.

Therefore, we can safely disregard various opinions while critically re- assessing the opinionated individuals and assessing the situations at hand with a resolve to move forward deliberately.

4

THE CONNECTION

It is necessary to dot the i(s) and cross the t(s) – or else we would be leaving the important stones unturned for the proper understanding of the angst about this country which seems to consume the bearers.

First of all, the connection of the people to one another is undeniable, though the half baked Nigerian historian may do so, for the convenience of their talking points.

There was a statement credited to the then Premier of the Northern Region of Nigeria, Alhaji (Sir) Ahmadu Bello, the Sardauna of Sokoto, to the effect that the Caliphate would extend its Islamic rule to the Lagos and the Atlantic Ocean. There was indignation and anger at the time at the Premier. The effontery of such statement was questioned. But it was laid to rest without further exploration but with a rebut by the then Premier of the Western Region-Chief Obafemi Awolowo that rather than surrender to the Northern Hausa-Fulani rule, the Yorubas would rather die! It became a North Versus the Yorubas duel and everything carried political overtones. The resistance was mostly from the Neo-Christian Yorubas who were lost to the historical connection and kinship of the Yoruba with the Hausa-Fulani cousin in the North. Such threat of Jihadism was never to the East. This is because there was never a kinship of the Igbos with the North historically.

For the record, there were four brothers who came in via the Southern Egypt-Nubian now Sudan namely, Uthman Dan Fodio, Abdullahi Gogobir, Muhammadu Limroid (Lamurudu) and Abdullahi Mustafa Raji. They were princes and Muslims who immediately set up shops to fulfil their missions. Uthman Dan Fodio chose to stay in Sokoto while Gogobir took to the East setting up shop in Borno and Muhamadu Limroid (Lamurudu) moved to Yorba setting up shop in Ile-Ife. How they chose their pads would remain their secrets. Investigation of cultural depth allude to the "Ifa oracle" which they all shared as guide. Yorba later became Yoruba probably because of the heavy diction or the twisting of the tongue from the soil minerals of the Yorba enclave.

The sharing of Ifa oracle needs to be mentioned since it all came from the Southern Egyptian origin consisting of the cowries shell. The shells are diced on the white sand of the sea and its appearance sequel to the dicing, requires special training and attribute in the reading and interpretation of the messages that show thereafter. The oceanic sand (white) was used as the platform on which the shells land. The North continues to use the rosary given by the Prophet Mohammad (SAW) and some special Quoranic verses for the interpretation of the messages of instructions.

Meanwhile, after the demise of Muhammadu Limroid (Lamurudu), his only son Y'Adua (Odua) or Oduduwa, perhaps not accessible to the clean white sand of the ocean beach and not wanting to loose the cowries shells during the hectic days decided to string them for easy reach and application when needed. Interestingly, the oracle was consulted during the time of the Pharaoh-the kings of Egypt for directives before the Islamic religion intervention ruled the practice as paganism. The practice nonetheless continues covertly but paying homage to the Almighty God, Allah to bless whatever directive is shown by the oracle. Even the new system viz the counting of the rosary by the Alfa's (the Muslim clerics) is practised by the two ethnics/tribal groups, the Muslims among them. Besides, more than fifty percent of the Yoruba language come from the core Hausa - Fulani lexicon.

Some people with less knowledge and huge personal frame of references would deny the relationship. The Edo ethnic and Itsekiri evolved from the Yoruba central. The first Oba of Benin City was Ewedemi who was one of the sons (third son) of Odua (Oduduwa). The subethnic resulting, is now of historical records, especially regarding the Ijaws who are kinsmen of the other riverine ethnic extension.

Adua (Odua) or Oduduwa had seven sons and a daughter, the one legend revealed brought a crown to Owu town before her father passed on. After Odua passed on, Oranyan (Oranmiyan) the first son moved the reign of authority and built the palace of Oyo leaving the youngest son to continue to care for the idol gods, as he did when their father was alive, and named him the Onirisa of Ile-Ife. Oduduwa remained the Ooni-Ile! You don't need rocket science to notice the similarity of the cultures of the Hausa-Fulani and that of the Yorubas. Their mode of dressings both for the male and female is very similar with very minor differences. They both have facial tribal marks coming from the present-day Sudan (Nubians). Besides, being both mostly Muslims in their origin, from before the advent of colonialism, and the influx of the returnees (the newly emancipated, freed slaves and the Christian expedition and invasion into Nigeria via Lagos, and the Delta region of Warri, Sapele, some Edo Kingdom (Yorba) areas), I dare say it included Rivers and Bayelsa too before the influx of the Igbos from the hinter landlocked areas of the East.

It was the blatant diversion and polytheism that evolved, which angered Abdullahi Raji the fourth brother in Sokoto backed by his Nephew Mohammadu Bello, the son of Uthman Dan Fodio who had established the Caliphate overall of the North, to set up an incursion by an army of Jihadists to assault /invade Yorbaland. His war cry was to return the Yorbaland of his late brother to Allah's religion, i.e. Islam. They came with the infantry from Bida – the Tapa ethnics and Igala.

The Jihad was so successful that it shocked and shook the Yoruba people. They succumbed to the religion – Islam - threatened with death, should they refused.

The Oyo dynasty gave way and alluded to the kinsmanship. Hence the adage: "it was in the world we met the Ifa oracle, the same goes for Islam, the advent of Christianity came in recently from foreign people not related to us (Yoruba). From then on, the rest became historical – record. I should add that the confusion of polytheism and atheism with force with no guaranteed peaceful existence without Islamic practice, paved the way for Christianity through the foreigner's intervention with the freed slaves as willing tools teachers. Christianity became the alternative to worshipping one God, the same Allah, albeit foreign and colonial. The freed slaves of Yoruba descent could no longer avail themselves to the discipline of worship required by Islamic observance. Christianity was presented as easy, hence the alternative.

The returnees were our brothers and sisters coming from the diaspora on the freedom promulgation for the American. Portuguese and British slaves of the time and being the ones who spoke the language of the colonialists, dictated the norms of civilization to the children of the indigenous natives of Lagos. Hence, they set themselves up as the replacements of the colonial rulers, enjoying the benefits their association with them. The indigenous natives looked up to them with regards to how to relate with the foreign colonialists.

The returnees told us what the mores and good behaviour was. The indigeneous children of Lagos through their parents took the lessons and ran with them, some even adopting the biblical names and manipulating it to reflect affiliation with the new families of the elites, having aquired the education i.e., the English language necessary to be counted in. This method came back to bite them as the indigenous children eventually realised their difference from the returnees. The indigenous children seized the advantage of their numbers, but could not completely rid themselves of the colonial indocrination and mentality.

Christianity was the in-thing and Islam was for the uneducated and backward. Only the stubborn and commited faithfuls remained muslims despite their colonial education and knowledge of the English language.

These include the Elias, Augusto, some Williams' lineage, Salawu (Dr); the aforementioned were lawyers. It was a case of over-emphasizing the superiority of the colonial mentality and de-emphasizing the intelligence of the Africans and their cultures and ways of life. Young children who grew to be adults under this yoke, had been so brain washed, that their upbringing was totally based on the illusion of what they thought they were and not what they actually were. This could be real torture to the intellect and it was. This created an ongoing conflict of self reflection though not physically seen, but mentally imbibed.

Unfortunately, the scenario kept repeating itself from generation to generation and it has extended to the various parts of the indigenous people of the country. It exacerbated the conflict in the interaction of the so-called "educated" elites of the North and the South with the former being belligerent and the latter being the rejectionist. Individual personalities seem to be the norms in navigating the landscape of existence as we find ourselves for survival. Many in the Southern part of the nation would rather identify with the foreign whims and caprices, though they would live as second class citizens in the Western European and American capital cities! Along the way, many talents have been lost due to different causes, traceable and not!

It started with their half-commitment to the Yoruba tradition and the giving of their children abbreviated Yoruba names, This did a lot to down- play the importance of the African identity, nay Nigerian by name. With the Yoruba names, the sentimental "oriki" such as Aremu, Akande, Ajao, Ishola, Alamu, Ayinde etc., was mostly deemphasized and absent. Women of the Yoruba tradition enjoy such names as Ayoka, Aduke, Ashabi, Ashake, Amoke, Esuu, Odee, Ayinke, etc. Such names are usually absent from the names of the returnee children.

The overwhelming muslim population of Lagos saved the culture and tradition more or less.

Please, permit me to state the followings: To make progress that we can call our own, we must re-orient ourselves to making life easier for our people, rejecting colonial mentality of inferiority and superiority of the same people of the same nation. We must use our intellect to create a level playing field. There should be no more unnecessary references to erstwhile colonial model. A quiet assertion and self confidence must be displayed from the elementary schools, the uniforms devoid of European models, to the high schools or secondary schools. We don't have to appear European in outlook as we have compelled our children to be, in order of display discipline, uprightness or neatness. No, our children do not have to be European or Americanized to be progressive, but we must be authentic and respectful of our ways of life and teach this to the children.

The narrative above, was part of the run-up to the independence quest for the colonial rulers. The South West Yoruba with its attending delta area citizens and the Eastern Igbo indigenes with the heavy colonial influence were hoping to replace the colonialists with the likes of Chief Obafemi Awolowo. These individuals were shocked by the colonialists who, hoping to hold on to the power by clandestine method, chose the leaders of the North to continue their influence of governance . This, they termed "maintaining the friendship" through the Northern political elites.

To the Yoruba political elites, devoid of the knowledge of their own history of kinship with their Northern cousins, this was unacceptable. Instead of accepting it as a victory over machination of colonial rulers' tactics of divide and rule, they allowed the scheme to fester and further divide the people with misgivings.

THE QUESTION OF WHO ARE THE YORUBA IJEBUS?

If I didn't put it to rest, it would continue to swirl around with so much unfounded conspiracy theories and baseless mythology. There had been the question of how the Ijebu ethnic became part of the Yoruba larger ethnic. It could be by assimilation. Many of the Yoruba historians' work had pegged the question, perhaps, not to infuriate or annoy the affected people should they tap into incorrect diatribe. But still it must be recorded however, imperfectly. These brave and intelligent ethnic people are our compatriot and cannot be discerned from the general Yoruba population. Their descendants are fully integrated Oodua children with all the glories of the founding dynasty.

Now, migration of people in those days was dynamic with no perfect path. People came in and out of different enclaves with no definite borders. The original Ijebu (meaning – people coming through the creeks of the ocean) were the off-shoot of the rebellious group from Ethiopia which refused to accept the new mode of worship of the Christian God introduced at the time in that part of Africa. They were worshippers of the River-god, a little different from the Osun/Yemoja in the post Oduduwa (Oodua) in Yorubaland. The same group (Ijebus) moved through the red sea spilling into the Atlantic ocean of the delta region through the creeks with some of them berthing in the now, Warri, Sapele, Burutu, Bayelsa town and the people share the same affinity of love of the Ifa and the worship of the deity with the Ese-odo of Okitipupa who share the Yoruba religious worship in addition to their worship of the sea-god. Traces of common dialects and pronunciation of similar words and objects identification could be detected with Ijebu dialect.

The arrival of the Ijebus into Yorba Land as stated earlier, through the creek into the domain of the Egbaland was welcome by the Alake of Egbaland after consulted with the Alaafin Oyo, compassionately seeing a deprived impoverished population washed up from the ocean. They (the Ijebus) needed the solace. They quickly seized upon the hospitalliy and quickly acclimatized with the environment and showed affinity with the Ifa oracle which they seemed very familiar with. They were good farmers and artisans while re-establishing their river-god worship (aiye-la-la). Similar worships were established of the river-god in the delta and riverine areas of the Yorba enclave. Oyo later sent an Oodua grandson to be crowned as the Oba in the ensuing rebellion against the rulership of Alake, the Ijebus having carved the areas where they were farming and claiming the ownership. There were indications that the colonialists had a hand in this rebellion. The Alaafin and the other Yoruba Obas of the Oodua lineage tried to shelve the uprising and backed by the might of the Ibadan warriors, should the Ijebus reject the armistice.

They had to shut out the colonial interference in their affairs. Some of the Alake domains include the present Sagamu, Ode-Remo, Remo and Ikorodu and Epe apart from Ijebu Ode and Ijebu Igbo which encroached Ibadan and other creeks areas and villages. I believe I didn't forget to mention the resourcefulness of the Ijebus.

Withthecolonialistscamethecreatedlinesofdemarcationswhichdenotethe modern day territories of the various ethnics and by extension, the countries. Without these demarcations, the Ajases or Beninoise who historically are Yorubas would not need to obtain a visa to cross to the Nigeria's Yorubaland. The creation of ECOWAS has made the movements somewhat easier now.

Inter-ethnic strifes, rivalries and war notwithstanding, the streak of Islamic religion running through the same ethnic brothers and sisters is a telling connection of their relationship before the advent of European "christian" intervention. All controversial accounts of ethnic intertribal strifes and wars are here left to those who would care to delve into them.

5

CHIEF OBAFEMI AWOLOWO'S ROLE IN FOSTERING AMNESIA OF HISTORY

No doubt, Chief Obafemi Awolowo was a political face in Yoruba land. He was ambitious as well as calculating to a fault. He bestrode the Western Region of Nigeria "like a colossus" that other men of his time had to be looking for ways to be relevant with such handicap, created by his followers. He was a cult figure!

He had brilliant vision and in a hurry to show the colonial rulers how much he would like to follow their footsteps in the administration of Western Region with the meager funds generated by the economy of the time. Awolowo was able to develop the roads from major towns and linking them to the adjoining villages to hasten development and enlightenment.

The free education of the rural children was a credit to his doggedness. As much as he thought he was helping the rural farmers, they were short- changed on the sales of their cash crops of cocoa, palm kennel and by- products.

His bias against the traditional rulers, and arrogance and haughty character became his undoing. Moreover, his favoritism of one ethnic group over the others based on whether they accepted or disagreed with his style of administration created disaffection for him; it might have been the remedy for political success of the time. He wanted yes-men, in everything he proposed, with no one under his tutelage expected to take any independent initiative without his blessing, no matter how progressive such initiative might be.

This last demerit of his (Chief Awolowo) became his undoing and unraffled the myth of the Action Group (AG) of Nigeria with him at the helm. Chief S.L. Akintola the Premier of the Western Region and deputy leader of the Action Group Party dared to accommodate the august visitor, the premier of the Northern Region in Ibadan, the capital of Western Region. This would have been the rapproachment of the two warring political parties then. But alas, it deepened the antagonism with Chief Awolowo playing into the hands of Northern "enemies" with his intolerance of the opposition.

Chief Awolowo could not find any connection to the Hausa-Fulani north of the country. Though some members of his family were muslims, he nonetheless maintained a studious distance unless there's something to lord over such individuals politically or cult-wise. Chief S.L. Akintola spoke hausa fluently!

No one should forget that Chief Awolowo was a prominent officer of the Ogboni fraternity cult, whose members were bound by allegiance of faithfulness and never to fault one another in any dispute against a non- member. This membership became the Achilles heel for him and cited by the Northern leaders, branding him as an atheist (Kafir). He was a cheerleader of the slogan "kaka ka dobale fun gambari, karoju ka ku" (we would rather die than accept the leadership of a Hausa man). This was the illusion held by the Yoruba of the West being the early Western or European educated in the country, courtesy of the early returnees (the emancipated slaves from America, Britain, and Brazil). Chief Awolowo fostered the amnesia of the Yoruba Christian and some ignorant Muslims believing that they have no kinship with the Northern Hausa Fulani clans. Some ignorant, European educated Northern Hausa-Fulani believed the same, and it showed in their behaviour towards their cousins from the Yoruba land. When I say European educated, I mean, brainwashed by western education as to not pay attention to their own history conveniently. Every attempt by these ill-educated Nigerians to circumvent their respective backgrounds to suit their whims and caprices proved futile. No one exists in a vacuum! Afterall, decades of interactions of the North and Yoruba before the advent of the colonialists had not been just a happenstance. The same goes for the Edo State people and some part of the present Delta State. All being part of Yorubaland.

For reasons unknow, nature and indeed the Almighty God made the minor differences in the ethnic dialectic tongues, while they decide their ethos and morals. This appraisal of Chief Awolowo's person should not be taken as an indictment of his eminence and character, by any means. He remained a formidable and visionary leader at the time of his reign. None has matched him in the North, South, East or West of this nation. Being human, everyone of us is vulnerable! His own brand may be what was needed at the time!

He made modern infrastructural roads for cars and lorries of the time- however narrow. He brought in television, first in Africa and a football stadium (Liberty Stadium) with floodlit electrics for night football competition; again, first in Africa. To top it all a free primary school education to be copied by the Northern administration, but not enforced!

6

THE PRESENT NIGERIA OUTLOOK AND THE IDENTITY QUESTION

I wrote in the beginning about the various events which led us into this debacle and the pitfalls which we have not learnt from, to date. There is no other way than to point out the failures of the political players who laid down these erroneous "do or die" maxim of the game. I have tried to look into the colonial rulers' way of playing politics in their own country but failed to see the same principle abiding. Unfortunately, this odious principle has slowed or even reversed the progress of the nation. And with hypocritical populist fan fair, they claim (the so-called politicians) they were serving the people.

Amassing of financial and material wealth at the expense of the ignorant population, has been the modus operandi and ethos of the so-called public servants with the exception of a few obscure unsung heroes. This obsession is so rampant, even now that it has gone beyond the necessary need of these "public servants". Sadly, this pattern of course had been set by the politicians at the beginning of the independence and exacerbated by the military dictatorship which intervened supposedly to check the excesses of the politicians. Never should a Republic allow a military dictatorship for correctional purposes. When it works for the people, it is a matter of pure luck. But then, the corruption excesses of the politicians should be checked by the population at large. The people should be so empowered to sack an administration without enabling the politicians to employ the security forces to allow their hold on power. For the maintenance of law and orderly transition of power, an amendment to the constitution would be necessary.

In the matter of the rampant embezzlement of public funds, young people continue in the footsteps of their fathers and women in the footsteps of their men and sometimes further in the neglect of their responsibility to the environment and the society. At this juncture, most of the present day politicians regard their ventures into the area of politics as some kind of investment to reap personal gains and rewards with a do or die energy. They employ miscreants of the society and create more, to kill or maim their opponents or those who call them out. They bribe the law enforcement agents to support their inglorious acts. The remaining hapless members of the society settle around to give them room to continue with the plundering of the resources only to complain with a hush away from the ear shot of the plunderer.

Now, you tell me, which section of the nation is spared of the plunderers in whichever ruling political party they are.

Forget the political party(s), none of which is guided by any concrete philosophy about governance. Each player copies manifestoes of any and every other political party from anywhere and try to make it his own without understanding it let alone believing it. And this is the same for most of the active political party(s) from any part of the country. Tell me, if the outlook of most of these active players is not similar as to wear the same character symbol.

When any of the above players complain about the ineptitude of the other, it is with an angst and lamentation that he or she is out of the plundering party. The aspiring youths have not been given any laudable image to look up to and their growth has been without specific focus, safe getting money by "hook or crook". After the swindling of others, for the acquisition of the riches, they would join the club of the "political" public fund plunderers. Before then, they engage in "see me" events with uses of philanthrophy- which is without any real feeling but with a mind of investment for the big pay-day off from the public cofers. They pretend to be clean like their elder brothers with distinct tastes in fashionable clothes and attire while their insides are as dirty as the gutter of filth. They are also united ethnically and tribes, apart from language differences from region to region, the philosophy of empty swagger and internet fraud and plunder reign supreme in their brain matrix regarding get rich quick!

Please don't get me wrong; there are still clean, dutiful young Nigerians quietly praying for the emergence of the right mentors. Great mentors when and if they emerge, would be subjected to varying degrees of assault and because they are not likely to have amassed the kind of financial resources to withstand the tearing down unless the down trodden, the clean upright youths would go to battle for themselves to allow them (great mentors) to clean up the land. Besides, the seed of suspicion and lack of trust of compatriots have wrecked a grievous havoc on the population. Who can be trusted?

7

LET THE WORK BEGIN

There is a lot of work to be done. The villages need to be brought up to modernity. The roads leading to them need to be constructed or reconstructed for easy access to the main roads which have all broken down by neglect and corruption. Homes with minimum comfort and hygienic surroundings, are to be constructed. All these besides the qualitative education at minimum costs to the average citizens.

When the above itineraries are attended to, the cry of ethnic differences would be minimal. The problems are universal in this country, cutting across every ethnic lines, north to south, east to west and especially south-south too.

The problem is the same the world-over except that it is exacerbated in Nigeria because the poverty level has reached such state of emergency that the memory of the population regarding the characters of those who pretend to lead the country become fuzzy at best. Such is the commonality of the character outlook of the citizens of Nigeria regardless of their tribe or ethnic origins and letters of education.

Meanwhile, the intellectuals and postulators of what needs to be done would soon join the comic, political leadership which would not get the necessary quality advice for good leadership to emancipate the population. Papers upon papers of different impractical solutions to the problems at hand would be written until another round of "leadership" roll around.

On the sidelines are the lawyers, engineers, business compatriots who nonetheless are making their contacts with the politicians and bureaucrats at the helm of power for never-to-be-executed contracts and projects, intended for the smooth running of the country. No reprimand is expected for non-execution of such projects of course, because the booty of allocated fund would be shared among them by their own known formulae.

And when anyone of them had their fill, he or she may join the political ranks and the milking of the public funds would continue.

Once in a while, there is a young man or woman who had been successful in fraud tons of money to show for it. Then, they would throw their hats into the ring of politics. This has been the lot of this nation-country and hence, the cycle of failures that seem to breed more of the same.

8

HOME-GROWN AND BRED VS OVERSEAS TRAINED NIGERIANS

The line is forever drawn between the home bred and grown Nigerians and their overseas, mostly European and American trained counterparts. This unnecessary competition has been going on for a long time, and grown especially noticeable after the first set of trained Nigerians from overseas settled into the positions vacated by the colonial rulers.

The Nigerians who never got the higher training at the Western institution became restive and insecure of their esteemed positions at the various departments and ministry(s). This behaviour was so pronounced in the western region which had a larger portion of the overseas trained Nigerians more than any other part of the country. Egos were easily bruised by the return of Nigerians trained abroad with better qualifications than the locally bred groups of administrators with only grammar school and high school diplomas.

Undermining of the overseas-trained soon became the order of the day. The phenomenon soon spread to the East more virulently. The north was not into this practice except against anyone brought from the other parts of the country to head a department there, which they considered to be a slap in the face with a hint of hegemony. And sometimes, naked hostility(s) to the Nigerian trained overseas with better Western Europe education which is the basis of the administration of the country were often. Soon, the trained administrators would join the lackluster home bred against new arrivals with latest and better methods and ways of doing things. Frustrations and hampering of the new ideas combine to thwart the attempts progress. This pattern of sabotage continues to this day and no one has any clue as to how to get out of this quagmire of self-inflicted wound ravaging the country. In all, individual egos and personal frame of references have a lot to do with the stuttering of progress made so far by the people of this country. So much bureaucracy has been created along the way that reining it in, and curtailing it, has become problematic without endangering the ethnic balance.

The reality is that, the education of the home-bred and grown Nigerians have been compromised by hegemony, nepotism and cultism initially introduced by the likes of Wole Soyinka a former student of University of Ibadan and his former classmates and school mates alike who were reacting to the hegemony or conservatism of other dialect ethnic leaders. Whereas, the hegemony and conservatism resided and endemic in their own ethnic community and spearheaded by the ethnic leadership they were following. Their (Soyinka's) ethnic leaders, disguised themselves as progressives! While some of the actions in the government house may record some economic stride, they were fanning the embers of ethnic division and discord.

Priviledge was assigned to the cult members of the leadership. The whole cover was blown when the crisis of the Western region erupted in 1963. Those who renounced the cultism aligned with the new leadership and those in the entrenched leadership went into battle. The entrenched original members of the cult aligned themselves with Eastern ethnic (the Igbos) who were their former sworn enemies before the independence. The Western Region was nearly destroyed by the Igbos who had nothing to lose at the time.

Destruction of properties by fire were so rampant and mayhem, championed by the likes of Soyinka and Bola Ige casting themselves as heroes, rented the air.

The cultists across the country would fight tooth and nail to proclaim nothing wrong with the country as long as their kind are in power and they are getting their own share of the national cake. However, money would be able to break their ranks later especially since the invasion of the boys from the barracks with the guns and armoured tanks. No sooner had they left, due to their own ineptitudes, had the so-called champions of the people's cause, gathered themselves together, and again continued with the plunder of the public resources. They keep showering praises on each other and whatever they considered the achievements which never changed the status quo of the common citizen and the children caught within. For the children today, it is the "survival of the fittest", both in the urban and rural areas. As it was then, so it is today, that the ambitious or otherwise uplooking youngster, would set his eyes abroad for solace.

Yet, there is still a blue sky within the clouds. Only when the positive minds find themselves can they muster the cohesion and force devoid of need for cultism and be able to move forward with progressive leadership, complementing each other's efforts rather than tearing them down. Leadership of a new political entity devoid of dependency on money bags to win hearts but comprising of principled clements with no envy of any one however financially enabled, would need to be inaugurated. Regardless of age or gender but ready to be ridiculed by the agents of regression and status quo, with the efforts of these individuals, we would determine their capabilities with their dogged determination in their private lives and enterprises. No hijacking of the party formed, would be allowed by the money bags and their surrogates. The party must screen the membership rigorously before embarking on this onerous mission of rebuilding the country. A litmus set of questions would be compiled, not too long, to determine the inner workings and philosophy of the would- be members. Expert determination would zero in on the psychological make-up of the leadership of the new party.

Acquisition of Western European education and their certificates (with no national contributions) has not benefitted us or transformed the landscape and improved the outlook of our people from the bottom up, in most instances. It has on the other hand, increased and expanded the bureaucratic nests to unmanageable extent. To reign it in, would result in mass unemployment than it is presently, of several cadres of the people without stemming measures put in place.

No more would it be necessary to give responsibilities or assign responsibilities to people on the basis of the secondary school or college or university(s) attended or graduated from, here in Nigeria, or overseas particularly in Britain or the United States of America. Instead, institutions would not make individuals but the other way round. I am here advocating decent environmental standards for our people, not making them in the image of European or United States of American Caucasians, but with their readiness to serve the country.

I have been rattling on the commonality of the Nigerian Citizen outlook in general. And I believe that most of the people would agree with this assessment of common dishonesty among the people, from the policemen to the lawyers and the judges adjucating criminal and civil cases.

We have to retrain and restructure the whole judicial system. We have to remove the cumbersome bureaucracy and establish for sure, the civil liberty and human rights as enshrined in our constitution.

THE BUILDING OF A VIABLE NIGERIA REPUBLIC

- A La The Late Chief Obafemi Awolowo

Too many of the lettered Yoruba leaders have always missed the point of Nigerian regression. Many of them would in fact quickly, without deeper inner soul-searching, even with the evidence glaring at them, lay the blame of Nigerian problems on the steps of the northern politicians. This is not an excuse of the ignoble role being played by some of these northern politicians in the name of politics or sheer ignorance, but we would not here excuse ignorance.

A brief visit to the beginning needs to illumine the role of that elder statesman, Chief Awolowo, in the wobbling movement of a people called Nigerians. The year 1953

Chief Obafemi Awolowo

will long remain significant in the Nigerian history. It was the year the Action Group Political Party of Nigeria formally asked the Colonial British Government ruler of Nigeria to grant independence to the country. The Action Group (AG) under the late Chief Awolowo formally, without consulting the two other larger political parties, Northern People Congress (NPC), and National Council of Nigerian and Cameroon (NCNC), asked for Nigeria's independence in 1953. There, the seed of discord and distrust was sown. Nonetheless, the open fissure between the Nigerian political parties notwithstanding, led to skirmishing of movements towards the eventual independence of Nigeria as a nation with the attending constitutional conferences in Britain.

This has been the saga of the Nigerian nation and the people who place themselves at the helm of its affairs for the independence from the British government. Let those who witnessed the council elections dispute the fraud committed by the Action Group in winning those seats in Lagos and many parts of Yoruba enclave. This fraud was later to be copied by the other political parties, making no saint of any of the political parties. Before the dawn of independence of Nigeria (12/12/59), the Action Group (AG) Party lost the general election into the Federal House of Assembly. Chief Obafemi Awolowo, having been disappointed despite the spirited campaign waged, and spurned by the Nnamdi Azikiwe's NCNC, decided that the only way to make Nigeria follow his whims and design was to seize the government by popular militant uprising. I dare say here, having looked over the whole preparation, it smacked of the half-read Bolshevick revolution under the great Vladimir Ilyich Lenin. The design failed and ended up with Chief Awolowo being prosecuted and found guilty of treasonable felony against a lawfully elected federal government of Nigeria.

Because the parties at the helm of federal government affairs proved to be inept at satisfying the yearnings of the masses, especially in the South (with better political enlightenment and sophistication), Chief Awolowo became a hero behind bars. Election to the Western House of Assembly was boycotted, leaving the field clear for Chief S.L. Akintola's Nigerian National Democratic Party (NNDP) to cruise to an unopposed victory. Thereafter, the AG thugs were summoned, and terrorism of their opponents escalated with each passing day. This wave of terrorism did not give the NNDP any breathing space to effectively implement its election pledges to the people of the Western region. This was the beginning of the subversion of the electoral process and hence, of democracy. With the escalation of the destruction of properties and the killing of political opponents of the Action Group, several clandestine calls were made for the military to restore order. Wole Soyinka, the erstwhile Professor of English Drama, and Bola Ige among the young turks, staged several dramatic exploits against the government of Chief S.L. Akintola. Little did those who were calling for the military intervention know of the military's own agenda. Any military regime brought into government without being under civilian control would run amok with its own agenda which never benefitted the unfortunate nations they governed. This was the naivete and ignorance of the military machine encouraged by Chief Awolowo and his cohorts. This naivete would be repeated, sadly enough, in the second republic, after it became apparent that the election was going to be lost the second time to the National Party of Nigeria.

Wole Soyinka

At any rate, one must not absolve the partisan judges, justices and magistrates of law courts of complicity in the subversion of democratic process either. Many of these sanctimonious officers of the court proved to be less deserving of the robes they put on themselves. They were too intimidated, partisan and corrupt to arbitrate election disputes. So it was then, and so it is now. But all these, as we've all learned, now pale against the military alternative. Let me hasten to add that no one would have been able to wrestle power out of any of the political parties once they have their stranglehold on power. Fraud and counter-fraud was committed in efforts to keep the parties perpetually in power while continuously intimidating their opponents. Any call for foreign or international observers of the conduct and count of electoral process was laughed at, or the callers called unpatriotic.

Such has been the fate of the Nigerian underclass which continues unabated. Calls of frauds and irregularities became so rampant, even from the perpetrators of the same, that it became a mockery. The dilution and irrelevance of such calls having been achieved leaves the ordinary citizen unattended to. One would have thought that the enlightened citizenry would have learned something from this inglorious behaviour perpetrated by members of their own class. This so-called enlightened group have dubbed themselves the political class. Being enlightened has come to be synonymous with the ingenious ability to embezzle the public funds. These embezzled funds were left for the poor, toiling masses to pay back to creditors who loaned the funds to the country for projects which were supposed to be developed to improve the lives of the masses and which never saw the light of day. The funds had been shared among the political, military and senior civil servants who were privy to the disbursement of such funds.

The fear of Chief Awolowo's hold on power, stated or not, had to do with his connection and presiding presence on various cults and fraternities which would be dispensing favouritism for the privileged, selected few. In other words, it was feared from the South to the North that he would become the worst dictator within any civilian annals of history.

But, just as Chief Awolowo dispensed ignorance to help ambitions of the military when he invited them to help redress what he perceived as injustice to him, the same ignorance was displayed by Chief Moshood Kashimawo Olawale Abiola in 1994.

Chief M.K.O. Abiola, believed that his ties to the military establishment would exempt him from being run over if he invited them to redress the wrong done to him by General I.B. Babangida's regime. General Babaginda nullified the election process which would have installed Abiola president of the Nigerian Republic at the last minute. Even with this action, one would have thought that Abiola would be the wiser about trusting the military with power. No, he never learned.

M.K.O Abiola

He would be the man to help plan the coup against the interim civilian government headed by Chief Ernest Shonekan. The coup was to be the ruse that would declare Abiola the victor of the presidential election of 1993. Instead, the coup enthroned General Sani Abacha, plunging Nigeria deep into the abyss of terrorism never before witnessed in the history of the country. The plot to unseat Shonekan is a subject of another discussion.

The same stupidity displayed by Chief Awolowo in trusting that General Yakubu Gowon would make it possible for him to lead the country was also shown twice by Chief M.K.O. Abiola. Those who never learned the lessons of history are condemned to perpetual failure.

CHIEF AWOLOWO'S ACTION GROUP PARTY OF NIGERIA

Within the Action Group Party which Chief Obafemi Awolowo owned, headed and controlled, there was little if any democratic collegiality. Chief Obafemi Awolowo had core inner circle of loyalists within the inner circle of the party. These core members were largely individuals from his ethnic speaking areas of the Yoruba tribe, namely the Ijebus. They received preferential treatment. Discipline of erring or questioning members were never ruthlessly extended to them, no matter their transgressions. This Ijebu-core inner circle was never really known for any great service to the people of western Nigeria, nay Nigeria as a nation, but they accepted without question Chief Awolowo's leadership. They formed the majority in any Ad-hoc Committee of the Action Group for any disciplinary case brought by the leader against any member and would deliver judgement in accordance with the wishes of their party leader. It was this partisanship and uneven handedness which later destroyed the Action Group Party of Nigeria.

The year 1962 will forever be remembered in the Nigerian history. This was the year Chief Awolowo's impatience with the leadership of the Federal Republic of Nigeria came to desperation. It was the year Chief S.L. Akintola ignored the hint and paid no attention to the developing machinations. After all, he was duly elected, and he was the principal campaigner for the position. Actually, Chief Awolowo had shown his irritation with the chants of S.L.A. competing with the Awo chants. He felt that the two chants were capable of confusing the constituency of the party with regards to the boss of the party. Since Chief Akintola paid no attention to this irritation, Chief Awolowo decided that he would deal with him, but first, he had to do it in such a way that his weakness with adulation would not be exploited by his opponents. Chief Awolowo's irritation, although concealed, was further compounded as Chief Akintola never sought his advice before taking action he deemed appropriate for the government of Western Region. Finally, Chief Akintola played into the Action Group Leader's hand, and Chief Awolowo seized the moment with reckless glee.

CHIEF AKINTOLA AND THE SARDAUNA OF SOKOTO – ALHAJI (SIR) AHMADU BELLO

A letter written by the Premier of the Northern Region, Alhaji (Sir) Ahmadu Bello, to Chief Akintola, his counterpart in Western Region, proved to be the culprit document and the weapon of seed of destruction. Alhaji Ahmadu Bello, the Sardauna of Sokoto wrote and enclosed with his letter, a copy of a letter written by the City of Ibadan Muslim community inviting the Sardauna of Sokoto to come and lay the foundation stone of an impending Central Jumat Mosque at Oja-ba in Ibadan. The Sardauna, in his letter, wanted to inform his western counterpart that his acceptance of the invitation had nothing to do with politics, and he sought the approval of the Premier of Western Region to visit the region to lay the foundation stone of the mosque.

Sardauna of Sokoto

Chief Akintola replied to the Sardauna of Sokoto that he felt deeply touched by his magnanimity. He opined that the Sardauna never really needed his approval to visit Western Region, as Sardauna was a free citizen of Nigeria, and as such could travel freely within the federation. He added in his reply that he would be at the airport to welcome him to the region on his one-day assignment. So, as it was customary for Chief Akintola, at his next briefing meeting with Chief Awolowo, he added the exchange between him (Chief Akintola) and the Sardauna of Sokoto. It is this

manner of reportage Chief Awolowo hated so much about Chief Akintola, which the AG party leader thought of as insubordination. Chief Awolowo demanded the actual date of the event in Ibadan by the Sardauna of Sokoto. When he was told, he never gave a hint of disapproval, if any.

After the Premier of Western Region returned to Ibadan from Ikenne where he had gone to brief his party leader, he was surprised to receive a letter from Chief Awolowo informing him of the next party convention scheduled to take place in Jos in the north and covering the date of the impending visit of the Sardauna of Sokoto to Western Region. Chief Akintola was the more stung since, as the deputy leader of the party, Chief Awolowo never raised the possibility of the Action Group convention with him when he had just visited with him in Ikenne. He felt slighted that he would receive the information of the date of the party's convention in the same manner as the general convention members. He was by no means privy to those who would be invited as he was to find out that the invitation was selective. Nonetheless, like a good soldier, he was going to keep his appointment with the opening date of his party's convention though acceptance of the date was mandatory and binding on members of the party.

Unknown further to Chief Akintola was the private meeting by the core inner circle of the Action Group presided over by Chief Awolowo. At this meeting, Chief Awolowo laid bare his mind and what he thought should be done. They counselled only that it would be too glaring for him to reclaim the mantle of Premiership of Western Region. They settled for a 'docile' and 'subservient' member with no clout in the party. That person must also be outside the Ijebu ethnic area. In this person was found Alhaji (Chief) D.S. Adegbenro, from Owu-Abeokuta. Having hedged their bets, they proceeded to implement the leader's wish at the convention.

Awolowo's inner core was sworn to secrecy. The loose cannon of this group who was equally uncomfortable with this dictatorial tendency, was Professor Sanya Onabamiro, a zoologist by training and parasitologist by specialty. He hailed from Ago-Iwoye, an Ijebu section of the region, but his foreign education (British) and the level of his educational attainment made his acceptance of such dictation rather difficult. It was the account of this professor and his rejection of the totalitarian dictatorship style of Chief Awolowo that proved decisive in the conviction of the AG leader in the ensuing treasonable felony charge. This individualism and nationalistic instinct would also earn the professor the label of traitor to Chief Awolowo's ambition and cause.

THE ACTION GROUP CONVENTION OF 1962

The convention had started with all the pomp and pageantry ably coordinated by the Action Group inner circle members. A parade of speakers spoke mostly of Chief Awolowo's accomplishments for the party and what more would be attained with Chief Awolowo being at the helm of affairs. New convention adhoc committee members were chosen to deal with subjects of confidence in members, retainance and expulsion from the party. Many of the members, particularly those from Ibadan, Oyo, Osun and Oyo North were confused by this turn of events. Why was it necessary now to create a new ad-hoc committee, and why were the committee members not voted for but had to be chosen by the esteemed leader, Chief Awolowo, who had just been given the vote of confidence by the rank and file of the party?

The fact that Chief Akintola was kept in the dark of this charade got him miffed, but he decided he would wait and reflect about what it all meant before he would mount any challenge. And if he had any objection, he would take it up with the leader himself without making any public scene. Little did he know that the convention was designed to oust the Premier of Western Region in the name of Chief Samuel Ladoke Akintola, the Deputy leader of the Action Group Party of Nigeria.

The date of visit of the Premier of Northern Region was drawing near, and Chief Akintola, well known for keeping appointments, would excuse himself from the convention to play host to his Northern Premier counterpart. The visit was memorable. Chief Akintola, the true politician donned the turban at Ibadan Central Mosque Jumat and won over quite a following with chants of S.L.A.!!!

The Premier of Northern Region was very impressed and grateful for the cordial and courteous reception accorded him and his entourage. He returned to the North with warm memories. He wrote so quickly to express his profound gratitude to the Premier of Western Region. This was to be the beginning of the thaw of distrust and animosity between the Northern Hausa-Fulani and their Yoruba cousins of the Western part of Nigeria.

Chief Akintola returned to the floor of the Action Group Convention only to have a vote of no confidence passed on him as the Premier of Western Region and the convention replacing him with Alhaji Dauda Soroye Adegbenro. With

**Otunba T.O
Shobowale Benson**

these developments the honourable Premier of Western Region walked out of the convention followed by members mostly of the core Yoruba tribe of Ibadan, Oyo, Ogbomosho, Iwo, Ede, and Oshogbo, Ibarapa areas and Ijesha. With Chief Akintola and his followers out of the hall, the convention followed swiftly to expel them forthwith from the party. When the convention completed the task it had set out to accomplish, it adjourned to begin the selling of the leadership of D.S. Adegbenro as the new Premier-designate which would be confirmed by the next House of Assembly Session to be called by the governor (the Premier still smarting at what happened at the convention and pondering the next move), a twist of order of official duty. The governor of Western Region was an Awolowo crony by the name of Oba Adesoji Aderemi, II, the Ooni of Ife.

THE WESTERN HOUSE OF ASSEMBLY – 1962

Without belabouring the point, the Western House of Assembly had the majority members belonging to the Action Group Party and the opposition minority members belonging to the National Council of Nigerian Congress (formerly Cameroon,), N.C.N.C. With the news of A.G. Convention events breaking and tongues wagging and the uncertainties floating around, Chief Akintola made the last effort at reconciliation. He tried to rally the Obas (traditional rulers) with sympathy towards Action Group to appeal to Chief Obafemi Awolowo to retreat his move at ousting him as the Premier of Western Region. The appeal was rejected outright by Chief Awolowo, even with Chief S.L. Akintola told to swallow his pride and apologize, though he was convinced he did nothing wrong. He was further told to accept Chief Awolowo's superiority unconditionally. What a way for Yorubas to settle a dispute! Chief Akintola did as told against his own better judgement, but in the interest of peace and tranquility in the country, and particularly Western Region. Still, Chief Awolowo refused to bulge! There a line was drawn in the sand. It remained for Chief Akintola to redeem whatever dignity was left for him in the eyes of the populace which elected him. Chief Akintola rallied. The opposition party expressed their support and confidence in his ability to govern and lead the Western Region. The leader of opposition, Chief Remi Fani-Kayode pledged his loyalty to Chief Akintola. Chief Akintola refused to vacate the Premier's Office at Secretariat and also the Premier's quarters at Iyaganku. Blocked and locked out, he gave orders to handymen to unlock the doors of these quarters. The 'Daily Times' of Nigeria came out with the now famous heading "Akintola Taku" (Akintola Refused To go). In the ensuing saga, the House of Assembly was convened to put an end to the confusion only to compound it further. No one actually knew what happened at that second. As the governor, Sir Adesoji Aderemi, was reading the order of the Assembly, a wooden chair was thrown from the back and landed on the head of Alhaji D.S. Adegbenro who was to be named by A.G. Party as the new Premier. Chief Adegbenro sustained a bloody head injury and a melee erupted with everyone looking for escape from the free-for-all fight. The Prime Minister of the Federation, hearing of the turn of events, ordered the House of Assembly closed down with members suspended until further notice. With the House closed down, Chief Akintola was sent off to a village to cool off and Chief Awolowo also was ordered to a southern village town and ordered to cease from making political utterances. The same gag order was imposed on all the principal members of the dispute, including Chief Akintola.

The Federal Government appointed a non-political Administrator, Dr. M.A. Majekodunmi, a physician from the Federal Government, Executive Council. He was to stay in that position for six months while tempers cooled off. Chief Akinyemi a.ka. Obe from Mushin had saved the day for the Premier.

Meanwhile, the Premier of Western Region challenged the constitutionality of Chief Obafemi Awolowo and the Action

Chief R.O Akinjide

Group Party of Nigeria in removing him from office at the Supreme Court of the Federation. He told the court that he was legally and lawfully elected premier of the Western Region of Nigeria. The Supreme Court upheld Chief Akintola's submission, saying that the Action Group Party did not show a "prima facie" before taking a vote of no-confidence in the Premier. The court ruled that the Premier should return to the State House as soon as the ban on him was lifted by the Federal Government. He could form a new party as he wished as long as he had enough delegates in the House to back his programs. The Premier Chief S.L. Akintola hastily formed United People's Party (UPP) in coalition with N.C.N.C. led by Chief Remi Fani-Kayode and Chief R.O. Akinjinde, who had emerged as the spokesman of the coalition government. Many of the former A.G. delegates who were removed by the convention, having been reinstated by the court, joined forces and threw their support for UPP. Together, the coalition formed the majority in the Western House of Assembly. Chief Fani-Kayode from Ife-Ila was named Deputy Premier.

THE U.P.P. AND THE N.C.N.C. COALITION GOVERNMENT OFWESTERN REGION 1962

The new government started with much good will and prayer for success by the general population of the region. The skeptics were the A.G. diehards and those who knew nothing of the workings of the Action Group inner circle of Chief Obafemi Awolowo. These individuals, mostly members of the Ijebu ethnic group and a few from the northern part of the region (Ekitis and Ondo's) ethnic areas were forever grateful for the free primary school education initiated by the interim Premier of the West, Chief Obafemi Awolowo. These groups would see nothing good in any leadership which did not include Chief Awolowo. They call this principled partisanship and loyalty to the point of blind followership.

The Action Group Party had created a reputation for its leader as a disciplined visionary. The propaganda of a selfless, sympathetic leadership was successfully disseminated. Hence, to overcome that image, however fake, the new party in government had its work cut out for it. Unfortunately, the UPP/NCNC coalition party failed to do this.

A grateful Premier S.L. Akintola repaid his new found loyalists by giving them a free ride with public funds with no accountability to anyone. Suddenly, the opposition and former A.G. back benchers who never had a taste of power became the power brokers and insiders within a ruling party. There was total lack of focus and programs for development of the state. This was shelved in favour of winning new loyalists to the party. The UPP immediately became the butt of jokes at ordinary people's social gatherings. Chief Akintola had to do something. He persuaded the coalition to adopt a common party platform in order to face the Action Group Party at the next election. This was a good strategy to prevent the splitting of their votes at the poll. Suddenly, the Nigerian National Democratic Party (NNDP) was born. That was a new political party's name, but the leadership and composition remained the same. The same absence of focus and developmental programs continued. Those were replaced by pre-occupation with holding onto power by whatever means possible.

The NNDP under Chief Ladoke Akintola started to display the same irritation with criticism which was the hallmark of Awolow's Action Group Party. He started to behave exactly like the Action Group Party leader before he could consolidate his own followership. These were periods of turmoil and fracas with the Action Group and its henchmen.

THE KWAME NKRUMAH ANGLE/AWOLOWO FLIRTATION

Meanwhile, the frequent travel and invocation of Kwame Nkrumah by the AG leadership was attracting attention and suspicion by the British and American Intelligence operatives disguising as reporters in all forms. Interviews and discussions were granted by the AG leader and Dr Kwame Nkrumah, sometimes simultaneously. The convergence of views was unmistakable. Nkrumah, the President of the Republic of Ghana, had discussed at length his dreams for a Pan-African Military High Command which would rid the entire Africa of colonial rule. Nkrumah called for the training of militias from African countries with Ghana as the training centre. The Abubakar Tafawa Balewa's government of Nigerian People's Congress (NPC) was not symphathetic with Nkrumah's call. The Prime Minister thought that Africa was not ready for this venture. Besides, the feudal Islamic north of Nigeria which he represented equated Nkrumah's socialist embrace with atheism and, therefore, saw it as unworthy of being associated with. Chief Awolowo, ever the smart opportunist, rushed to Nkrumah's side proclaiming himself a socialist, an African Socialist, which is synonymous with acquisition of private wealth and financial empire. Never mind, Awolowo had found a perfect place to start his quest of an armed takeover of the Federal Government.

This spectre had been discussed in jest at an executive committee meeting of the Action Group shortly after the loss of the federal election of December 12, 1959, by Chief Awolowo. He had fought strenuously and was almost assuring himself in-road during the campaign to the Northern territories. He was devastated when he lost. He offered to unite with the Nnamdi Azikwe's NCNC to form the federal government under Azikiwe's Prime Ministership. He was too late. Sardauna of Sokoto, the leader of the NPC, had reached Dr Nnamdi Azikwe first and reached an agreement of a coalition federal government with Sir Abubakar Tafawa Balewa as Prime Minister and Nnamdi Azikiwe the Ceremonial First President of the Federal Republic of Nigeria. With this in place, Awolowo thought there was no way he was going to fulfil his dream of one day becoming the Prime Minister of the Federal Republic of Nigeria short of staging an armed insurrection by the Yoruba ethnic south where his popularity knew no bounds. He was later to divulge his yearnings to his most ardent Turks in the party. These young men had already accepted unconditionally Chief Awolowo as their saviour. After all, everyone of these Turks owed him for whatever they had become. There was Michael Omisade, Lateef Jakande, Samuel Oredein, Anthony Enahoro, Sanya Onabamiro, Bisi Onabanjo and Josiah Olawoyin.

The British Intelligence community in Nigeria had expressed their horror at Awolowo's hiring of the Socialist Russian helicopter for his ill-fated federal election campaign of 1959, and he had come under increasing, scrutiny as he aligned himself with Ghana's Nkrumah government and his association with the Russian and Chinese Socialist governments. Another battle line was drawn in the sand, this time with foreign, western governments against Chief Obafemi Awolowo, who at this desperate period, displayed poor judgement. His every movement from then on was passed to the federal government. So also was the movement of any of his associates. The federal government was here presented with a dilemma of either to arrest Chief Awolowo and his boys, given all the facts of his transgressions, or wait for his intending plan to mature and hatch into government hands. The former option would risk making a martyr Chief Awolowo and his fellow militia leaders; and the latter might not be that easy to predict in terms of outcome. Who knew how many people within the rank and file of the armed forces would sympathize with him? Remember this was Chief Obafemi Awolowo. The government chose the former and hoped the sympathetic popularity would be short lived.

CHIEF OBAFEMI AWOLOWO, THE MASTER CALCULATOR

He was born poor. His animist/Muslim parents were from a little village outside Ikenne, too small to really make the identification on the Nigerian map. Chief Awolowo chose to abandon it as a birth place, but instead opted for Ikenne in his autobiography, which was his wife's birth place and home town. He married the social status of his wife's family which actually launched his career, not as a lawyer, but as a politician with clout and money, arriving from England where he stayed a few years to attain his law degree and always knew the smell of money. After all, he was an Ijebu ethnic person, synonymous with preoccupation with material wealth which was never displayed for others to see. In fact, he was modest with his vast financial acquisitions. None of his associates really knew the extent of his wealth. It was the late Chief S.L. Akintola who knew more by virtue of his position as the Premier of Western Region after he took over the reigns of office from him. It is this modesty which endeared him (Awolowo) to the Yoruba population as a disciplined leader. This discipline, it is sad to state, is not extended to his children who were garrulous and untamed save for perhaps 0his eldest son, Segun Awolowo to some extent. Segun Awolowo was everything his old man wanted to be professionally, but who, because of lack of funds, had to settle for business law which he started via correspondence and completed off campus in London. That notwithstanding, he was determined to be successful in life.

After the elder Awolowo returned from England with his law degree, and having been set up for corporate representation of various companies, with his wife's business disposition, which was profitable, afforded him the luxury of political forage. He still needed to be known among "who is who" in Lagos Island where the crème-de-la-crème of Nigerian political movement resided. Young Obafemi Awolowo decided to team up with a notable socialite in Lagos' political circle susceptible enough and unwary of his moves. In this individual he found Chief

Bode Thomas, a well regarded Lagos lawyer who hailed from Oyo, the ancient city capital of Yoruba tribe of Western Region. Chief Bode Thomas was to serve as Awolowo's conduit to the corridor of power and acceptance into the class of leaders of thoughts in the independence movement party being led by Herbert Mobolaji Macaulay, a Yoruba slave child returnee after the emancipation and abolition of slavery in the United States of America. The General Secretary of the movement was Chief Adeyemo Alakija. Other members were J.K. Randle, Olorunimbe, Mayor of Lagos, Dr Akinola Maja, Dr Doherty, Dr Akerele, Dr Salawu, to name a few, were the professionals lending competence and legitimacy to the movement. There were other men of importance and persuasions who, because of their religious affiliation and lack of Western education, the history of Nigeria has not been too kind to mention. Among them were Chief Nuru Oniwo, Chief Augusto, Alhaji Elias, the father of a former Chief Justice of the Federation of Nigeria, Imam Abdulahi Popoola Raji, in Lagos Central near Faji Court, his son Alhaji Bello Adeniji Raji from a ruling house in Ibadan, the modern Western Region capital city. Mention must be made of the Assistant General Secretary of the movement, Nnamdi Azikiwe. Nnamdi Azikiwe must be credited with the rekindling of fervour with which the movement gained attention through the works of the likes of Rev. Ransome Kuti, Mrs Kuti, J.J. Ladipo, Madam Tinubu and Chief H.O. Davies of Oyo. The editor of West African Pilot, Nnamdi Azikiwe was incredible.

AWOLOWO AND INJECTION OF TRIBALISM IN THE POLITY

Chief Awolowo knew, however, that it would be difficult to challenge the pre-eminence of Nnamdi Azikiwe and the high regard the people of Lagos had for his tireless and humble devotion to duty. Nnamdi's personality was too towering and the only way to cut him to size was too attack his roots. There, tribalism as a political classification and identification was introduced into the Nigerian movement character. Rather than join the National Democratic Party, Chief Awolowo persuaded Chief Bode Thomas to join him in forming the Action Group Party of Nigeria. The rest is history.

The preceding lines served merely as an illustration of events that led to the formation of political parties. He formed the Egbe Omo Oduduwa, the prelude group to the Action Group Party and appealed to tribal sentiments. Nonetheless, formation of this party injected keenness and fervor in the demand for independence of the nation. Nnamdi Azikiwe reached homeward, bringing into the movement the Igbo citizens' participation and helping to hasten their Western education if they would be relevant in the emerging Nigerian nation. In doing so, he also sustained his own relevance against the bulwark onslaught of Awolowo and his followers.

Justice Sowemimo

AWOLOWO AND HIS DEFENSE AGAINST IMPRISONMENT

Chief G. Fawehinmi

Lest anyone read this piece like an autobiography of personalities in the Nigerian history, it is not. This is shedding the light on how we as a people got into this mess that we find ourselves in. That Chief Awolowo knew what he always wanted and how to get it, was an understatement. But more importantly, he brought to bear on whatever he decided to do, his entire personality and energy. He was only matched with that forcefulness and single mindedness by the Sardauna of Sokoto, Alhaji Ahmadu Bello, the Premier of the Northern Region.

Chief Awolowo, underestimating his opponent or those he wished to descend on as his hallmark, became virtuperant and exasperated by the squandering and complete lack of focus of resources demonstrated by the Federal Government under Alhaji Abubakar Tafawa Balewa. He was later arrested and the celebrated trial brought to the open the clandestine preparation of the Action Group Party of Nigeria to topple the federal government by armed insurrection. Whether the method would succeed or not was too risky to condone. Chief Awolowo opted to get his defense lawyer from Britain, named Dingle Foot Q.C. Mr Foot was denied entry to the country on the ground that it would constitute interference in the country's internal affairs and also that there were enough competent Nigerian lawyers who were also British Queen's Counsel to defend the politician and his cohorts.

Justice K. Eso

The trial and subsequent appeal which was going to be led by his son, Segun Awolowo, who had then been qualified as a barrister-at-law, and international jurist at that, became the emotion of immense proportion of the time. It did not help the matter when Segun Awolowo died of a ghastly motor vehicle accident on his way to Lagos during the period of his spirited defense appeal against the conviction of his father, Chief Obafemi Awolowo. Emotion and sympathy which was lukewarm before the accident, swung decidedly to the Chief's side. From then on, nothing could be done right by any sitting government in the eye of an average Yoruba person. Chief Awolowo was then regarded as the victim of machination and connivance of the Fulani-Hausa north and the Akintola and Oyo Yorubas of the southern part of Nigeria. Obafemi Awolowo was charged and convicted for treasonable felony and intent to overthrow the elected federal government of Nigeria.

It was not what Chief Obafemi Awolowo said at his conviction trial that mattered, but the fact that the various governments from the Federal government to regional governments lacked focus in improving the lives of the average citizen which lent credence to his speech at his conviction. Apart from the free education in Yoruba and Hausa-Fulani areas of the federation in primary schools, nothing else was going on. The eastern part of the country was so lax that there was no road to call modern. Even where there were markets (modern) built, access roads to them were non- existent. Most of the lawmakers and members of the executive cabinets of the various governments were busy helping themselves through the public coffers and neglecting the people they were elected to serve. In the end, it became the way of life for every successive administration which took over except for two of the military interventionist governments, which genuinely tried to stop the slide of the country to bankruptcy. They included the Murtala Mohammed-Obasanjo regime which rescued the country from the floundering and laissez-faire government of General Yakubu Gowon, and Mohammadu Buhari-Tunde Idiagbon regime which tried to bring back sanity to government after Shehu Shagari's NPN-NPP coalition party at the centre and UPN state's level management made a mockery of democracy as we had it.

Try as the two mentioned regimes might have done in their brief periods in the spotlight, they still were not equipped to rule a civilian population requesting dialogue and sense of direction from their leaders. The military was never elected, even if there were calls for their intervention from self-serving quarters. They were ill at ease to give accounts of their stewardship. They could not engage in dialogue necessary for the civilian sense of belonging.

NIGERIA 1966 – 1975 WITH YAKUBU GOWON

The period between July, 1966 to June, 1975 was both the best of times for Nigeria and the worst of times. It was the time of missed opportunities supplanted by cosmetic progress and reckless implementation of the unnecessary and half-thought out commission of inquiry report on the need to improve the wages and conditions of the average Nigerian worker. It was the best of time when the country started to realize revenues from one of her many natural resources – the crude oil natural gas deposits.The oil deposit which was explored and found in sizable amount became the focus of exploitation for misdirected development projects.

General Yakubu Gowon

General Yakubu Gowon, who was the military head of government for these periods, was singularly responsible through ill-advised, early pronouncements over the Nigerian air-waves, for plunging Nigeria into the civil war. The Nigerian civilian cabinet members he put together would later spend several months to allay the fears of the nation that the rulership was not ethnically oriented or directed. Up to now, the damage has not been completely corrected. The notion that the rulership of the nation must always come from the northern part of the country was the worst wound still capitalized on by some half-baked and self-anointed nitwits from the northern section of the country – notably, the Hausa- Fulani clique elements.

Yakubu Gowon started the calculated opportunism by the Nigerians in military uniform. He may have meant well, but he was ill-equipped as a leader of most populous nation in Africa. He represented the worst in our people, because he could not objectively appraise his own capability to lead. Instead, he substituted handsome appearance in military uniform, flashy smiles and region of origin for readiness to lead the nation.

He and his fellow Tiv ethnic soldiers who staged the coup d'etat to topple the General Aguiyi-Ironsi's unitary government may have saved the country from an imminent tribal war which would have been worse than the civil war of 1967 – 1970. But, because of the opportunism represented by Gowon and his need to gain acceptance by the dominant Hausa-Fulani ethnic group of the North, he resorted to careless statements which were seized upon by another calculating opportunist, Igbo ethnic member in military uniform, Odumegwu-Ojukwu, resulting in the inevitable civil war.

Odumegwu Ojukwu

Mention must be made of those careless statements of Yakubu Gowon on toppling the military government of General Aguiyi-Ironsi in a bloody military coup. Yakubu Gowon enjoined the northern Nigerian citizens to be happy and to remain calm and refrain from the ongoing civil unrest and ethnic strife with the Igbo ethnic people living in the North because, as he put it, the government was again in the hands of another Northerner. He also happened to tell the Nigerian population that the "basis of our unity" was not there. These statements were later to be taken out of context and seized upon by Chukwuemeka, Odumegwu-Ojukwu as the reason why he thought that the Eastern region, which is not all of Igbo ethnic speaking people but was nonetheless dominated by the Igbos and which encompasses the areas of initial crude oil exploration, should secede from Nigeria.

Gen. Olusegun Obasanjo
(Head of State 1976-1979)

Gen. Shehu Yar' Adua (Chief of Staff- Defence
Headquaters & Deputy Head of State 1976-1979)

The civil war was relentlessly prosecuted and the statesmanship and maturity displayed by Yakubu Gowon at the end of this unfortunate period saved the Nigerian nation as an entity to be envied by other nations of Africa and the world if the Western Europeans and United States would admit to the facts. Unfortunately though, every fool in the Nigerian military uniform felt that it was his right to plunder the nation's wealth, convinced that he had earned that right. Little did the military care about the brunt of the hardship borne by the Nigerian population, too disorganized and impoverished to claim its stake in the nation's economic pie. The civilians who joined the military leadership because of greediness and selfishness relinquished their birth-right of leadership to the military machine but saving the regime from the rebellion of the populace. Yakubu Gowon was sensitive enough to save the regime. But the neglect of the infrastructures viz education and total overhaul and re-orientation of the masses was to prove the point of the unsuitability of the military government over a civilian population during and after the war.

THE MURITALA MOHAMMED –Olusegun Obasanjo Administration 1975-1979

The military government of General Muritala Mohammed which replaced the Gowon regime was set out to correct the lax, floundering and indulgent psyche left on the Nigerian consciousness. His pace was breathless, and his actions were done with military precisions. He was the very opposite of Yakubu Gowon, in many ways. Mohammed had vision of purpose. He was secure and regarded every Nigerian as a worthy compatriot. He paid attention to the corrective criticism of Nigerians living in technologically advanced Western European nations and the USA. He made room for the contributions of these foreign trained compatriots. But his belief that being good and patriotic alone would keep him safe from enemies

Muritala Mohammed

within was his ultimate undoing which he paid for with his life in an abortive coup d'etat which was engineered by the loyalists of Yakubu Gowon from the Tiv ethnic northern part of the country. Murtala Mohammed was a Nigerian Patriot, a civil war hero. The nation was shocked and plunged into disarray. His deputy, General Olusegun Obasanjo who, with equal credentials as a patriotic, civil war hero, took over the reigns of power, having foiled the coup attempt for a Gowon comeback. Nigeria as a nation was once again saved.

General Muritala Mohammed's breathless speed to correc the anomalies of corruption, he thought was hindering the progress of the country from taking root nonetheless, mistakenly punished the innocent civil servants by leaving them in the hands of the corrupt bosses who seized upon the mistake and so, quickened the retirements of such efficient administrators with no blemish in their records of service.

Obasanjo kept to Murtala Mohammed's agenda. He further kept the timetable of the government to return the reign of power to the duly- elected civilian leadership for better or for worse in 1979. Being a military government, he could only rule by decrees and being devoid of duly elected legislative civilian body, the military decrees could not stand the test of time. He was convinced the country belonged to all, irrespective of ethnic background. He had no tribal bone in him, and this singular attribute marked Olusegun Obasanjo and Murtala Mohammed as the duo with impeccable patriotic credentials rising head and shoulders above their compatriots in uniform.

It would never be, and it must never be compared, with the advent of Nigerian military rulers, the exploits of Major Kaduna Nzeogwu, Major Ifeajuna Emanuel, Lt. Colonel Banjo and Lt. Colonel Chukwuemeka Odumegwu-Ojukwu, who were the forerunners of military travails into the arena of Nigerian civilian life. These young military Turks had their agenda, and by their composition and actions witnessed, it was not doubtful that ethnic chauvinism was on their minds. We would leave the judgements to subsequent historians with no prejudice and good introspection.

Yakubu Gowon had the best opportunity to correct the previous anomalies of the country at the end of the Nigerian Civil War of 1970. But he neither had that vision nor the sense of direction or the understanding of what was to be done. He was a soldier with a short list and having been exhausted, he proceeded to enjoy the spoils of the war. The economic boom brought about the crude oil sale on the international market. The Arab-Israel war and subsequent oil embargo had proven to be an economic blessing for Nigeria with the lightest crude oil devoid of impurities in the world.

Gowon started a lot of white-elephant projects without first correcting the damage of the infrastructures brought about by the civil war – namely, the interruption of electric power supply, access roads repairs of the interland to farmers' produce and the strengthening of educational sectors for unity and progress of the country. No, he could not do all these. He was after all, a soldier with limited vision besides fighting a war of attrition. That this conjecture is true was borne out by the fact that after the regime was toppled by a bloodless coup d'etat in 1975, he proceeded to Britain to enroll as an undergraduate student of political science at the Warwick College with the vast amount of financial windfall from his helmsmanship of the Nigerian military government.

The pattern of behaviour and appointments of the military dictators must be read, understood and discredited. Apart from the Aquiyi-Ironsi and Sani Abacha regimes which are similar and at the opposite ends of the strip, the other regimes were careful and calculating. The Aguiyi-Ironsi regime which was the first military government was naïve and innocent, and it paid dearly for it. The Abacha regime was pugnant, reckless and ruthless, daring anyone to question his handling of the affairs of the nation.

MUHAMMADU BUHARI- TUNDE IDIAGBON ADMINISTRATION 1984-1986

The period of 1984 to 1986 needs a little mention as it relates to the injection of the military power into the polity of the Nigerian civilian lives. It was not the place of the military to inject itself into the civilian politics. The first term of the civilian so-called second republic had been shaken at best. The civilian rulership had taken leave of their senses and were oblivious to the history of what happened to the first republic. Having been out of power for so long, the civilian governments both at the centre and state houses indulged themselves with monetary allocations for projects intended for the country. Open display of currency holdings became commonplace among the politicians. Even Chief Awolowo was handsomely paid by the state government his Unity Party of Nigeria controlled.

Muhammadu Buhari

Many of the state and federal members of the legislative bodies were caught with money laundering. The same behaviors would repeat themselves by the interim civilian state governments under the military dictator president Gen. Ibrahim Babangida in an experimental stage of return of the federal government to the civilian leadership. This kind of reckless disregard for probity exhibited by the civilian political class may have convinced the military of their lack of admission of guilt in squandering the finances of the nation with ignominy.

Yet, one must pay tribute to the works embarked upon by the corrective military government of Muhammadu Buhari-Tunde Idiagbon. The Buhari Idiagbon's government wanted to correct the indiscipline it thought had consumed the nation. They decided to re-orient the civilians to observe the civilized and egalitarian, disciplined code of conduct for the country.

However, the veering of the duo in its crusade to bring the finances of the country in order involving the military leadership members did not go well with the other military leaders used to doing whatever they wanted, regardless of the law of the nation. Most members of the military leadership felt very strongly that the law courts and laws of the nation were not meant for them, and would dare any civilian or military administration to bring them to book. There were also rumours of cocaine trafficking by the army chief of staff and his friends. For this reason, the Buhari-Idiagbon administration was short-lived. They were accused of high handedness and strict discipline and therefore, of human rights abuses.

What followed the coup d'etat spear-headed by the chief of staff, Nigerian Army, Gen. Babangida and Gen. Abacha, the principal military leaders the previous administration was gong to bring to book, has been the state of calamity, terror, unparalleled corruption and malaise to descend on the national psyche. Unparalleled disregard and the bursting of the Central Bank vault became the norm, converting the nation's money for personal spending at will.

THE BABANGIDA-ABACHA MILITARY DUO

Everyone, including those who benefited materially from the military regimes of Ibrahim Babangida and Sani Abacha, agreed that both regimes will go down in the Nigerian history as the worst regimes, civilian or military ever to impose itself on the Nigerian populace. The regimes saw to the plundering of the public funds and open corruption of civilian recruits brought in as face-savers. The Babangida regime was only a little better in civility, style and direction. The Sani Abacha regime had none of the above, but was exemplary in brutality and dared anyone to ask for accountability of his stewardship. Both military leaders were brought into the arena of governance by the connivance of none other person but the man who had to suffer from the same brutality he invited upon the nation because of lack of vision, planning and sense of understanding and/or plain foolishness –M.K.O. Abiola. By his close association with these hoodlums, Abiola had shown himself as a bird of the same feather. I doubt if the country would have been any better under Abiola, given his own personal lifestyle and his general disposition with the military.

Ibrahim Babangida

Chief Moshood Olawale Abiola was not given to dialogue either, and just because he is a civilian politician, his general being lacked focus other than his business acquisition. We might have sooner be prepared for a civilian dictator backed by the military muscle.

Sani Abacha

Until the valuable lessons of service and dedication are learned by our elite and learned population, corruption and self-service would continue to block the march forward because the largely uneducated population is yearning for leadership in the mode of progressive humanism. That hope has not been fulfilled. The politicians seen around clamoring for positions at this time from the first republic through the sojourn of the military interventions to the present horror are personified by Sani Abacha.

Alhaji Dasuki

Incompetence and pretence seem to be the order of the day. Paper qualification if worked for, while necessary and a yardstick for future measurement of discipline and dedication to service and orderliness, must not be the sole measurement of human personality. Because of the legacy of disservice and followership by dogma and civil service by rote, most lettered or literate Nigerians have had this inordinate ambition to rule or lead in any sphere of their lives within the country. This phenomenon which must be changed, crept into the psyche, almost becoming the norm, if not already the norm, because of the dulling of the senses from being able to appraise oneself critically as to one's real capabilities and why higher position of authority is desired. The patience, discipline, perseverance, tolerance and considerate deliberation, the same attributes exercised by Nigerians working and educated abroad, especially in the United States, Canada and the rest of Western Europe must be brought into practical use, if Nigeria will be rescued from falling into a bottomless abyss. We would go through a walking tour of our situations as we have them physically staring at us right now from more than two decades to the present.

PROGNOSIS FOR THE FUTURE

Now that we have diagnosed the problem, we have to look at the various symptoms presented by the patient – Nigeria. The following presentations, offering what needs to be fixed and how it could be, depends on the willingness of the citizenry, from all walks of life and endeavors. Let us take a few steps back two decades hence and visualize what it would take in terms of determination and resolve to right the wrongs that have been done to this great nation, to its people by a few pretending "leaders."

I wish to state here that to look for the scapegoats and bicker about the righteousness of the rulership is not the answer. Such was embarked upon by the Sani Abacha regime. To do that would also bring Abacha and his entire family to question, and we would be going around the problem without getting to the solution.

Let us take a hard look at the situation at hand and put forward concrete plans devoid of ostentation and social-climbing solutions to the re-orientation of the nation. There's the African adage which states that we must chase away the fox to enable to chicken to thrive. A nation with no standardized health care plan, retirement plan for its citizens, despite the years of their service and no good housing and urban planning has no mouth in the comity of nations, let alone a chest to beat in proclaiming its greatness among equals.

Ken Saro- Wiwa
Early victim of Abacha's rule

Chief Ernest Shonekan

Coomassie, Abacha's Inspector
General of Police

As a first, the people must be willing to converge their thoughts and resolve. The people must take the reigns of government and instrument of power away from the guards – viz the armed forces whose job in the first place is for the security of the government of the people by the people and our borders. Any citizen in uniform if he or she desires to rule, must first remove the uniform of a security personnel and join the citizens at large before presenting himself for the position.

Lt. Gen. Diya

Our constitution must emphasize the above in no uncertain terms. Suspension of the nation's constitution must not be accepted by any law court in the nation. No one, I mean no citizens should dance to the whims and caprices of the armed forces because the military leadership is not the citizens' leadership. At the worst, the constitution must emphasize the steps that should be taken should our nation be thrown into turmoil of a constitutional crisis, as are taken by progressive nations all over the world. Even if a situation should arise as to cause the revulsion of the armed forces leadership, it could arrest the culprit, flagrant leadership and allow for temporary civilian management which should be barred from taking part in a new election that would install a new progressive leadership within a three month period. What is the situation we find now?

Maj. Gen. Olanrewaju

Maj. Gen. Adisa

CATALYSTS FOR DEMOCRATIC REVOLUTION

This situation is still confused. This situation is filthy and the whole business we call government is disappointingly uncoordinating. I've traveled through the country from the cities to towns and from the towns to villages, and there seems to be dismally lacking the presence of government. I know that the average conservative of the Western World would read this writing with a wonder in his mind as to why invite the government into the affairs of the people. To these I say thanks and no thanks for their comments of alarm. This place lacks the orderliness of purpose. The preparedness or the sign of it that we would witness in most Western and Eastern countries of this part of the century is not here! The newspapers are full of childish headlines and routine gossips about nothing.

The towns and the cities lack the planning expected of a modern nation. The villages and towns are chaotic in their settings. Bushes of brush- type spring up here and there, and as one travel from one town to the other, one is left with the feeling of travelling through one jungle to the other. To be sure, there are some unkempt farms a little distance from the so-called major roads. What is this? Would anyone contest this fact that this place is orderless? I have not spoken about the situation of our people. At this juncture, I feel nauseated and mad at the corrupt, blind and callous leadership of our country. Most of them have traveled out of this country, and I challenge them to tell the people that this way in which our people live is the way they would want to live. I know that most of these "leaders" grew up under these circumstances and having achieved the paper qualifications, they have moved into the neocolonial quarters and have damned the living conditions and situations of the so-called common people.

I saw the condemnation of the people to the mercies of the ruthless exploitation of the big and petty landlords who now form the upper and middle class strata among the unlettered masses. The white-collar workers are of course the immediate middle class and affluent workers of our society.

But one needs to point out that no one is looking for perfection as obtained in the Western countries. The landlords in Nigeria, having grappled with the living styles of our people, allowed any number of people to live in the rooms cut like cells, without any vocal indictment, although the rents paid seem to atone for this silence – of the situation. When we look at the rents paid, especially in the cities, compared with the cost of living of these unemanicipated workers, one feels a sense of disillusionment at the establishment of the institutions on the countries. The catchy slogans are so empty that they stink! By God! Whatever this mean, things are going in the completely wrong direction. Exploiters are enjoying the spoils of the people and the government – whatever government there is, seems to be operating in isolated stances and carrying out the suppression of anyone who dared criticize its performances. Criminal courts are jokes, and the judgements delivered are funny. The cases presented smacked of a people very close to nature in 1978! I have heard of complaints upon complaints, about how everything is going wrong and the fear expressed of the unknown calamities or disaster, if you will, which periodically visit with the people who live according to the natural law of chaos and disorderliness. Fools have been given the reins of power, and the wise, being timid or arrogant or chauvinistic, have been reduced to servants of the former's order. Misplaced priorities are commonplace. And, if you put this up to the so-called authorities, you will be labelled as the one to be harassed.

Nothing seems to work here. The hydroelectric plant left by the whites and built by their designs now give trouble, and we have not been able to effect proper troubleshooting techniques. As a result, electric power supplied by the National Electric Power Agency (Authority) depends on sheer luck for the population.

Frequent and incessant power failure is a common occurrence and part of power failure is a common occurrence and part of the routine life we lead here. Now, can anyone claim the contrary to our living very close to nature in 1978?

The preceding note constitutes the one aspect of the disorderliness of our nation. The other aspect and most profound and fundamental in the life of a nation and her inhabitants is health.

This place is unhygienic and sickening! How can anyone imagine that everything is all right here when a family of six ill-clad people with varying ailments huddle in a room in which they seem condemned! Any wonder that the country products so many dunces and raw heads called the members of the professions. Any wonder that the so-called academicians have abandoned researches and indulged in plagiarism and copy-writing for cheap and quick promotions up the ladder of academic institutions. All of this stems from the tired brains and useless and fatigued faculty which, unable to meet the challenge of academia, has turned to cheap thoughts of acquiring money and property. The health of this nation is at stake. Any wonder that our leaders, though relatively young, are fatigued and uninspiring?

The diagnosis has been nothing more than the ill-health that has accompanied and eaten through us from birth (thanks to the multiple development of immunity) to adulthood. But, immunity has not helped us overcome the unfortunate incapability of our brain cells which perhaps due to disease (viral or otherwise) or to social pressures have been deprived of acute alertness and development and agility in combating the present woes and decay of the present development. We shall refrain from arguing about a handful of individuals who constitute an extremely negligible percentage of this vast population. Those individuals will be the privileged few. Now, let me bring us to the simple illustration which we all know and the so-called modern health care embodied in government health institutions. Do we have adequate and modern health care? How about the number of the sick; is this reasonable?

Too much has been written on the quality and organizational set-up of our hospitals. Somehow, for the complaints to be effectively settled or satisfactorily corrected, there's need for the disbandment of the present bureaucratic machine. How confused could a nation be! A "developing" nation at that, without the proper focus on the development priorities? If we at this period of the 20th century still have misplaced priorities, we had better invite recolonization, which, of course, is an ominous and disturbing statement. The nation is sick, and the leaders are ignorant. The masses, though more intelligent and of better capabilities than their "leaders," are disorganized and lack the clear thinking capabilities and training required for effective take over. I know I will incure a barrage of insult from the disgruntled academicians who will feign "unfairness" on their characters and their "unearned" integrity. I ask for revulsion and admission of guilt and a willingness to rise to combat the filthy situation.

PROVOCATIVE REASONINGS OF OUR EDUCATED, CERTIFICATED MEMBERS OF THE PROFESSIONS AND INTELLIGENTSIA

A brief digestion of the recent history of our people since the colonial period to the present situation may suffice to throw the much needed light on the darkening shades of our behavior and reactions to situations and problems which have arisen and have been devoid of understanding by the simple-minded members of the so-called intelligentsia. But, before I continue on this aspect of decay of our society, I want my reader to note that I do not intend to lay all the blame on the imperialist British colonialists and the bourgeois-minded feudalists of our societies. But, most importantly, I wish to state that the exploitation of this character in our people is to the detriment of our progress politically and socially (by our people I am going to make categorical generalization), I mean the people of Africa.

Because primitive feudalism had existed, the colonialists substituted selective education of the "elite" family to dominate over the rest of the masses. Now the Britons are gone; yet we still have colonial yoke all over us – the selective education still continues and this time shows itself along the line of economism. Our members of intelligentsia, fashionable and with pomp, state that amass education is "impossible," "ridiculous" and will deny them of their hold on the society. We would be opening too much of the coveted "prestige" to the lowest member of our society. But, who are these new "elite" who cry about Socialist form of government as being the enemy of the Nigerian people? Who are these "nouveau riches" in our societies? Were these people not the upstart of yesterday who, by a stroke of luck, survived the malicious exploitation in the hands of the British and American, and German and French racists? Were thee not the same people who performed manual labor in the capitals of the imperialist West in the name of paper education? Were these not the same people who now cry about opening educational opportunities to the masses but now find it too open? Let us tackle the initial history of the colonial period and examine how far we have moved since 1955 – the beginning of the internal self-rule at the whim of British liberalism. By the date and period stated above, I am referring to the Nigerian self-rule or self-government under the supervision of the British appointed governors.

I dare anyone to disprove the facts that are stated below that this period represented the modern raping of our society by the neo-colonialist stooges of the society of which they are members. The period, of course, started the beginning of the cliques of opportunist of wanton creation of their much dreamed of feudal society. It would not have struck with amazement these people being members of the rich "elite" in the traditional setting. But these "nouveau riches" were people who had stowed away on the ship, people who had been subjected to the worst treatment before they could have the "education" in the white-esteemed institutions of higher learning. These upstarts now found themselves loving their exploiters more than the exploiters love themselves. They now love the system created to benefit the rich left by the imperialists. Needless to say, from all these accounts that these people, these so-called leaders of the people, lack imagination of their own on how to improve the lot of their people.

We will devote more time to this situation of brain-washing in a later writing.

WHAT MEANING ADVANCED EDUCATION SHOULD HOLD FOR A BACKWARD PEOPLE

For a backward people, education and, in particular, advanced education should mean more than the mere acquisition of a piece of paper called diploma or degree. I advance this notion because what is obtained here is self-evident and, unless our philosophy and reason for the acquisition of the advanced Western scientific education chan+ge, it is meaningless for our ding-dong race to acquire it. If that acquisition will reflect nothing of our contribution to improve the lot of our people in Africa, I think very passionately it is useless work as we theorize in physics to strive for the piece of paper called certificate of achievement.

First of all, what has been our general attitude to this Western-oriented education? I will reply that our educational aspirations have been limited to the acquisition of the certificate after which we settle down to rot and fool ourselves by calling ourselves "educated". You ask an average college student of our nation what his/her aim is, the reply would make you blush, if you can, at the limited and narrow scope of his interpretation of his educational attainment.

The goal is limited, and therefore, the honest inquirer does not have too far to go or explore. Our average college or university student wants to obtain his Bachelor of Arts of Science degree for a bigger slice of money. He may proceed to obtain a post graduate degree after which he starts to "enjoy life." No element of creativity is left in him after that acquisition of the "ivory tower" they call education. Listen, I never refused to explore the other reasons for his problems and why his determination has not been expanded beyond this narrow path. But, I say, whatever his reasons, they do not justify his reactions.

ON RELIGION DOGMA OF EVERY PERSUASION

Point to a simple-minded, brain-washed individual and show him his method of thinking and his ways of action merited the adjectives above, and you will find yourself mortally locked in a combat. If Bishop Muzorewa accepts that he is a puppet of the Ian-Smith and British colonialists, there would be no problem in Zimbabwe. But, we have problems in Zimbabwe because Bishop Abel T. Muzorewa does not accept the facts recognized by the rest of he world, even by the most backward leaders of Nigerian government that he is brain-washed, simple-minded and a neo-colonialist stooge of the British government who must obey the whites to murder and hold his people in servitude to the white man. No, has anyone seen the picture of combat that has ensued between the Muzorewa, Sithole, Chirau clique on the one side and the forces of progress led by Mugabe and Nkomo, the patriotic front, on the other?

The same argument above is advanced here. Tell an African Christian of his ignorance for following Christianity, and you will hear arrant nonsense never been told before even by the white men who brought the religion in the first palce.

Tell a Muslim of our continent or, in fact, of Nigeria that his Islamic beliefs have out-lived their usefulness, and you will be insulted for calling him ignorant. Now, we have dealt to some extent on the colonial character of the Christian religion. We will now deal with the outdated Islamic philosophies from the beginning of its inception to the outdated usefulness and consequently why its character seems to smack of Christianity and why the philosophies are similar and merited rejection along with Christian faith – that neither is the answer to the current economic problem facing the people.

This invariably drags us into a question that will be asked by the simple- minded, one-track-minded, certificated member of the profession who should know better, but is more confounded than the ordinary people, the cause of whom he claims to champion. Let me state here categorically and for the education of the masses that I am not a religionist, and I have no belief in any organized religion. I have read the Koran and the Bible and have grounds to disagree with the mysteries both books seem to emphasize. But, disbelief in any of the two existing organized religious doctrines does not mean being an atheist. I believe in the supreme God Almighty by whom man is created and endowed. This supreme conscious mind enables man to affirm or reject a proposition. This same consciousness has for duality a subconscious disposition which allows for his (man's) creativity.

Let any religious leader bring home his challenge against our position, and we shall examine his careful thoughts (if they are original thoughts). We shall answer him upon his merited presentation. The reason for our rejection has, to some extent been advanced partially with regard to Christianity, but the rejection of Islamic philosophy has not been fully explained, and its interpretation by the ordinary people has not been fully explored here before – if there are backward instances. I am not running a cheap popularity contest, therefore, I think I owe it to the people of this continent to enumerate our thoughts on this matter without fear or favor having cognizance for the arguments this unpopular piece may generate. The Islamic religion and its philosophy should be looked at from the following three general areas. (1) Socialism, (2) Economic and (3) Social effects.

The fact that Islamic religion preaches and seems to have stressed and enforced selflessness, irrespective of the individuals' cleverness at amassing wealth, makes it a candidate for a free enterprise philosophy. The equally of worship and its total relegation of personality safe spirituality in practice argues well for the identification of the common man with the religion to a greater or lesser extent. But, this aspect enumerated yet leaves the individual open for dogmastic servitude of the self-styled knowledgeable clergy – of the faith.

The enforcement and preaching of a visit to Mecca in the Middle East and its enshrinement in the five laws of Islam makes one wonder at the design. Poor people's money and foolish government leaders, or deceptive government leaders, which encourage the Hadji have made Saudi Arabia a rich country from tourism. The fact that since the oil-exploration and discovery, the visit of the believes has been curtailed by the authorities demonstrates the realities which were never thought of before. Now the Saudi, realizing more money from the oil revenue would soon ban the influx of the pilgrims from the poor countries so that the new-found wealth may not be drained or over-burdened in the face of welfarism or swindled which may rob the country (Saudi Arabia) of its hard and esteemed monetary system.

The people (ordinary or low intelligent or emotional) of all creeds still purporting significance of the Hadji pilgrimage need fierce re-education. One at any rate and in all fairness must consider the basic reasoning behind the religious fervor of all types. Where governments or leadership have failed to improve the lot of the people, despair and a state of hopelessness set in and the people, looking for salvation or relief of their economic burdens, grapple for religion.

We try to show that attack is not merely on the Christian religion which was given strength by the ineptitude of 'headers' and governments which sought refuge under the yoke of these various religious dogmas to hide their lack of resolve and courage. We shall state here that it these leaders led by the consent of the led, they must not condone the ignorance of the people but show the people the path of truth and enlightenment, however unpopular they may seem from some quarters of their societies. It is a well-known dictum that a leader by his nature is ahead of his people. He is apt and acute in in-depth thinking of the solution to the general malaise of his people and usually enhances their respect even in posterity.

I wish to state here that I am yet to find a true Socialist, a true believer in people, who would be so faint-hearted as to become a religious puppet. Action of leaders of the people and those especially progressive ones are not immediately reasoned by the populace, hence, the necessity of leaders to adequately explain their programs honestly and with clarity to the people they lead, pointing out the merits and requirements of the programs for full realization of their goals.

To the extent that Islamic leaders use Islam as an instrument of instability and backwardness to the stone Age exposes them as exploiters of human sentiments and emotions for their own selfish ends. In Africa, we cannot and we must not allow these sentiments to continue to hold us down in servitude to the colonialism of the Western Europeans and America and the colonialism of our brothers of Middle Eastern sphere of Arab descent or Persian descent. I declare that no one holds exclusive rights to the Creator's presence. No one can interpret the Creator's will for the people than the socialist-minded who strive for full emancipation of God's of Allah's own people. To the extent that the gulf between the people is irrationally widened economically in the name of religion or any other pretentious disposition is to the extent that we reject it wholesomely.

Until the people of Africa start to believe in themselves and not in some colonial Western investor and/or some shelks or religious fervor for salvation, we will continue to be pawns in the hands of the super powers, most especially those of the West. Because this state of backwardness exists in our people, it makes it a catalystic situation that must be changed by socialist-minded leaders of the people.

THE INFRASTRUTURE AND OUR FEUDAL CHARACTER

We have dealt with religion, I mean organized religions of various creeds, to a length, and we have examined the colonial and feudal characters in all and the generating economic impact and the bane to progress engendered in all. Now, let us deal in substantial terms with 'modern' African feudal characteristics which, combined with Western European imported bureaucracy and its genealogy, which has endured hitherto our changing lives and changing geopolitical stance of our time.

We must deal with this aspect and examine it with clarity of mind its contribution to our progress in this latter part of the twentieth century. Let us look at its merits and its demerits and call ourselves both individually and collectively to attention and judge ourselves with a personal progress chart using not our village environment but the progressive world as a point of reference, or we would not need to complain and have acute or chronic sense of frustration. We shall present three events of recent times in Nigeria, and we will reason with the term of these events whether they inflame our conscience and heighten our revolutionary aspirations or they beat us to servitude and acquiescence.

1. The Agbekoya Uprising of 1968

The catalyst which manifested itself in the uprising of the farmers of Yoruba land is an accumulation of chronic neglect of the plight of the poor

A PARADE OF OKADA OPERATORS 1978

and down trodden. This actually marks the first revolutionary uprising in the country. The poor farmers took up arms and demanded redress having been disillusioned by the Farmer's Trade Union Organization which took a bourgeois character with limited demands from the government. The farmers' uprising took about four weeks to put down. It forced the government to negotiate limited settlement, having failed to forcefully quench the uprising. But, lack of organized revolutionary vanguard brought down the armed insurrection of the people. Alas, the revolution failed to garner the necessary far-reaching stance, plus the compromising corruption of the leadership.

2. The Incessant University Uprising and Riot of 1971 – 1981

Let us look at the student uprisings and disrespect for the bourgeois and feudal governments of Nigeria in the proper perspective. These uprisings were results of heavy-handed and autocratic attitudes of the people in the governments. Policies and enactments of them were never discussed with those affected, and all actions smacked of spontaneity and had no regard for the affected people's disposition. Seeing no other way for redress, the students resorted to violence and because of a lack of proper training and youthful exuberance, their demands were thrown out by the better organized bourgeois members of the elite class which form the bulk of the people in government. Judiciary is for the rich and the elite. The system is bourgeois-oriented, and that's saying it all for the verdict or judgments that will be passed on the situation.

In this decade, the student uprising started with the pronouncements and insults showered on the students of the Benin Institute of Technology by the then Commissioner for Education in the then Mid-West State, Mr Edwin Clark, over the provision of adequate meals for the undergraduate students. This was the same reason which led to the death of a university undergraduate of Aberdeen University in the Military Administration.

Then came Col. Alli's turn – a medical doctor by training, and we shall not say that this gentleman is not well read if we go by the letters, yet his action leaves much to be desired. The measures taken were almost apocalyptic. The actions showed heavy-handedness in all facets.

Let us, for a moment, ponder on the reason for these various uprisings in Nigeria. If the disposition of the people were economically viable or stable, they could easily have confidence in the future, I doubt if these occurrences would have the various magnitudes exuded. The selective education and the accompanying nepotism makes the acquisition a privilege rather than a right of every citizen or the under-privilege to be in this circle of "elite" of the society.

Here lies the dubious continuity of action that has been guiding this nation before and since "independence" from the colonial rule. That arrogance of power constitutes the feudal character in us. It is in the privileged "educated elite" of our society and the smart, fast money-maker and not so educated elite of the same society. All in one, acquisition of wealth has become the yardstick of measurement of the worth and intelligence of any member of that society fundamentally, if I may say, but I have not yet seen us moving away from it.

THE VIEWS OF THE SO-CALLED CONSERVATIVES OF SOUTH AFRICA

Mr M. Buthelezi, the Chief of Zulus, would want the people to believe that he's not a white conservative puppet. He will argue that he has an independent thinking mind. Yes, like everyone that is alive, we all have independence from other people or events. But the mark of greatness is when an individual could realize that his thinking is flawed by many factors, most especially the realities of situations and an admission that one is lacking in the assessment of his strategy.

People could be blinded by inordinate personal ambition or the need to prove that they posses or have some following or influence to be reckoned with. That personal ambition has driven quite a few men to destruction of their people and themselves too. The failures of these men to realize their puppet roles have left them distasteful to right and deep-thinking populace over whom they wanted to rule. We have had such individuals in Mobutu Sese of Zaire, Jones Savimbi of Angola, Moise Tsombe and a host of others to mention a few. Gusu Buthelezi has now joined the first of the infamy.

Nelson Mandela

There was no African in South Africa who was conservative and not a white puppet. The view of the black conservative was the apartheid's or disciple of that horrendous system which the West was treating with kid gloves. As long as the people oppressed are non-white, the West will continue to look the other way. The vitriolic Margaret Thatcher would, of course, find something kind to say about apartheid. The progressive and freedom-fighters of the ANC, of course, met with Maggie's wrath and disgust. How dare African people fight for freedom and independence? This was not the first time the British conservative Prime Minister would hypocritically cry or acquiesce to the cry of apocalypse whenever African freedom fighters take up arms to fight for the control of their own destiny. Even then, after the struggle is won, various acts of connivance, intrigues are contrived to dash the hopes of the oppressed people – remember Zimbabwe's struggle for freedom from the white settles and the subsequent civil unrest that was created and fueled by the unseen hands of the West. Thank God for the wisdom and management displayed by Robert Mugabe, the Zunbabwe president.

For smooth reviving of the country, a lot depends on how the people themselves are willing to work hard, reduce Western interference and Western dependency. So far, the government of Robert Mugabe has shown itself up to the task. Essential infrastructure is being maintained and a people who had been neglected over the centuries have now taken their position among the comity of nations.

THE COMING TOGETHER OF THE EAST AND WEST: I FEAR FOR THE FUTURE OF THE AFRICAN CONTINENT AND HER DESCENDANT THIRD WORLD NATIONS

It would have been a thing of joy. It could have been an occasion for celebration, despite the breathless pace it assumed. How joyful it would have been had it not been the shades and colours it all assumed. I am speaking of the coming together of the East and West and the attending ramifications when all gauntlets are thrown down.

For the not-so-informed and the swim-along, small-minded bureaucrats of the Third World, there's more than meet the eye for his/her future in the final analysis. But, what does it all mean? What lies ahead? What will be the gain of the Third World governments? What will be the interest of the individual Third World person? Who cares about the future of these people who call themselves people of color? How are they going to grapple with this new dawn? We could ask thousands of questions without one common answer to satisfy the yearning of the people. But, ask we must or leave ourselves in quandary.

When we talk about people of color, we have included all people different and culturally so, from the Caucasians. The unification of people of color is of paramount importance before they are divided against themselves by their common enemy – the imperialist West. This point will addressed in the next article.

First of all, I want to state that the existence of the Socialist Russia paved the way for the quick release of the colonies from the Western imperialists. The so-called independent Third World nations of Africa owe so much so that existence bred the emergence of a socialist order. The "independence" of the Latin American countries, which never before now were thriving, will now be doomed to deep freeze. With the people acutely paralysed educationally and assaulted by cynicism and penetrated by the C.I.A. and enormous brain-washing the picking apart of each of the nations was all but an easy exercise. Anyone who doubts the above statement should recount Chile and lately Panama. The new leadership enthroned and aided by the C.I.A. now sounded like the quasi-capitalists drumming out capitalist themes of economics which they know so little about and which they are powerless to control. So far, the exception to this rule in the Latin Americas and the Caribbean is the Socialist Nation of Cuba. But, even this has not escaped the negative machination of the U.S. Witness the C.I.A. arranged assault or invasion of Cuba in 1962 to kill the emergence of the strong Cuba in its infancy of revolution. When that failed, there has been the staging of various economic blockades and sabotage to the point that most puppet regimes of the other Latin American countries were forbidden to trade with Cuba. Anyone of these regimes that dared disobey the master to the North risked, and risks destabilization and removal from office through the all-pervading machinery already mentioned. The North American government and press would conveniently ignore the various barriers they have put in the way of any progressive national leadership of the Latin American aspiring to be truly independent, while pointing to the "economic failures" and "repressive" natures of such countries. These blatant frauds could only convince the ill-formed conniving collaborator.

The antagonism with which the US. and the Western imperialists look at any dissenting nations of the Third World knows no bound. It does not matter how big or small that nation is. Here with one hand, it would preach democracy with the Western European countries, but will refuse to aid or grant the same status to the Third World countries. If the Third World nations have illusions as to where they stood with the Western imperialist, the advent of the Reagan Administration should dispel that notion forthwith. More than any administration before it, the Reagan Administration bared its hand and teeth.

The coming together of the East and West never quite caught insightful people off guard. We have always been suspicious of the ineptitude of the practitioners of socialism since the departure of Vladmire Hyich Lenin and the cultist Stalin took up the mantle recruiting various inept sycophants. But, the paranoia of Stalin helped "free" the colonies from the grip of the colonial Western rules. And this is when the help ended. Otherwise, how can inept masters help any upcoming young leadership? The departure of V.I. Lenin left a big gash in the wound of the world – and the misery of the down-trodden, ordinary people of the world.

Now, the world has to contend with the hypocrisy of the U.S. and Britain–always a willing tool in the plunder of Third World resources. A case in point of the blatant hypocrisy is the opposition mounted against the Heng Samrin government of Cambodia in favor of the murderous Khmer Rouge regime of Pol Pot and a lackluster Prince Sihanouk who was previously deposed by the C.I.A. during the infamous expansion of the Vietnam War when Lo1 No1 was put in power. The claim against Hend Samrin was that benevolent government or not, progressive government or not, he was helped to power by a foreign military power. What is the US. doing not in Panama? Who certified Endara as the winner of any election? The complicity of the US. in the election was well known. But, what is a defeated, invaded people to do but pretend by all means to love the occupying invading power?

The background to the seemingly getting together of the Eastern and Western powers has been hinted or predicted. The East has to capitulate in the face of economic impossibility. The West has been accusation to the hypocrisy of life more abundantly. Never mind the increase in timelessness, large school drop-outs and all, as long as a few continue to make it, that number will be made the representative affluent of the entire society. The defense budget was set so high that in the attempt of the Soviet government to match it, the planned economic system crashed. With the Soviet Union unable to get her economic house in order, she soon lost the confidence of most of the Third World nation who must endure the continuing economic assault set forward by the Reagan Administration which did away with the caution of the previous administrations before it.

The destruction set on the Third Word nations was not a rash decision. It was a calculated, well-orchestrated design. Progressive thinking leaders of the Third World, even in the mode of the Western capitulation, were replaced by inept and corrupt ones – who, through greed and selfishness, destroyed the fragile economy but were allowed to sustain an illusion by the West giving or granting loans to these corrupt leaderships in the name of a people not allowed to participate in the planning of their economic future. The cost of debt-servicing is weighing heavily on the people of the Third World nations and derided by the white Westerners that this is what they should have known in their fate (appendages to the Western government). The eighties were then designated the decade of pride for the West, and the opposite terminology must be applied to the Southern impoverished nations of the Third World.

The Third World of the yellow pigmentation was left to some extent to their own fate (because of difficulty of understanding their culture and moves). Stumbling measures were erected to limit their advancement one way or another. Those Asians, being not wholly colonized by the Western imperialist over a great period of time, maintained and continue to maintain their ancient culture and religion to a larger degree. Assaults on these institutions continue, nevertheless, through the same old route–Christian religion Japanese, Chinese and the rest of the Southern East Asians must guard against this imposition, or their discipline – a la culture –will be eroded and dismantled. No one will ever find a Caucasian bearing an African or Chinese or Japanese name for that matter. Few may be less demagogic, but with these negligible few, one must wonder about the motive if it is not part of the grand design for "intelligence gathering."

Western (I mean people of European descent) people never really allow African people or their dependents to live in peace wherever they (the Europeans) ate in majority. It is, therefore, short-sighted and stupid for any African people, or for that matter any people of colour in the world, to allow the Europeans to establish a beach on any of the native territory. The principle of expropriation of other people's land has never been abandoned by the Europeans. The rise (you would say and come back to it) of the Socialist doctrine or ideology which became an alternate avenue where oppressed people could obtain ammunition for modern warfare weapons en masse pave the way for the rapid independence of most African nations after World War II. Now, the East and the West are coming together, blurring ideologies and making the world order to return to status of Now, our religion as being ridiculed (a la Noriega with voodoo practice). The same religion which President Reagan practiced and is still practicing for years is being used as a pretext to brand the African who practices the religion of his forefathers as a bad man worthy of death by the hypocritical moralists. Am I to tell you her that witchcraft was not new to the Western World? Astrology is an outgrowth of such practices and is very much revered today in these capitals.

THE CASE AGAINST NORIEGA OF PANAMA

Manuel Noriega was supposed to be stupid. He was supposed to be selling out his fellow down-trodden barrios of Latin America. For a long while, he seemed to play that role well. He was then moved up the ladder for informants. He became the connector – connecting the Latino leaders with the powerful movers and shakers of Washington. Then came the drugs. Afterward Omar Torrijos, the general commanding the Panamanian Defense Force, forced the Panana Canal treaty on the U.S. The treaty was signed for Panana to take charge of the canal from 1997–and consequently her destiny. Even though this did not go down too well with the right-wing while supremacists of the U.S.A., the overriding concern was money and how to get a piece of the action, of the new gold–cocaine from Latin America. General Omar Torrijos was too nationalistic in the view of the C.I.A. and its influential members (employees). Torrijos must be eliminated. Noriega would not do the job. He could not organize any successful putsch against a popular Torrijos. Therefore, he must be helped Besides, Noriega was loyal to Torrijos sometimes. Torrijos' place was blown up in the sky, and this paved the way for General Noriega to take command of the P.D.F. In this new position, General Noriega became the conduit for drug money laundering for the movers and shakers of Washington, California and Texas. They had more than their full at the onset of the Reagan Administration. Money was everywhere. Meanwhile, the domino effect must not be allowed to materialize in Latin America. Nicaragua must be harassed until she abandons her progressive march. Washingtong needs more of General Noriega. The Somosa family was a good one. Duvalier in the Caribean was another good one to Washington. The cover-up was, and is still, democracy. El Salvador, Honduras, Nicaragua and, yes, Panama must remain squalid and impoverished, with pockets of corrupt puppet military officers who push for power for the drug trafficking money to be amassed from the company, the C.I.A.

Actually, the case against General Manuel Noriega is not so much about drugs or anything else, but an example to other ill-prepared Third World leaders that they can forget any notion of independence of thoughts or opinions as they govern their respective states or nations. They must take as gospel truth the directions they are being led by the nit-wits in Washingtong, D.C. One should only wonder about the intent if not the aforementioned, considering the proliferation of drug distribution and selling inside the United States of America. If the U.S. government could have no regards for Pananma's sovereignty and the human rights of the people there, in the name of the "war against drugs," the same reasoning should be applied to internal clean up. No, it could not. The imperialist government needs the home support to continue its aggression abroad. Especially if the drug trafficking is largely carried out by the WASP drug lords. The point of the matter is which Anglo-Saxon America needs for whipping boys. If it is not the non-white Americans, nor the African- Americans, then it must be the foreign non-Anglo-Sacon nations under one pretext or another.

No nation is angelic in their policies, but there are ways these national governments could be nudged to open up their systems for their people's benefit and progress, especially economically. No, these poor, oppressed people of the Third World classification must be kicked in the groin while they are down because their unchosen leaders refuse to play lackeys one way or another. These poor people with no weapons and organization are called upon to overthrow the tyrant who happens to hold all the cards, with weapons, organization and you name it. If they would not, they are to blame.

But, let me give credit where it is earned. There have been occasions where the West, nay the US., Britain, has risen to the occasion like after the massive slaughter of Muslim citizens of Bosnia. The rationale to help here again is economic self-interest. Fearing that the Moslem people of Bosnia would be badly radicalized and consequently cause untold havoc in Western Europe to businesses which may be moved by the barons in Britain, Germany, the U.S. and France – through sabotage and all. Until the selfish ways are abandoned and selflessness and "food Christian" conscience takes over, the world would never know peace. Life is different now, and, yes, turmoil and distrust will continue.

Finally, the consequences of the East meeting the West will unfold as we move along, and the trouble is borne by the poor people of the world. Their economic plight will determine the survival or destruction of the world order as it should be. But there is still hope somewhere – if greed, selfishness and would domination philosophy do not snuff out the ray.

REAGAN'S LIBYAN ACTION BRINGS BACK THE COLONIALBULLY, AGGRESSION MEMORY

It is nothing new. It has been going on for years, i.e., the subjugation and intimidation of the developing world people, including their leaders. Only the providence of nature and sheer population explosion have rescued otherwise peaceful people from the throes of the so-called developed. Western European democracies, championed by the United States of America. Unfortunately, few of the Third World people, including their leaders, fully learned the dangers posed to their very existence by these Western democracies. Secretly, it almost feels that the Western government would wish the people of the Third World, where natural resources abound, disappear from the face of the earth and allow them to enjoy the bounties. Otherwise, the occupation of these lands and the expropriation and exploitation of the resources would not have been for so long, nor so severe.

Libya and its leader, Muamma Quadaffi, should have known that in the absence of strong defense capabilities and development comparable to the super powers, you cannot thump your chest and champion the cause of your downtrodden and oppressed fellow Third World, where natural resources abound, disappear from the face of the earth and allow them to enjoy the bounties. Otherwise, the occupation of these lands and the expropriation and exploitation of the resources would not have been for so long, not so severe.

Libya and its leader, Muammar Quadaffi, should have known that in the absence of defence capabilities and development comparable to the super powers, you cannot thump your chest and champion the cause of your downtrodden and oppressed fellow Third World brothers and sisters. This is by no means the championing of

Muammar Quadaff's cause. A better way could be devised to have dialogue with the military ruler of Libya. What we disagree with is the arrogance and callous manner with which the plight and frustrations of the Third World nations are treated.

In the past, there might have been some kind of trepidation, but with the newly-found conservative revolution, all caution and considerate feelings are thrown to the wind. Many of the Third World countries are experiencing tremendous brain drain which, if unchecked, might prove to be catastrophic in the long run.

Even with the death (murder) of his daughter during the US air raid on Quadaffi, there was no apology given. The US considered a display of remorse for the death of that innocent child to be a sign of weakness rather than strength.

Unfortunately, now Third World countries' leaders, because of their thirst for personal material acquisition, have put service to their people in the far back seat. Their countries continue to rot away while they live a lie and illusion. Individual riches within a sea of rot is translated to rot. Before I degress further, the US should realize that should Africa be treated with ignominy further and be allowed to rot away, the stench may yet travel across the Atlantic and envelope all those who would prefer the life of illusion to reality.

LET ME ADD MY TWO CENTS: DISCUSSING AFFIRMATIVE ACTION IN THE US.

Caucasian Americans and the "Oreo" African Americans always make me laugh. Not because they are necessarily conical, but because they live in delusion and believe in the correctness of their flawed argument on affirmative action. The Caucasians lead and their "Oreos" follow. Their argument from day one of assault is already won, and even when renewed, could only attract the following of the idiotic masses of the nit- witted, selfish, conceited, ignoramuses which unfortunately populate this great land mass.

President Bill Clinton

Therefore, the rejection of further appearances of opponents to affirmative by John Hope Franklin, President Clinton's Chairman of Advisory Panel, should be applauded. He did away with hypocrisy and charade for the first time in the annals of bureaucracy. Now he is vilified for not continuing the charade and illusion of listening to the opponent of Affirmative Action in a "debate" of argument. (See New York Times, November 22, 1997).

Now, Abigail Thernstrom, the "genius," Oreos or Caucasians for all I care, must lead the change against affirmative action. She tried to be impressive by citing several derogatory statistics about the drop out rates of African Americans in a California college. She never mentioned any statistics in Massachusetts. Of course,

Massachusetts never admits a less deserving African American to its colleges, therefore, that citation may negate her argument.

But for reasons best known to California college admissions officials, they have been coached on how to survey the vast majority of Caucasians and away along the otherwise well-meaning African Americans into an outrage against their less privileged compatriots. The orchestration and assault on the sensibilities of this unsuspecting black intelligence having been successful is allowed to unravel and divide the people against themselves. Here's the trick! You pack the college with low-grade African American youths with nothing in place to upgrade their preparedness for a college education. With robotic counseling, the youth are thrown to the full blow of college courses which they are ill-prepared for. The advice may be to the contrary before the students were admitted. It is no accident that these young people, given their disposition, could succumb to the drop- out statistics.

With the anticipation in place, a young or older Caucasian would be resurrected to fight a "hero" battle of a victim of reverse discrimination, having been told that his or her rejection for admission the previous year was to make room for that African American in order for the college to comply with the government-ordered affirmative action. What a splendid connivance and manipulation – (sic) Allan Bakke and Taxman, the former case in California and the latter in New Jersey. How wonderful this concoction we mix to be accepted as the ideal potion to be swallowed by all, including the "learned" justices of the American Supreme Court. Apart from the fact that these judges are politically appointed, they often fail to question the kinds of evidence they are presented and the methods for the gathering of such evidence. Neither did they ever question the motif behind the design and the reasoning behind the evidence offered to the plaintiff by the various institutions in resolving these affirmative action cases.

I think enough is said for now! I will add my two cents in the future or at any other time when outraged enough. Everyone living in U.S.A. is not fooled by the process of its law.

THE GULF WAR: SUPPRESSION OF IRAQ AND THE LARGER RAMIFICATIONS FOR THE DEVELOPING AND NON-WHITE NATIONS OF THE WORLD

The Gulf War between the active Western powers and the tacit support by the US surrogate government of Saudi Arabia, Omar and Egypt on one side and the government of Iraq on the other side, rather than being a principled war or one fought over high morals, was a war based on the manifestation of the culmination of a 30-year-old plan by the US imperialist power to affect a presence military in the Gulf and using a perfect alibi – Saddam Hussein – to implement such design.

It all escalated by the snarling tongue of George Bush, the imperialist coalition leader ordering the withdrawal of the Iraqi troops from Kuwait, knowing full well that no such order would be obeyed quickly by any leader of any country without a showdown. They (Western, especially US leaders) knew perfectly well that such an ordering tone was provocative and would meet a recalcitrant stance. Having set the tone, they proceeded to twist arms in the Arabian peninsula. With different tactics of belligerence, rewards and threats, a coalition was formed, based on forced alliance and with the support of blackmailing propaganda against the Iraqi leadership. All of a sudden, Saddam Hussein did everything from raping of every man's wife to the damaging of every man's toilet bowl in the US. No one could breathe without thinking of Saddam's power of manipulation of the air. The hate mongering against the Iraqi leadership, having been personalized by Mr Bush, set the stage for the onslaught against the people of Iraq. The events that led to the invasion of Kuwait were ignored and totally blanked off the pages of the US and Western newspapers. The events that followed saw the blatant extortionist tactics against the governments of industrial powers which tried to be reasonable. Protection money was demanded from Germany and Japan unless they were willing to commit troops to the Gulf – and participate in the destruction of Iraq.

Having manipulated the Soviet leadership into accepting an illusory promise of consumer commodities in abundance once it dropped its defense of the Socialist principle and noting that it had wrought damage and driven a wedge against the Soviet people and its leadership, the US realized that a determined response to its hegemony and expansionism in the Gulf could go forward unchallenged. The Soviet Union was blackmailed into accepting the Western-style dictatorship which the leadership (Soviet) is ill-equipped to master and introduce to a people who for decades have been socialist oriented. Before the Soviet leadership realized that the smoke screen was towards the dismembering of its parts, it was almost too late. Luckily they recouped, but it would not be completed until Gorbachev was removed and fresh leadership was introduced.

The events which led to the war are well known. Though Saddam Hussein had been known to be the most brutal of the military dictators in the Middle East, the United States had closed its eyes to the atrocities the man was committing against his own people in order to stay in power. He had wasted or squandered the resources of his nation pursuant of non- benefiting causes in the strengthening of his hold on power. As long as Saddam was a tool to be used to destabilize any government in the region which did not dance to the economic tune of the West, he was allowed to grow to the extend that he felt comfortable enough to threaten his neighbors on his own without any prompting. This behavior and tactics have often been displayed by previous U.S. and Western puppets of Third World nations. Remember Mobutu Sese Koko of Zaire Preparation and fortification for war against their neighbours are tactics of destabilization employed by these leaders against their own people in the name of non- existing national pride. Saddam Hussein now would want to assume the role of the extortionist West – the US. This was an affront that would not be condoned by the US. Therefore, Saddam must be stopped! Besides, Saddam enjoyed this attention from the US because they provide a distraction from his own ineptitude to improve the lives of the average Iraqi citizen, supplanting their yearnings with nationalistic pride.

This type of behavior was not new. In fact, this is the norm for ruthless dictators of the Third World. These militants would rather chase their own shadows than to fulfill the promise of abundance to the citizens of their own countries. Some would stage a war on corruption to divert their countrymen's attention from the real goal of their those countries would be made scapegoats of their machinations. Some may even decide that change of name of the country or personnel at the helm of their country's affairs is a major battle for identifying with the country. Others may just stage diversionary schemes to strengthen their hold on power with allegations of fictitious plots to overthrow their administration – witness Mobubu Sese Koko of Zaire, Chilumba of Zambia and Abacha of Nigeria, to name a few.

The lessons of this maneuver should not be lost on the people of the Third World. The U.S. should help these poor people remove these dictators by hook or by crook. Why should this writer call for the removal of these brutal dictators? For a starter, the general citizenry of the respective countries are so beset by age-old blases and ethnic struggles, that any organization formed within the country lacks cohesion and force of section. Besides, the majority of the people lack the necessary preparation and military precision to overthrow these dictators on their own. Rather than continue this cycle of armed aggression on these wayward dictators to the destruction of the country and unnecessary billing of the innocent citizens, the US and the Western nations should help foster democratic institutions everywhere and refuse to recognize any regime seizing power by force of arms or elected civilians not opening the democratic process for the world to see.

Most unfortunately, the language of the US especially in negotiating with Iraq as a country, suggested a master-servant or superior-inferior diatribe in the name of the United Nations. Until the US and its officials learn the proper tone of dialogue with the rest of the non-white world, conflicts not worthy of the light of day will continue to be emblazoned on the pages of world newspaper and electronic media. There should be civility in answering or discussing a world problem on the electronic media by officials of the U.S. government. Using vitriolic language capable of incensing the other side to recalcitrant responses must be checked.

I do understand the need of most US officials to have their fifteen minutes on the world stage or the seizing of a window of opportunity to appear tough for the domestic political agenda. But this would not fly without an immediate ability to back such pronouncements. Even in the event of losing face because of a prior tough statement, the impact of rash action should be seriously weighed, lest the lives of innocent children, women and men be wasted needlessly. These Third World citizens are defenseless and are mere pawns in their ego-maniacal game. Like Macbeth in Shakespeare's play, both the official who inflames the conflict and his ardent supporters would murder sleep and their "Cawdor" would sleep no more. There is no number one citizen in this world. What is good for the geese is also for the gander, good!

A GOLDEN OPPORTUNITY

With providence and the will of the Almighty God, an opportunity once more was provided to the Nigerian nation. Disregarding the hapless rumours surrounding the deaths of the principal actors in the confusion which descended on Nigeria – viz, the death of Gen. Sani Abacha and his nemesis, Chief Moshood K.O. Abiola, I believe that Nigeria has come a full cycle and presented with the opportunity to take the leap forward or descend into a hopeless abyss. The gesture displayed by the sudden administration of Gen. Abdulsalam Abubakar to free the political prisoners across the nation was matched by his desire to return the country to civilian participatory democracy.

Gen. Abdusalam Abubakar

Equally required and expected of the civilian political class is a sense of collective responsibility to move the country forward, devoid of the bickering of the yester-years which brought in the adventure of the country's armed forces. The enemies of Nigeria will now be identifiable by their actions and utterances. One of the identifying markers would be the careless call for separation and division of the country along ethnic lines which to date is blurry at best – setting in a new confusion. Another would be the utterances of some cliques in the northern part of the country to want to arrogate a "divine" order of leadership to themselves, thereby deepening the suspicion of the rest of the people of the country of their hegemony. Nigeria belongs to all. Actually, any group of leadership bestowed on them would by now have exposed their ignorance and disregard for the Almighty God which they claim they revere and believe in. Every man and woman is created equal before the Almighty. He wills and commands all with no exception.

Actually, those who thought they must rule by any means necessary have shown Nigeria that their wanton desire for power is for corruption and not to serve. Service requires a lot of sacrifices in the midst of plenty. To serve requires a lot of personal self-denials of the luxuries and the lavish good life.

The military government must not, because of the need to please anyone, shirk its responsibilities to the nation. With a civilian interim government installed in accordance with the proclamation effective October 1, 1998, the military supervised a new electoral process in conjunction with a horde – of international observers in order to spare the nation of finger pointing irregularities. All elections must be conducted with the previous sham abolished and squashed. Electoral laws must not stifle any Nigerian because of/or lack of personal wealth or ethnic origin. The election process must be free and fair for all Nigerians to participate in. The process must exclude any sitting member of the interim government who would otherwise enjoy advantage of incumbency. Such member, if desiring to contest for an office must resign his position forthwith once he or she makes his or her intention known, and be replaced by another non- partisan member. Finally, the term of his interim civilian government must not extend beyond a six-month period once the political parties formed and streamlined to prevent chaos have been put into place.

There are several members of the society who could be drawn into this interim government. There are those who have served with distinctions in both previous civilian and military administrations who have served with distinctions in both previous civilian and military administrations who have not gotten their hands soiled with the decadence of the immediate past. Alas, there's so much to do, and the people in the leadership of the nation have done so little.

This is not the time to galvanize the ordinary people into frenzy partisanship. This is not the time to echo disruptive and destructive utterances. Nigerians are not interested in ethnic divisions but collective progress. It is the sordid behavior which had created the void we have now and the same which had brought about the wanton behavior of the likes of the dictator, Gen. Sani Abacha, and his unworthy and partisan advisers.

Finally, a new and permanent national constitution must allow for progressive and collective endeavors which must ensure a Nigerian consensus moving forward collectively. The constitution must forbid and discourage an adventure by any group of armed forces personnel in uniform to overthrow an elected government by the people of Nigeria. A corrupt civilian government could be sacked by the armed forces with its replacement by another civilian interim government for another election, conducted as the last resort. Otherwise, a simple process of recall of any corrupt government by provisions in the constitution must be vested in the people through the representatives duly elected and vested with such powers. As a safeguard, the open invitation for foreign observers during electioneering period must be a standing one.

Conclusion

In the end, I wonder if all is not lost to posterity as I write these thoughts! I wonder if we would be able to get the selfless young people again. I wonder if the love of money has not consumed every fabric of our being in our country. Most of the people I have been priviledged to share my thoughts of optimism with, have returned it with pessimism and skepticism at best of its achievement without huge amount of money.

Relationships are not as firm as before unless the one person would derive financial gains without returns from the other person. People don't often return calls to cement bonds of friendship unless financial rewards would result. Perhaps, a change of heart would come; but I will continue to trudge on the journey. Maybe there would be sojourners to pitch my tent with. My wife who is of some short fuse when it comes to this frustrated outlook, advised me to quit and exhibit less incurable optimism but I won't.

Bibliography

Adeniji, Bello, O.B Pendulum… Works like a Boomerage: An Odyssey of the Nigerian Nation

Ajayi, J.F. Ade: Milestones in Nigerian History 2nd Edition, Longman, 1980. Ajayi, J.F.Ade, K.E. Lamek, Gomah and G. Ampah Johnson.

The African Experience With Higher Education. Longman, 1966. Arnold, Guy. Modern Nigeria Longman, 1977.

Daily Express December 15, 1964.

Daily Times. July 30, 1966.

Daily Times. August 19, 1966

Daily Times – Nigeria. March 21, 1962 Daily Times – Nigeria. March 27, 1962 Daily Times – Nigeria. April 4, 1963

Eyo, Ekpo and Willet, Frank. Treasures of Ancient Nigeria. Knofp, 1980.

The New Nigeria April 29, 1966

The New York Times. November 22, 1997 The West African Pilot. January 1950.

Walter, Rodney. How Europe Underdeveloped Africa. Ikenga, 1966

INTRODUCTION

How the Green Mountain Wood Pellet Grill Works

Essentially, pellet grills are high-performing outdoor cookers that combine elements from smokers, ovens and charcoal or gas grills. They run on 100 per cent hardwood pellets and can provide direct and indirect heat to your grilling.

The hardwood pellets are poured into a storage container, or hopper, in the grill that moves them into a cooking chamber. Through combustion, the pellets ignite and heat the cooking chamber. Fans bring in air which is dispersed throughout the cooking area. You'll want to be sure you can position your grill near an electrical outlet, as these functions are powered by electricity.

Much like an oven, these grills are capable of tracking precise temperatures. You can control these digitally or with a dial to ensure your food is cooked just the way you want.

Wood pellet grills pack a big flavour and allow users better temperature management than traditional grills. You also have the added benefit of choosing the wood you use to grill with — a factor that can impact flavour, cooking time, and maintenance.

Five Significant Reasons to Choose the Green Mountain Wood Pellet Grill

1. TASTE

If the taste of your food is one of the most important reasons that you grill, then BBQ pellets should be your first choice. They provide a much better flavor than charcoal, especially when charcoal burners use lighter fluid to start then coals. When you grill with wood pellets, you give your food a strong, smoky flavor. There is also a lower chance of overcooking using a wood pellet grill, and it locks more of the natural moisture into the meat or fish.

Americans are very familiar with the taste and flavor of charcoal. However, when given a chance to barbecue with wood pellets, they find the food is delicious and tender, and it's hard to beat that wonderful flavor.

2. CONVENIENCE AND EASE-OF-USE

When you grill with charcoal, it can be a pain to start and once started it requires your constant attention because you don't want your food to burn or the charcoal to flare up too much. When you use a wood pellet grill, you push a button to start then set your temperature where you know it will give you the flavor that you want and the tenderness that you desire. You can leave the grill and prepare other food that you may be serving at your barbecue. A wood pellet grill burns with consistent heat, so you never have to worry about the grill getting too hot or the wood pellets flaring up and burning your meat or fish, making it tough and unpleasant.

3. VERSATILITY

When you buy a wood pellet grill, it's like you're getting a smoker for free. You can use your wood pellet grill to barbecue, grill, roast, bake, smoke, and even sear. That's because the ability of a wood pellet grill to cook your food at a consistent temperature allows you to use all these different methods.

Most charcoal grills will smoke, barbecue, grill, and sear and that's about it. Charcoal grills lack the versatility of a wood pellet grill. This is especially important if you like to experiment with your barbecue and use it for cooking in a variety of ways.

4. SAFETY

With a charcoal grill, even when you're finished grilling, you still need to keep an eye on the hot coals. When you use a wood pellet grill, you simply turn the grill off, and there are no more concerns or wasted fuel.

5. COST

It would be foolish to say that you can't get a charcoal grill for a reasonable price. Small grills sell for as little as $30. But most people prefer larger grills. In the past, wood pellet grills were more expensive than charcoal grills. But with the advances in technology made by wood pellet grills, along with competition, the costs are relatively similar. The actual difference in price depends on which model you choose. For instance, you can buy a pellet grill where you could use your smartphone to control the temperature.

Then there's the question of fuel. Lump charcoal is relatively inexpensive, but if you barbecue frequently, the cost of charcoal adds up quickly. If, on the other hand, you purchase a 20-pound bag of wood pellets, it can last five times longer than a comparable bag of charcoal because wood pellets burn more slowly.

Tips for Making the Most of Your Green Mountain Wood Pellet Grill

(1) Take time to give your grill behind-the-scenes TLC. A clean smoker grill produces flavorful recipes without any lingering oiliness or staleness. We know cleaning's not exactly as fun as whipping up award-winning ribs or deep dish pizzas. Still, it's a necessary component to owning a smoker grill that's going to serve up mouthwatering meals.

(2) Store your wood pellets properly. Wood pellets that have been exposed to humid conditions won't give you the burn you need. Plus, they'll lose their freshness. So keep your wood pellets safe and dry.

(3) Pick the right wood pellet for the job. Want a nice smoke ring around your beef brisket? Choose cherry wood pellets for a predictable presentation. Want strong smoke flavor that stands out? Choose hickory or apple wood pellets for their intensity.

(4) Remember to cold smoke, too. At low temperatures, you can cold smoke foods like cheese, fish, cream and even butter, infusing them with the flavor of food-grade wood pellets made from hardwoods like pecan and oak. Get creative and go the distance by cold smoking ingredients to liven up your cooking.

Tips and Tricks on Cleaning Your Green Mountain Wood Pellet Grill

1. Make sure the grill is cold.
2. Place the grill rack and the chimney dome in the hot soapy water.
3. Remove foil from the drip pan and flame reflector and brush off debris; put these parts in the tub only if they're still very dirty after brushing.
4. Remove solids from the grease bucket and place in the tub.
5. Scrub all parts, then air-dry completely.
6. Use the paint stirring stick to clear the grease chute.
7. Use rubber bands to secure the scrubby to the end of the spoon, brush handle or stirring stick and wipe the (often surprisingly disgusting) inside of the chimney.
8. Give the inside of the lid a good scrape with the brush.
9. Vacuum the grill interior and the firepot, being sure to clear the holes in the firepot.
10. Wipe the interior with a scrubby dampened with water or a natural cleaning product.
11. Carefully wipe the temperature probe.
12. Give any stainless steel parts a wipe with stainless steel cleaner.
13. Replace the grease bucket; line it with foil for future easy maintenance.
14. Keep things easy and flavors clean by maintaining your pellet smoker all year. All you'll need: your brass wire brush, a damp rag, and heavy-duty aluminum foil.
15. Run on high for ten minutes, then brush the grates.
16. Switch off and cool the smoker according to your grill's instruction manual.
17. Carefully remove the grease bucket and put it out of the reach of animals.
18. Wipe any drips off the grill exterior with a damp rag.
19. Allow to cool overnight and replace the foil on the drip pan.

BAKING RECIPES

Quick Baked Dinner Rolls

Servings: 8
Cooking Time: 30 Minutes

Ingredients:

- 2 Tablespoon quick-rise yeast
- 1 Teaspoon salt
- 1/4 Cup sugar
- 3 1/3 Cup flour
- 1/4 Cup unsalted butter, softened
- 1 egg
- cooking spray
- 1 egg, for egg wash

Directions:

1. Combine yeast and warm water in a small bowl to activate the yeast. Let sit until foamy, about 5-10 minutes.

2. Combine salt, sugar, and flour in the bowl of a stand mixer fitted with the dough hook. Pour water and yeast into the dry ingredients with the machine running on low.

3. Add butter and egg and mix for 10 minutes gradually increasing the speed from low to high.

4. Form the dough into a ball and place in a buttered bowl. Cover with a cloth and let the dough rise for approximately 40 minutes.

5. Transfer the risen dough to a lightly floured surface and divide into 8 pieces forming a ball with each.

6. Lightly spray a cast iron pan with cooking spray and arrange balls in the pan. Cover with a cloth and let rise 20 minutes.

7. Supply your smoker with wood pellets and follow the start-up procedure. Preheat the grill, with the lid closed, to 375° F.

8. Brush rolls with egg wash and then bake for 30 minutes until lightly browned. Serve hot. Enjoy! Grill: 375 °F

Baked Molten Chocolate Cake

Servings: 4
Cooking Time: 20 Minutes

Ingredients:

- all-purpose flour
- butter
- 4 Ounce butter
- 6 Ounce Chocolate, Bittersweet
- 2 eggs
- 2 egg yolk
- 1/2 Cup sugar
- 1 Pinch salt

Directions:

1. Supply your smoker with wood pellets and follow the start-up procedure. Preheat the grill, with the lid closed, to 450° F.

2. Butter and flour four (6oz) ramekins. Tap out excess flour. Place ramekins on a baking sheet and reserve.

3. Melt butter and chocolate in a double boiler over simmering water. In a medium bowl, beat eggs and yolks with sugar and salt on high until thick and pale.

4. Whisk in chocolate until smooth and quickly fold into the egg mixture along with flour.

5. Spoon the batter into prepared ramekins and bake for 20 minutes or until sides are firm but centers are soft. Grill: 450 °F

6. Let cool for 1 minute, then cover each with an inverted dessert plate. Carefully turn each over, let stand 10 seconds, then unmold.

7. Serve immediately with Maple Ice Cream with Candied Bacon. Enjoy!

Spiced Carrot Cake

Servings: 10
Cooking Time: 35 Minutes

Ingredients:

- 1/2 Cup Apple Sauce, Unsweetened
- 2 Tsp Baking Powder
- 1 Tsp Baking Soda
- 1 1/2 Cups Brown Sugar
- 1/2 Cup Butter, Room Temp
- 3/4 Cup Canola Oil
- 3 Cups Carrot, Grated
- 1 1/2 Tsp Cinnamon, Ground
- 2 (8-Ounce) Packages Cream Cheese, Room Temperature
- 4 Egg
- 2 Cups Flour, All-Purpose
- 1/2 Tsp Ginger, Ground
- 1/4 Tsp Nutmeg, Ground
- 1/2 Tsp Salt
- 1/2 Cup Sugar
- 3 Cups Sugar, Icing

Directions:

1. Supply your smoker with wood pellets and follow the start-up procedure. Preheat the grill, with the lid closed, to 350° F.

2. Line the bottom of 2 9-inch cake pans with parchment paper and spray the sides with cooking spray. Set aside.

3. In a large bowl, combine flour, baking powder and soda, spices and salt.

4. In a smaller bowl, combine oil, eggs, sugars, and applesauce and whisk together. Add carrots and stir until well combined.

5. Pour the wet ingredients into the dry. Stir until combined but take care not to over mix. Pour the batter evenly between the two cake pans. Bake for about 35 minutes in your Grill, rotating the cake pans halfway between the cook. Remove once a toothpick is inserted in the middle of the cake and comes out clean.

6. While the cake is cooling, prepare the frosting. Beat the cream cheese until smooth with a hand mixer. Add the butter and icing sugar and mix until fully combined.

7. On a clean plate or cake stand, place one half of the cake and top with a good layer of cream cheese frosting. Place the second half on top and cover with the remaining frosting. Icing tip: try not to lift your knife while icing. Instead make long, smooth strokes. Lifting the knife often make cause crumbs to get into your icing. Top with pecans if desired.

Pull-apart Dinner Rolls

Servings: 8
Cooking Time: 10 Minutes

Ingredients:

- 1/4 Cup warm water (110°F to 115°F)
- 1/3 Cup vegetable oil
- 2 Tablespoon active dry yeast
- 1/4 Cup sugar
- 1/2 Teaspoon salt
- 1 egg
- 3 1/2 Cup all-purpose flour
- cooking spray

Directions:

1. Supply your smoker with wood pellets and follow the start-up procedure. Preheat the grill, with the lid closed, to 400° F.

2. In the bowl of a stand mixer, combine warm water, oil, yeast and sugar. Let mixture rest for 5 to 10 minutes, or until frothy and bubbly.

3. With a dough hook, mix in salt, egg and 2 cups of flour until combined. Add remaining flour 1/2 cup at a time (dough will be sticky).

4. Prepare a cast iron pan with cooking spray and set aside.

5. Spray your hands with cooking spray and shape the dough into 12 balls.

6. After shaped, place in the prepared cast iron pan and let rest for 10 minutes. Bake in Traeger for about 10 to 12 minutes, or until tops are lightly golden. Enjoy! Grill: 400 °F

Baked Peach Cobbler Cupcakes

Servings: 8
Cooking Time: 30 Minutes

Ingredients:
- 2 Large Peaches, fresh
- 3/4 Cup sugar
- 2 Teaspoon lemon juice
- 1/2 Teaspoon ground cinnamon
- Yellow Cake Mix, Boxed
- 1 Can vanilla icing

Directions:
1. Bring a pot of water to a boil. Turn peaches upside down and cut a small shallow X across the bottom. Put peaches in boiling water and boil for 1 minute to help loosen the skin.

2. Drain the peaches into a colander and rinse off with cold water. Peel skin off peaches.

3. Filling: Dice peaches and place into a large pan. Cook peaches over medium heat. As it starts to sizzle, add sugar, lemon and cinnamon. Cook mixture on medium heat for 10-15 minutes until a majority of the juice from the peaches evaporates leaving a thick syrup.

4. Transfer to a bowl to cool.

5. Supply your smoker with wood pellets and follow the start-up procedure. Preheat the grill, with the lid closed, to 350° F.

6. Cupcakes: Follow the directions on box cake mix and put the mixture into cupcake pan with liners.

7. When grill has preheated, bake cupcakes for 13-16 minutes, until a light golden brown. Grill: 350 °F

8. When cupcakes have cooled, use a piping bag to pipe the peach cobbler mixture into the middle of the cupcake.

9. Ice with your favorite vanilla icing. Enjoy!

Baked Cheesy Parmesan Grits

Servings: 4
Cooking Time: 60 Minutes

Ingredients:
- 4 Cup chicken stock
- 3 Tablespoon butter
- 3/4 Teaspoon salt
- 1 Cup quick grits
- 1 Cup shredded cheddar cheese
- pepper
- 1/2 Cup Monterey Jack cheese, shredded
- 1/2 Cup whole milk
- 2 Large eggs

Directions:
1. Supply your smoker with wood pellets and follow the start-up procedure. Preheat the grill, with the lid closed, to 350° F.

2. Butter an 8" baking dish or a 10" cast iron pan.

3. Bring the chicken stock, butter, and salt to boil in medium saucepan. Gradually whisk in grits.

4. Reduce heat to medium and cook until mixture thickens slightly, stirring often about 8 minutes. Remove from heat.

5. Add cheeses and stir until melted. Season with pepper and salt to taste.

6. Whisk together milk and eggs in small bowl. Gradually whisk mixture into grits.

7. Pour the cheese grits into the buttered cast iron pan. Bake until grits feel firm to touch, about 1 hour. Grill: 350 ˚F

8. Remove from grill and let stand 10 minutes before serving. Enjoy!

Anzac Coconut Biscuits

Servings: 4
Cooking Time: 30 Minutes

Ingredients:
- This recipe makes a dozen biscuits.
- 1 cup rolled oats
- 3/4 cup raw sugar
- 3/4 cup desiccated coconut
- 1 cup plain flour, sifted
- 125 g butter, melted
- 2 tablespoons Golden Syrup
- 1/2 tsp bicarb soda
- 3 tablespoons boiling water

Directions:
1. Combine and mix thoroughly sifted flour, oats, sugar and coconut in a large bowl.

2. Melt the butter and Golden Syrup over low heat.

3. Add boiling water to the bicarb soda, once dissolved add into the butter/syrup mix, it will bubble/fizz up a bit.

4. Add the liquid into the dry ingredients and mix throughly.

5. Rolls the mix into golf ball size balls and layout on grease proof paper on baking tray and flatten the tops just slightly.

6. Space the balls with about 3 fingers between each ball as they will flatten to about triple the diameter as they cook.

7. Supply your smoker with wood pellets and follow the start-up procedure. Preheat the grill, with the lid closed, to 350° F. Cook for 25-30 minutes until golden brown.

8. Rest on cooling rack until at room temperature then store in air-tight container.

Butternut Squash Macaroni And Cheese

Servings: 2
Cooking Time: 50 Minutes

Ingredients:
- 1 Medium butternut squash
- 2 Cup macaroni, uncooked
- 1 Small yellow onion
- 1/2 Cup chicken broth
- 1 Cup milk
- salt
- pepper
- 1 Cup cheese, grated

Directions:
1. Supply your smoker with wood pellets and follow the start-up procedure. Preheat the grill, with the lid closed, to 225° F.

2. Puncture butternut squash with a fork several times and place on grill grate. Cook until tender, about 40 minutes to an hour. When cooked, scoop out meat and discard seeds. Grill: 225 ˚F

3. Cook elbow macaroni according to package instructions. Drain and set aside.

4. In a medium skillet, sauté chopped onion until fragrant and golden. Add broth, milk, salt, onions and butternut squash to a food processor. Puree until smooth and creamy. Add salt and pepper to taste.

5. Pour pureed sauce over cooked noodles and add the shredded cheese. Stir to melt the cheese and add milk to reach desired consistency. Serve warm. Enjoy!

Green Bean Casserole Circa 1955

Servings: 6
Cooking Time: 30 Minutes

Ingredients:
- 1 1/2 Pound Green Beans, fresh
- 1 Can cream of mushroom soup
- 1/2 Cup milk
- 2 Teaspoon soy sauce
- 1/2 Teaspoon Worcestershire sauce
- 1/2 Teaspoon black pepper
- 1.334 Cup French's Original Crispy Fried Onions
- 1/4 Cup red bell pepper, diced

Directions:
1. In a mixing bowl, combine the beans (trimmed and cooked until tender, or may use 2 16 oz. cans), soup, milk, soy sauce, Worcestershire sauce, black pepper, 2/3 cup of the onion rings, and red pepper, if using. Transfer to a 1-1/2 quart casserole dish.

2. Supply your smoker with wood pellets and follow the start-up procedure. Preheat the grill, with the lid closed, to 375° F.

3. Cook the casserole until the filling is hot and bubbling, 25 to 30 minutes. Top with the remaining onions and cook for 5 to 10 minutes more, or until the onions are crisp and beginning to brown. Grill: 375 °F

Vanilla Chocolate Bacon Cupcakes

Servings: 12
Cooking Time: 120 Minutes

Ingredients:
- 1 Lb Bacon
- 1 1/2 Tsp Baking Powder
- 1 1/2 Tsp Baking Soda
- 1 Cup Cocoa, Powder
- 2 Egg
- 1 3/4 Cups Flour
- 1 Cup Milk, Whole
- 1/2 Cup Oil
- 1 Tsp Salt
- 2 Cups Sugar
- 2 Tsp Vanilla

Directions:
1. Supply your smoker with wood pellets and follow the start-up procedure. Preheat the grill, with the lid closed, to 250° F.

2. Once your grill is preheated, place bacon strips on the grates. Smoke for 1hr-1 ½ hours or until desired crispiness is achieved.

3. Remove the bacon from the grill and set aside.

4. Increase set the temperature to 350°F and preheat.

5. Mix the rest of the ingredients in a bowl with an electric mixer until it is nice and smooth.

6. Pour the mixture into a cupcake tin.

7. Transfer the tin to your grill and bake for about 20 - 25 minutes.

8. Allow the cupcakes to cool on a wire rack. Once cooled, top with your favorite premade icing and a half of strip of the bacon. Serve and enjoy!

Old Fashioned Cornbread

Servings: 4

Cooking Time: 25 Minutes

Ingredients:
- 1 Cup all-purpose flour
- 1 Cup Cornmeal
- 1 Tablespoon sugar
- 2 Teaspoon baking powder
- 1/2 Teaspoon salt
- 3 Tablespoon butter
- 1 Cup milk
- 1 Whole egg, lightly beaten

Directions:

1. In a mixing bowl, combine the flour, cornmeal, sugar, baking powder, and salt.

2. Melt the butter in a small saucepan. Remove from the heat, and stir in the milk and the egg. (Make sure the mixture isn't hot or the egg will curdle.)

3. Add the milk-egg mixture to the dry ingredients and stir to combine. Do not overmix.

4. Spread the batter evenly in a greased 8 or 9-inch square baking pan or pie plate.

5. Supply your smoker with wood pellets and follow the start-up procedure. Preheat the grill, with the lid closed, to 375° F.

6. Bake the cornbread until it begins to pull away from the sides of the pan and the top is beginning to brown, 25 to 35 minutes. Cut into squares (or wedges, if you used a pie plate) for serving. Grill: 375 ℉

Eyeball Cookies

Servings: 20

Cooking Time: 35 Minutes

Ingredients:

- 2 Packages Candy Eyeballs
- Green, Blue And Purple Food Coloring
- 1 Box Of Yellow Gluten Free Cake Mix
- 1/2 Cup (Optional) Granulated Sugar
- 2 Large Eggs
- 1/3 Cup Powdered Sugar
- 1 Teaspoon Pure Vanilla Extract
- 6 Tablespoon Melted Vegan Butter (Unsalted)

Directions:

1. Supply your smoker with wood pellets and follow the start-up procedure. Preheat the grill, with the lid closed, to 350° F.

2. Line two large baking sheets with parchment paper. In a large bowl, combine cake mix, melted butter, eggs (or egg substitute), powdered sugar, sugar (optional), and vanilla and stir until combined. (substitute 2 flax eggs for Vegan – 1 tbsp flax seed meal and 5 tbsp water per egg).

3. Divide dough between 3 bowls and dye each bowl a different color.(We used green, blue and purple).

4. Roll dough into tablespoon-sized balls.

5. Place about 2" apart on the baking sheet and grill until tops have cracked and the tops look set, 8 to 10 minutes. – Turn half way through baking, after 4-5 minutes.

6. Immediately, while the cookies are still warm, stick candy eyeballs all over the cookies.

7. Let cool completely before serving.

Pizza Bites

Servings: 6

Cooking Time: 20 Minutes

Ingredients:
- 4 1/2 Cup Bread Flour
- 1 1/2 Tablespoon sugar
- 2 Teaspoon Instant Yeast

- 2 Teaspoon kosher salt
- 3 Tablespoon extra-virgin olive oil
- 15 Fluid Ounce Water, Lukewarm
- 8 Ounce Pepperoni, sliced
- 1 Cup pizza sauce
- 1 Cup mozzarella cheese
- 1 Whole egg, for egg wash
- 1 As Needed salt

Directions:

1. For the Pizza Dough: Combine flour, sugar, salt, and yeast in food processor. Pulse 3 to 4 times until incorporated evenly. Add olive oil and water. Run food processor until mixture forms ball that rides around the bowl above the blade, about 15 seconds. Continue processing 15 seconds longer.

2. Transfer dough ball to lightly floured surface and knead once or twice by hand until smooth ball is formed. Divide dough into three even parts and place each into a 1 gallon zip top bag. Place in refrigerator and allow to rise at least one day.

3. At least two hours before baking, remove dough from refrigerator and shape into balls by gathering dough towards bottom and pinching shut. Flour well and place each one in a separate medium mixing bowl. Cover tightly with plastic wrap and allow to rise at warm room temperature until roughly doubled in volume.

4. When ready to cook, set the grill temperature to 350°F and preheat, lid closed for 15 minutes.

5. After the first rise remove the dough from the fridge and let come to room temperature. Roll dough on a flat surface. Cut dough into long strips 3" wide by 18" long.

6. Slice pepperoni into strips.

7. In a medium bowl combine the pizza sauce, mozzarella and pepperoni.

8. Spoon 1 TBSP of the pizza filling onto the pizza dough every two inches, about halfway down the length of the dough. Dip a pastry brush into the egg wash and brush around pizza filling. Fold the half side of the dough (without the pizza filling) over the other the half that contains the pizza filling.

9. Press down between each pizza bite slightly with your fingers. With a ravioli or pizza cutter, cut around each filling- creating a rectangle shape and sealing the crust in.

10. Transfer each pizza bite onto a parchment lined cookie sheet. Cover with a kitchen towel and let them rise for 30 minutes.

11. When ready to cook, preheat the grill to 350 ⌧ F with the lid closed for 10-15 minutes.

12. Brush the bites with remaining egg wash, sprinkle with salt and place directly on the sheet tray. Bake 10-15 minutes until the exterior is golden brown.

13. Remove from grill and transfer to a serving dish. Serve with extra pizza sauce for dipping and enjoy!

Italian Herb & Parmesan Scones

Servings: 8

Cooking Time: 20 Minutes

Ingredients:

- 2 1/2 Cup all-purpose flour
- 2 Teaspoon baking powder
- 1 Teaspoon baking soda
- 1/2 Teaspoon garlic salt
- 1 Tablespoon Italian Seasoning
- 1 Cup Parmesan cheese, grated
- 2 Large eggs
- 1 1/2 Cup buttermilk
- 1/4 Cup olive oil

Directions:

1. In a large mixing bowl, combine flour, baking powder, baking powder, soda, garlic salt, Italian seasoning, and 1/2 cup of the cheese. Make a well in the center.

2. In a smaller bowl, whisk together eggs, buttermilk, and olive oil.

3. Pour into the well in the dry ingredients, and stir batter just until it's combined. It will appear lumpy.

4. Oil 12 muffin cups, spray with cooking spray, or line with disposable paper liners.

5. Divide the batter evenly between the cups. Sprinkle the tops of the muffins with the remaining Parmesan cheese.

6. Supply your smoker with wood pellets and follow the start-up procedure. Preheat the grill, with the lid closed, to 400° F.

7. Arrange the muffin tin directly on the grill grate and bake the muffins for 20 to 25 minutes, or until a toothpick inserted in the center of the muffin comes out clean.

8. Cool for several minutes before removing from the muffin tin. Serve warm with butter or olive oil. Enjoy!

Basil Margherita Pizza

Servings: 6
Cooking Time: 25 Minutes

Ingredients:
- Basil, Chopped
- 2 Cups Flour, All-Purpose
- Mozzarella Cheese, Sliced Rounds
- 1 Cup Pizza Sauce
- 1 Teaspoon Salt
- 1 Teaspoon Sugar
- 1 Tomato, Sliced

- 1 Cup Water, Warm
- 1 Teaspoon Yeast, Instant

Directions:

1. Combine the water, yeast, and sugar in a small bowl and let sit for about 5 minutes.

2. In a large bowl, stir together the flour and salt. Pour in the yeast mixture and mix until a soft dough forms. Knead for about 2 minutes. Place in an oiled bowl and cover with a cloth. Let the dough sit and rise for about 45 minutes or until the dough has doubled in size.

3. Roll out on a flat, floured surface (or on a pizza stone) until you"ve reached your desired shape and thickness.

4. Supply your smoker with wood pellets and follow the start-up procedure. Preheat the grill, with the lid closed, to 350° F.

5. On the rolled out dough, pour on the pizza sauce, cheese, and then tomatoes and basil. Place in your Grill and bake for about 25 minutes, or until the cheese is melted and slightly golden brown.

Smoked Vanilla Apple Pie

Servings: 6
Cooking Time: 45 Minutes

Ingredients:
- 1 1/2 cups of self-raising flour
- 3/4 cup of sugar
- 0.3 lbs of butter melted
- 1 tsp of vanilla extract
- 1 egg
- 0.9-lb tin of pie apples
- sugar & cinnamon for dusting

Directions:

1. Supply your smoker with wood pellets and follow the start-up procedure. Preheat the grill, with the lid closed, to 350° F.

2. Combine the self-raising flour, sugar, melted butter, vanilla, and egg in a large bowl until a golden dough texture is formed.

3. Spread half the mixture in a pie dish and press the bottoms and up the sides of the dish.

4. Pour pie apple tin into the pie and spread out evenly.

5. Sprinkle the remaining mixture over the top of the apple evenly and place in the smoker.

6. Leave for 45 minutes or until the golden crust forms on the top.

7. Dust with cinnamon and a little sugar if desired.

8. Serve warm with custard, ice cream, or both.

Baked Chocolate Brownie Cookies With Egg Nog

Servings: 6

Cooking Time: 12 Minutes

Ingredients:

- 16 Ounce Bar bittersweet chocolate, finely chopped
- 4 Tablespoon unsalted butter, room temperature
- 4 eggs
- 1 1/3 Cup granulated sugar
- 1 Teaspoon vanilla extract
- 1 1/2 Cup all-purpose flour
- 1/2 Teaspoon baking powder
- 1 Cup semisweet chocolate chips

Directions:

1. Supply your smoker with wood pellets and follow the start-up procedure. Preheat the grill, with the lid closed, to 350° F.

2. Line two baking sheets with parchment paper.

3. Put the finely chopped chocolate and butter in a heatproof bowl and set over a saucepan of barely simmering water; stir occasionally until chocolate is completely melted and smooth. Set aside and allow to cool to room temperature.

4. Whisk together eggs, sugar and vanilla extract in a medium bowl. Set aside.

5. Sift together the flour and baking powder in a small bowl. Add the melted chocolate mixture to the egg mixture and stir with a rubber spatula until completely combined.

6. Add the flour mixture in three batches, folding gently into the batter with a spatula. Once all of the flour has been incorporated, stir in the chocolate chips.

7. Scoop 1-1/2 tablespoons of dough onto prepared baking sheets. Bake for 10 to 12 minutes or until they are firm on the outside. Do not over bake. Grill:350° F

8. Leave to cool completely on the baking sheets. Enjoy!

Smoked Blackberry Pie

Servings: 4-6

Cooking Time: 25 Minutes

Ingredients:

- Nonstick cooking spray or butter, for greasing
- 1 box (2 sheets) refrigerated piecrusts
- 8 tablespoons (1 stick) unsalted butter, melted, plus 8 tablespoons (1 stick) cut into pieces
- ½ cup all-purpose flour
- 2 cups sugar, divided
- 2 pints blackberries
- ½ cup milk
- Vanilla ice cream, for serving

Directions:

1. Supply your smoker with wood pellets and follow the start-up procedure. Preheat, with the lid closed, to 375°F.

2. Coat a cast iron skillet with cooking spray.

3. Unroll 1 refrigerated piecrust and place in the bottom and up the side of the skillet. Using a fork, poke holes in the crust in several places.

4. Set the skillet on the grill grate, close the lid, and smoke for 5 minutes, or until lightly browned. Remove from the grill and set aside.

5. In a large bowl, combine the stick of melted butter with the flour and 1½ cups of sugar.

6. Add the blackberries to the flour-sugar mixture and toss until well coated.

7. Spread the berry mixture evenly in the skillet and sprinkle the milk on top. Scatter half of the cut pieces of butter randomly over the mixture.

8. Unroll the remaining piecrust and place it over the top of skillet or slice the dough into even strips and weave it into a lattice. Scatter the remaining pieces of butter along the top of the crust.

9. Sprinkle the remaining ½ cup of sugar on top of the crust and return the skillet to the smoker.

10. Close the lid and smoke for 15 to 20 minutes, or until bubbly and brown on top. It may be necessary to use some aluminum foil around the edges near the end of the cooking time to prevent the crust from burning.

11. Serve the pie hot with vanilla ice cream.

Cake With Smoked Berry Sauce

Servings: 12
Cooking Time: 90 Minutes

Ingredients:
- 12 Oz Blackberries
- 18 Oz Blueberries, Fresh
- 1/4 Cup Brown Sugar
- 2 Tsp Cinnamon, Ground
- 4 Eggs
- 2 Tbsp Flour
- 1 3/4 Cup Granulated Sugar
- 1 Lemon, Juice & Zest
- 1/2 Cup Unsalted Butter
- 3.4 Ounce Box Vanilla Instant Pudding Mix
- 3/4 Cup Vegetable Oil
- 3/4 Cup Water
- 1 Cup White Wine
- 1 Box Yellow Cake Mix

Directions:

1. Fire up your Grill and set to Smoke mode. If using a gas or charcoal grill, set it up for low, indirect heat. Supply your smoker with wood pellets and follow the start-up procedure. Preheat the grill, with the lid closed, to 450° F.

2. Place blueberries and blackberries on a sheet tray, then transfer to upper shelf of smoking cabinet. Make sure that the sear slide and side dampers are open, then preheat the grill, with the lid closed, to 375° F, to ensure the cabinet maintains temperature between 225° F and 250° F. Smoke for 30 to 45 minutes.

3. Place cast iron skillet on grill grate. Add sugar, lemon juice and zest, and wine to skillet. Stir with a wooden spoon until sugar dissolves, then add berries from smoking cabinet.

4. Simmer berries for 15 minutes, then remove sauce from grill to cool.

5. While berries are smoking, prepare cake pans and batter. Grease and flour 2 - 9-inch round cake pans. Set aside.

6. In a large mixing bowl, combine cake mix, brown sugar, granulated sugar, pudding mix, cinnamon, eggs, water, oil, and white wine. Using

a hand mixer, mix on low speed for 1 minute, then slowly increase mixing speed to high, and beat an additional 2 to 3 minutes, or until batter is smooth.

7. Evenly distribute batter among cake pans, then place pans on grill shelf and bake at 350° F, for 25 to 30 minutes, or until a toothpick inserted comes out clean. Remove from grill and set aside to cool slightly.

8. While cake is cooling, prepare glaze. Melt butter with sugar in a sauce pot on the grill. Stir for 3 minutes, then add wine. Remove from grill and set aside.

9. Turn out cake onto a sheet tray lined with parchment. Use a toothpick to poke holes in the cake, then slowly pour hot glaze over cake.

10. Spread half of smoked berry sauce on top of one layer, then place second cake layer on top. Pour additional sauce on top of cake and dust with powdered sugar, if desired. Serve warm, or room temperature.

Cast Iron Pineapple Upside Down Cake

Servings: 6
Cooking Time: 40 Minutes

Ingredients:
- 1/4 Cup butter, melted
- 1 Cup brown sugar
- 20 Ounce Pineapple, sliced
- 6 Ounce maraschino cherries
- 1 Whole Yellow Cake Mix, Boxed
- vegetable oil
- eggs

Directions:

1. Supply your smoker with wood pellets and follow the start-up procedure. Preheat the grill, with the lid closed, to 350° F.

2. Pour melted butter into a 12-inch cast iron pan. Sprinkle brown sugar on top of the butter. Arrange pineapple slices on brown sugar, squeezing in as many slices as possible. Place a cherry in center of each pineapple slice; press gently into brown sugar.

3. Make cake batter as directed on box, substituting pineapple juice mixture for as much of the water as possible, and adding in required oil and eggs. Pour batter into cast iron dish, over pineapple and cherries.

4. Place the cast iron pan on the grill grate and cook for 20 minutes. Rotate the pan a half turn to ensure it cooks evenly. Cook for an additional 20 minutes, or until toothpick inserted in center comes out clean.

5. Immediately run knife around side of pan to loosen cake. Place heatproof serving plate upside down onto pan; turn plate and pan over.

6. Leave pan over cake 5 minutes so brown sugar topping can drizzle over cake. Cool 30 minutes. Enjoy!

Smoked, Salted Caramel Apple Pie

Servings: 4
Cooking Time: 60 Minutes

Ingredients:
- 1 Cup cream
- 1 Cup brown sugar
- 3/4 Cup Light Corn Syrup
- 6 Tablespoon butter
- 1 Teaspoon sea salt
- 1 Pastry for Double-Crust Pie

- 6 Granny Smith Apples, Cut Into Wedges

Directions:

1. Supply your smoker with wood pellets and follow the start-up procedure. Preheat the grill, with the lid closed, to 180° F.

2. Fill a large pan with ice and water. Pour the cream into a smaller, shallow pan. Place the pan with the cream in the ice bath and place them both on the Traeger to smoke for 15-20 minutes. Grill: 180 ˚F

3. To make the caramel, combine the sugar and corn syrup in a saucepan and cook over medium heat, stirring constantly until it coats the back of your spoon and starts to turn a copper color, then stir in butter, salt, and smoked cream.

4. To assemble the pie, gather the pie crust, salted caramel, and apples. Place one of the pie crusts into the pie plate and fill with apple slices. Pour caramel over the apples. Lay the top crust over the filling, then crimp the top and bottom crusts together.

5. Make slits in the top crust to release the steam and finish by brushing with egg or cream. Sprinkle with raw sugar and sea salt.

6. When ready to bake, set the Traeger to 375˚F and preheat, lid closed for 15 minutes.

7. Place the pie on the grill and bake for 20 minutes. Grill: 375 ˚F

8. Reduce heat to 325˚F and cook for 25 more minutes. When ready, the crust should be golden brown and the filling, bubbly. Grill: 325 ˚F

9. Remove the pie from the grill and let cool. Serve with vanilla ice cream. Enjoy!

Chili Cheese Fries

Servings: 6
Cooking Time: 10 Minutes

Ingredients:

- 1 Cup Cheddar Cheese, Shredded
- 1 Cup Chili Con Carne, Prepared
- 1 Bag French Fries
- 1 Tablespoon Olive Oil
- 1 Tablespoon Sweet Heat Rub

Directions:

1. Supply your smoker with wood pellets and follow the start-up procedure. Preheat the grill, with the lid closed, to 350° F. If you're using charcoal or gas, set it up for medium high heat.

2. Bake the fries according to manufacturer's instructions. Once the fries are done, place them in a large bowl and add the olive oil and Sweet Heat Rub. Toss the fries to coat. Once everything is well coated with the oil and seasoning, spread the fries on a baking sheet.

3. Top the fries with the chili and the shredded cheddar cheese. Place the baking sheet on the grill and grill for 7-10 minutes, or until the cheese is melted and bubbly, and the chili is warm all the way through.

4. Remove the baking sheet from the grill and serve the fries immediately.

Smoked Lemon Cheesecake

Servings: 16
Cooking Time: 130 Minutes

Ingredients:

- For the crust
- Vegetable oil, for oiling the pan
- 12 ounces gingersnaps (about 36) or chocolate icebox cookies (about 36)
- 3 tablespoons light brown sugar
- 8 tablespoons (1 stick) unsalted butter, melted
- For the filling

- 4 packages (8 ounces each) cream cheese, at room temperature
- 1 cup firmly packed light brown sugar
- 2 teaspoons pure vanilla extract
- 2 teaspoons finely grated lemon zest
- 1 tablespoon fresh lemon juice
- 2 tablespoons (1/4 stick) unsalted butter, melted
- 5 large eggs
- Burnt Sugar Sauce (recipes follows, optional)

Directions:

1. Supply your smoker with wood pellets and follow the start-up procedure. Preheat the grill, with the lid closed, to 400° F. Lightly oil the springform pan with vegetable oil and wrap a sheet of aluminum foil around the outside.

2. Make the crust: Break the cookies into pieces and grind with the brown sugar to a fine powder in a food processor. You'll want about 1 3/4 cups of crumbs. Add the melted butter and run the processor in short bursts to obtain a crumbly dough. Press the mixture evenly across the bottom and halfway up the sides of the springform pan. Indirect-grill or bake the crust until lightly browned, 5 to 8 minutes. Transfer the pan to a wire rack and let cool.

3. Make the filling: Wipe out the food processor bowl. Add the cream cheese, brown sugar, vanilla, lemon zest, lemon juice, and butter, and process until smooth. Work in the eggs one by one, processing until smooth after each addition. (You can also use a stand mixer, beating the cream cheese mixture until smooth and beating in the eggs one at a time.) Pour the filling into the crust. Gently tap the pan on the countertop a few times to knock out any air bubbles.

4. Supply your smoker with wood pellets and follow the start-up procedure. Preheat the grill, with the lid closed, to 225 °F-250 °F.

5. Place the cheesecake in the smoker. Smoke until the top is bronzed with smoke and the filling is set, 1 1/2 to 2 hours. To test for doneness, gently poke the side of the pan—the filling will jiggle, not ripple. Alternatively, insert a slender metal skewer in the center of the cake; it should come out clean.

6. Transfer the cheesecake in its pan to a wire rack to cool to room temperature. Refrigerate until serving; the cheesecake can be made up to 8 hours ahead. Run a slender knife around the inside of the springform pan. Unclasp and remove the ring. (You'll serve the cheesecake off the bottom of the pan.) Let the cheesecake warm slightly at room temperature before serving.

7. If serving with the sauce, pour some of it over the cheesecake and the rest into a pitcher. Cut into wedges and pass the remaining sauce.

Tarte Tatin

Servings: 6
Cooking Time: 55 Minutes

Ingredients:

- 2 Cup all-purpose flour
- 1 Teaspoon salt
- 1 Cup butter
- 5 Tablespoon cold water
- 1/4 Cup unsalted butter
- 3/4 Cup granulated sugar
- 10 Granny Smith Apples, Cut Into Wedges

Directions:

1. Supply your smoker with wood pellets and follow the start-up procedure. Preheat the grill, with the lid closed, to 350° F.

2. For the crust: Place flour and salt in a food processer and pulse to mix. Add butter a little at a time while pulsing. Once it starts to looks like cornmeal, add the water until dough start to come together. Form a round with the dough, wrap in plastic and let it cool in the refrigerator.

3. While dough cools, place a pie dish or a 10-inch round cake pan on the grill; add butter and sugar to pie dish. Let it caramelize.

4. When the sugar caramelizes and has come to a dark amber color, take off grill. Arrange apple wedges in a fan formation covering the caramel.

5. Roll the pie crust into a circle big enough to cover the pan. Prick the pie dough with a fork and cover the pan with the pie dough. Trim the crust leaving room for shrinkage.

6. Place on the grill and bake for 55 minutes until apples are soft. Let sit for 3 minutes. While pan is still hot, place a plate over pie and flip over. Grill: 350 °F

7. Serve warm, topped with ice cream or whipped cream. Enjoy!

Baked Bourbon Maple Pumpkin Pie

Servings: 6-8
Cooking Time: 60 Minutes

Ingredients:
- 1/4 Cup Cocoa Powder, Unsweetened
- 1 Tablespoon Cocoa Powder, Unsweetened
- 3 1/2 Tablespoon sugar
- 1 Teaspoon salt
- 1 1/4 Cup all-purpose flour
- 1 Tablespoon all-purpose flour
- 6 Tablespoon butter
- 2 Tablespoon vegetable oil
- 1 Large Egg Yolk
- 1/2 Teaspoon apple cider vinegar
- 1/4 Cup ice water
- 1 Large egg, beaten
- 15 Ounce Pumpkin, canned
- 1/4 Cup sour cream
- 2 Tablespoon bourbon
- 1 Teaspoon ground cinnamon
- 1/2 Teaspoon salt
- 1/4 Teaspoon ground ginger
- 1/4 Teaspoon ground nutmeg
- 1/8 Teaspoon Allspice, ground
- 1/8 Teaspoon Mace, ground
- 3 Large eggs
- 3/4 Cup maple syrup
- 2 Tablespoon sugar
- 1/2 Vanilla Bean, halved
- 1 Cup heavy cream

Directions:
1. For the Chocolate Pie Dough: Pulse cocoa powder, granulated sugar, salt, and 1-1/4 cups plus 1 Tbsp flour in a food processor to combine. Add butter and shortening and pulse until mixture resembles coarse meal with a few pea-sized pieces of butter remaining. Transfer to a large bowl.

2. Whisk together the egg yolk, vinegar, and 1/4 cup ice water in a small bowl. Drizzle half of the egg mixture over flour mixture and, using a fork, mix gently just until combined. Add remaining egg mixture and mix until the dough just comes together (you will have some unincorporated pieces).

3. Turn out dough onto a lightly floured surface, flatten slightly, and cut into quarters. Stack pieces on top of one another. Placing unincorporated dry pieces of dough between layers, and press down to combine. Repeat process twice more (all

pieces of dough should be incorporated at this point). Form dough into a 1" thick disk. Wrap in plastic; chill at least 1 hour.

4. Roll out a disk of dough on a lightly floured surface into a 14" round. Transfer to a 9" pie dish. Lift up the edge and allow the dough to slump down into the dish. Trim. Leaving about 1" overhang. Fold overhang under and crimp edge. Chill in freezer 15 minutes.

5. When ready to cook, set the smoker to 350°F and preheat, lid closed for 15 minutes.

6. Line pie with parchment paper or heavy-duty foil, leaving a 1-1/2" overhang. Fill with pie weights or dried beans. Bake until crust is dry around the edge, about 20 minutes.

7. Remove paper and weights and bake until surface of the crust looks dry, 5-10 minutes.

8. Brush bottom and sides of crust with 1 beaten egg. Return to grill and bake until dry and set, about 3 minutes longer.

9. For the Pumpkin Maple Filling: Whisk together pumpkin puree, sour cream, bourbon, cinnamon, salt, ginger, nutmeg, allspice, mace (optional) and remaining 3 eggs in a large bowl; set aside.

10. Pour maple syrup and 2 tbsp sugar in a small saucepan. Scrape in the seeds from vanilla bean (reserve pod for another use) or add vanilla extract and bring syrup to a boil. Reduce heat to medium-high and simmer, stirring occasionally, until mixture is thickened and small puffs of steam start to release about 3 minutes.

11. Remove from heat and add cream in 3 additions, stirring with a wooden spoon after each addition until smooth. Gradually whisk hot maple cream into pumpkin mixture.

12. Place pie dish on a rimmed baking sheet and pour in pumpkin filling. Bake pie, rotating halfway through, until set around edge but center barely jiggles 50-60 minutes.

13. Transfer pie dish to a wire rack and let the pie cool. Slice and serve. Enjoy!

Pretzel Rolls

Servings: 6
Cooking Time: 20 Minutes

Ingredients:
- 2 3/4 Cup Bread Flour
- 1 Quick-Rising Yeast, envelope
- 1 Teaspoon salt
- 1 Teaspoon sugar
- 1/2 Teaspoon celery seed
- 1/2 Teaspoon Caraway Seeds
- 1 Cup hot water
- As Needed Cornmeal
- 8 Cup water
- 1/4 Cup baking soda
- 2 Tablespoon sugar
- 1 Whole Egg White
- Coarse salt

Directions:
1. Combine bread flour, 1 envelope yeast, salt, 1 teaspoon sugar, caraway seeds and celery seeds in food processor or standing mixer with dough hook and blend.

2. With machine running, gradually pour hot water, adding enough water to form smooth elastic dough. Process 1 minute to knead. (You could also knead it by hand for a few minutes.)

3. Grease medium bowl. Add dough to bowl, turning to coat. Cover bowl with plastic wrap, then towel; let dough rise in warm draft-free area until doubled in volume, about 35 minutes.

4. Flour a large baking sheet. Punch dough down and knead on lightly floured surface until smooth. Divide into 8 pieces. Form each dough piece into a ball.

5. Place dough balls on prepared sheet, flattening each slightly. Using serrated knife, cut X in top center of each dough ball. Cover with towel and let dough balls rise until almost doubled in volume, about 20 minutes.

6. When ready to cook, start the smoker on Smoke with the lid open until a fire is established (4-5 minutes). Turn temperature to 375 F (190 C) and preheat, lid closed, for 10 to 15 minutes.

7. Grease another baking sheet and sprinkle with cornmeal. Bring water to boil in large saucepan. Add baking soda and sugar (water will foam up). Add 3 rolls (or however many will fit comfortably in the pot) and cook 30 seconds per side.

8. Using slotted spoon, transfer rolls to prepared sheet, arranging X side up. Repeat with remaining rolls. Brush rolls with egg white glaze. Sprinkle rolls generously with coarse salt.

9. Bake rolls until brown, about 20 to 25 minutes. Transfer to racks and cool 10 minutes. Serve rolls warm or at room temperature. Enjoy!

Donut Bread Pudding

Servings: 8
Cooking Time: 40 Minutes

Ingredients:
- 16 Cake Donuts
- 1/2 Cup Raisins, seedless
- 5 eggs
- 3/4 Cup sugar
- 2 Cup heavy cream
- 2 Teaspoon vanilla extract
- 1 Teaspoon ground cinnamon
- 3/4 Cup Butter, melted, cooled slightly
- Ice Cream

Directions:
1. Lightly butter a 9- by 13-inch baking pan. Layer the donuts in an even thickness in the pan. Distribute the raisins over the top, if using. Drizzle evenly with the butter.

2. Make the custard: In a medium bowl, whisk together the sugar, eggs, cream, vanilla, and cinnamon. Whisk in the butter. Pour over the donuts. Let sit for 10 to 15 minutes, periodically pushing the donuts down into the custard. Cover with foil.

3. Supply your smoker with wood pellets and follow the start-up procedure. Preheat the grill, with the lid closed, to 350° F.

4. Bake the bread pudding for 30 to 40 minutes, or until the custard is set. Remove the foil and continue to bake for 10 additional minutes to lightly brown the top. Grill: 350 °F

5. Let cool slightly before cutting into squares. Drizzle with melted ice cream, if desired. Enjoy!

Smoked Sweet Beer Bread

Servings: 6
Cooking Time: 60 Minutes

Ingredients:
- 3 cups all-purpose flour, sifted
- 2 tbsp. sugar
- 1 tbsp. baking powder
- 1 tsp. salt
- 1 (12 oz) can or bottle beer (not too dark or bitter)
- 2 tbsp. honey or agave, warmed
- 6 tbsp. butter, melted

Directions:

1. Supply your smoker with wood pellets and follow the start-up procedure. Preheat the grill, with the lid closed, to 350° F.

2. Lightly grease a 9 ×5 inch loaf pan.

3. In a large mixing bowl, put in the flour, sugar, baking powder, and salt. Whisk to combine and aerate, using a wire whisk. Add the beer and honey and stir with a wooden spoon until the batter is properly mixed (Do not over-mix).

4. Pour half of the melted butter into the prepared loaf pan and pour in the batter. Pour the remaining butter over the top of the loaf.

5. Place the loaf pan on the grill grate and bake for 50 to 60 minutes or until the bread is golden brown.

6. Allow the loaf to cool slightly in the pan before removing it from the pan. Leftovers make great toast.

Baked Pumpkin Pie

Servings: 6
Cooking Time: 50 Minutes

Ingredients:
- 4 Ounce cream cheese
- 15 Ounce pumpkin puree
- 1/3 Cup Cream, whipping
- 1/2 Cup brown sugar
- 1 Teaspoon pumpkin pie spice
- 3 Large eggs
- 1 frozen pie crust, thawed

Directions:
1. Supply your smoker with wood pellets and follow the start-up procedure. Preheat the grill, with the lid closed, to 325° F.

2. Mix cream cheese, puree, milk, sugar, and spice. One at a time, incorporate an egg to the mixture. Pour mixture into pie shell.

3. Bake for 50 minutes, edges should be golden and pie should be firm around edges with slight movement in middle. Let cool before whip cream is applied. Serve and enjoy! Grill: 325 ˚F

Garlic Cheese Pull Apart Bread

Servings: 2
Cooking Time: 20 Minutes

Ingredients:
- 1 Loaf Bread, Sourdough Round
- 2 1/2 Tbsp Butter, Salted
- 8 Oz Fontina Cheese
- 1 Grated Garlic, Roasted
- 1/4 Cup Parsley, Minced Fresh
- 1 Tsp Red Flakes Pepper
- 1 Pinch Salt

Directions:
1. Start your Grill on "smoke" with the lid open until a fire is established in the burn pot (3-7 minutes). Supply your smoker with wood pellets and follow the start-up procedure. Preheat the grill, with the lid closed, to 300° F.

2. In a small bowl, add the soft butter, grated garlic, red pepper flakes, sea salt, and ¼ cup of the chopped parsley, and whisk together. With a bread serrated knife, cut 1-inch slices into the bread, not cutting all the way through the bottom of the load. With a butter knife, spread a thin layer of the butter mixture on each slice of the bread. Take the serrated knife again, and cut across the loaf to form 1 inch squares. Next, slice the cheese into small thin slices, then stuff one slice into each bread opening. Place the bread on a baking sheet, and cover tightly with aluminum foil. Place on the grill for about 10 minutes, remove the foil, and grill for a few more minutes until the top is nicely golden and the cheese is oozing. Remove from the grill, sprinkle with fresh parsley leaves, then serve.

Chicken Pizza On The Grill

Servings: 4

Cooking Time: 10 Minutes

Ingredients:

- 3 Boneless, Skinless Chicken Breast
- 5 Cups Flour, Strong
- 3 Cups Georgia Style Bbq Sauce
- 3 Cups Mozzarella Cheese, Shredded
- 1 Tsp Olive Oil
- 3 Cups Georgia Style BBQ Sauce
- 1 1/2 Cups Red Bell Peppers, Diced
- 1 1/2 Cups Red Onion, Diced
- 1 Tsp Sugar
- 1/2 Cup Water, Hot
- 1 1/4 Cup Water, Warm
- 2 Tsb Active Yeast, Instant

Directions:

1. Roll your pizza dough so it forms a base about a 1/2 inch thick. To impress your friends and family, you'll want to aim for a nice, pizza like shape. HINT: use a sprinkle of cornmeal on the countertop to aid in moving the dough.

2. Now for the toppings! Start by spreading 1 cup of Georgia Style BBQ sauce onto each base. Make sure to leave a small portion for the crust! Next, load up with sliced, cooked chicken breasts, diced red onions and red bell peppers before finishing off with a two cups of shredded mozzarella cheese.

3. Supply your smoker with wood pellets and follow the start-up procedure. Preheat the grill, with the lid closed, to 500° F. Place the pizza stone in your grill. Pick up your pizza using a flat surface like a chopping board and slide the pizza carefully onto the hot stone. Close the lid and let your homemade wood-fired pizza bake for 10 - 12 minutes. Remove once your pizza has a golden crust and the cheese is bubbling. Cut and serve for pizza you'll hardly want to share.

Smoker Wheat Bread

Servings: 6

Cooking Time: 60 Minutes

Ingredients:

- As Needed extra-virgin olive oil
- 2 Cup all-purpose flour
- 1 Cup whole wheat flour
- 1 1/4 Ounce Packet, Active Dry Yeast
- 1 1/4 Teaspoon salt
- 1 1/2 Cup water
- As Needed Cornmeal

Directions:

1. Oil a large mixing bowl and set aside. In a second mixing bowl, combine the flours, yeast, and salt.

2. Push your sleeve up to your elbow and form your fingers into a claw. Mix the dry ingredients until well-combined.

3. Add the water and mix until blended. The dough will be wet, shaggy, and somewhat stringy.

4. Tip the dough into the oiled mixing bowl and cover with plastic wrap.

5. Allow the dough to rise at room temperature-- about 70 degrees-- for 2 hours, or until the surface is bubbled.

6. Turn the dough out onto a lightly floured work surface and lightly flour the top. With floured hands, fold the dough over on itself twice. Cover loosely with plastic wrap and allow the dough to rest for 15 minutes.

7. Dust a clean lint-free cotton towel with cornmeal, wheat bran, or flour. With floured hands, gently form the dough into a ball and place it, seam side down, on the towel.

8. Dust the top of the ball with cornmeal, wheat bran, or flour, and cover the dough with a second towel. Let the dough rise until doubled in size; the dough will not spring back when poked with a finger.

9. In the meantime, start the smoker grill and set temperature to 450 F. Preheat, lid closed, for 10-15 minutes.

10. Put a lidded 6- to 8-quart cast iron Dutch oven - preferably one coated with enamel, on the grill grate.

11. When the dough has risen, remove the top towel, slide your hand under the bottom towel to support the dough, then carefully tip the dough, seam side up, into the preheated pot.

12. Remove the towel. Shake the pot a couple of times if the dough looks lopsided: It will straighten out as it bakes.

13. Cover the pot with the lid and bake the bread for 30 minutes. Remove the lid and continue to bake the bread for 15 to 30 minutes more, or until it is nicely browned and sounds hollow when rapped with your knuckles.

14. Turn onto a wire rack to cool. Slice with a serrated knife. Enjoy!

Baked Bourbon Monkey Bread

Servings: 6
Cooking Time: 40 Minutes

Ingredients:
- 3 Can Pillsbury Grands Buttermilk Biscuits
- 1 Cup sugar
- 3 Teaspoon ground cinnamon
- 1 Cup Butter, unsalted
- 1 Cup dark brown sugar
- Tablespoon bourbon

Directions:

1. Supply your smoker with wood pellets and follow the start-up procedure. Preheat the grill, with the lid closed, to 350° F.

2. Cut each biscuit into quarters. In a Ziploc bag, combine sugar and cinnamon and add quartered biscuits. Toss to coat in cinnamon sugar.

3. Dump coated biscuit dough into a bundt pan coated with non-stick spray.

4. In a small saucepan, combine the brown sugar, butter, and bourbon. Cook over medium heat until the sugar has dissolved.

5. Pour the butter mixture over the biscuits in the bundt pan.

6. Place in the center of the grill and cook for 40 minutes or until dark golden brown.

7. Let cool on the counter for 5-10 minutes, then flip out onto a serving plate. Enjoy!

Baked Pear Tarte Tatin

Servings: 6
Cooking Time: 45 Minutes

Ingredients:
- 2 1/2 Cup all-purpose flour
- 2 Tablespoon sugar
- butter chilled
- 8 Tablespoon cold water
- 1/4 Cup granulated sugar
- 1/4 Cup butter
- 8 Whole Bartlett Pear

Directions:

1. Supply your smoker with wood pellets and follow the start-up procedure. Preheat the grill, with the lid closed, to 350° F.

2. For the crust: Place flour and sugar in a food processor and pulse to mix. Add butter a little at a time while pulsing. Once it starts to looks like

cornmeal, add the water until dough start to come together.

3. Form a round with the dough, wrap in plastic and let it cool in the refrigerator.

4. While dough cools, make the caramel sauce. In a sauce pan, add 1/4 cup granulated sugar and 1/4 cup butter. Cook butter and sugar until it becomes a dark caramel, a couple minutes.

5. Pour caramel in the bottom of 10 inch deep cake pan. While the caramel is still hot, arrange pear wedges in a fan formation covering the caramel.

6. Roll the chilled pie dough into a circle big enough to cover the pan. Prick the pie dough with a fork and cover the pan with the pie dough. Trim the crust leaving room for shrinkage.

7. Place on the grill and bake for 45 minutes or until pears are soft. The pears will be soft and most of the juice will evaporate and thicken.

8. Let sit for 3 minutes. While pan is still hot, place a plate over pie and flip over. Slowly lift the plate.

9. Serve warm, topped with vanilla ice cream or whipped cream. Enjoy!

Sourdough Pizza

Servings: 4
Cooking Time: 12 Minutes

Ingredients:
* 1 1/2 Cup Fresh Sourdough Starter
* 1 Tablespoon olive oil
* 1 Teaspoon Jacobsen Salt Co. Pure Kosher Sea Salt
* 1 1/4 Cup all-purpose flour

Directions:

1. Supply your smoker with wood pellets and follow the start-up procedure. Preheat the grill, with the lid closed, to 450° F.

2. Mix together the fresh sourdough starter, one tablespoon of oil, Jacobsen salt and 1-1/4 cups of flour. Add more flour, a little at a time, as needed to form a pizza dough consistency.

3. Allow the dough to rest for 30 minutes, to allow for easier rolling. Roll the dough out into a circle, using a small amount of flour to prevent sticking.

4. Place on a pizza stone. Bake the crust for approximately 7 minutes Grill: 450 ˚F

5. Remove the crust from the grill; brush on remaining oil to prevent toppings from soaking into the crust. Add the desired toppings and return pizza to grill; bake until the crust browns and the cheese melts.

Caramelized Bourbon Baked Pears

Servings: 4
Cooking Time: 30 Minutes

Ingredients:
* 3 Whole Pears, fresh
* 1/4 Cup brown sugar
* 1/4 Cup bourbon
* 2 Tablespoon butter, melted
* 1 Teaspoon vanilla extract
* 1/2 Teaspoon salt

Directions:

1. Supply your smoker with wood pellets and follow the start-up procedure. Preheat the grill, with the lid closed, to 325° F.

2. Peel and core the pears. Arrange them in a buttered baking dish.

3. In a small bowl, combine the brown sugar, bourbon, butter, vanilla, cinnamon and salt. Pour the bourbon mixture over the pears.

4. Place the baking dish on the grill grate, close the lid and bake for 30-35 minutes or until the pears are fork tender. Grill: 325 °F

5. Transfer to a serving plate and spoon the caramelized bourbon mixture over the pears.

6. Serve warm over vanilla ice cream. Enjoy!

Baked Potatoes & Celery Root Au Gratin

Servings: 2

Cooking Time: 60 Minutes

Ingredients:

- 5 Tablespoon butter, softened
- 2 Large leeks, white parts only, cleaned and sliced into half moons
- kosher salt
- freshly ground black pepper
- 5 Small Yukon Gold potatoes, sliced 1/4 inch thick
- 2 Whole celery root, peeled and sliced 1/4 inch thick
- 2 Cup cream
- 1 Tablespoon minced sage
- 1 Cup shredded Gruyere or other hearty Swiss cheese, divided

Directions:

1. Supply your smoker with wood pellets and follow the start-up procedure. Preheat the grill, with the lid closed, to 400° F.

2. Butter a 9x13 baking dish with 1 tablespoon of the softened butter. In a medium frying pan over medium heat, melt the remaining butter. Add the leeks and a generous pinch of salt and pepper and cook, stirring often until softened, about 5 minutes.

3. Remove from the heat and allow to cool. Place the potato and celery root slices into a large mixing bowl. Add the cream, leek mixture, minced sage, 1 teaspoon salt, 1/2 teaspoon pepper and 1 cup cheese. Stir gently to coat.

4. Arrange a layer of potato and celery root slices so they're slightly overlapping in the prepared baking dish. Repeat two more times so there are three layers of potatoes. Pour remaining cream from the bowl over the gratin, then sprinkle the top with the remaining cup of cheese.

5. Cover the dish loosely with foil and bake on the grill for 45 minutes. Remove the foil and continue baking until the top is golden and bubbly and the potatoes are tender when pierced, about 30 to 45 minutes longer. Let stand for 10 minutes before serving. Enjoy!

Zucchini Bread

Servings: 6

Cooking Time: 50 Minutes

Ingredients:

- 1 Cup Walnuts, Chopped
- 2 Large zucchini
- 1 Teaspoon salt
- 1 Teaspoon ground cinnamon
- 1/4 Teaspoon ground cloves
- 1/4 Teaspoon baking powder
- 3 Cup all-purpose flour
- 1 eggs
- 2 Cup sugar
- 1/2 Cup vegetable oil
- 1/2 Cup Yogurt
- 1 1/2 Teaspoon vanilla extract

Directions:

1. Grease and flour two 9- by 5-inch bread pans, preferably nonstick.

2. When ready to cook, set the temperature to 350°F and preheat, lid closed for 15 minutes.

3. Spread the walnuts on a pie plate and toast for 10 minutes, stirring once. Let cool, then coarsely chop. Set aside.

4. Trim the ends off the zucchini, then coarsely grate into a colander set over the sink on a box grater (or use the shredding disk on a food processor). You'll need 2 cups.

5. Sprinkle with the salt and let drain for 30 minutes. Press on the zucchini with paper towels to expel excess water.

6. Sift the flour, baking powder, cinnamon, and cloves in a mixing bowl or on a large sheet of parchment or wax paper.

7. Combine the eggs, sugar, oil, yogurt, and vanilla in a large mixing bowl and mix on medium speed. (You can mix the batter by hand, if desired.) Add half the dry ingredients and mix on low speed; add the remaining dry ingredients and mix until just combined.

8. Stir in the walnuts and zucchini by hand.

9. Divide the batter between the prepared baking pans.

10. Arrange the pans directly on the grill grate and bake for 50 minutes, or until a bamboo skewer inserted in the center of the breads comes out clean.

11. Transfer to a wire rack and let cool for 10 minutes, then remove the breads from the pans.

For best results, let the breads cool completely before slicing.

Onion Cheese Nachos

Servings: 6
Cooking Time: 10 Minutes

Ingredients:
- 1 Pound Beef, Ground
- 3 Cups Cheddar Cheese, Shredded
- 1 Green Bell Pepper, Diced
- 1/2 Cup Green Onion
- 1/2 Cup Red Onion, Diced
- 1 Large Bag Tortilla Chip

Directions:

1. Supply your smoker with wood pellets and follow the start-up procedure. Preheat the grill, with the lid closed, to 350° F.

2. While you're waiting, empty a large bag of nacho chips evenly onto a cast iron pan. Start loading up with toppings - cooked ground beef, red onion, red pepper, cheese, green onions. These are just the toppings we had on hand, so feel free to add anything you like! Make sure you do a couple layers of chips so everyone gets a good serving of nachos. And don't be skimpy with the cheese - lay it on heavy!

3. Place your loaded nachos on the grill and let the hot smoke melt your toppings into one cheesy creation. Heat at 350°F for 10 minutes or until the cheese has fully melted. Remove and serve with sour-cream and salsa.

SEAFOOD RECIPES

Whole Vermillion Red Snapper

Servings: 6
Cooking Time: 20 Minutes

Ingredients:
- 1 Whole Vermillion Red Snapper, scaled & gutted
- 4 Clove garlic, chopped
- 1 Whole lemon, thinly sliced
- 2 Sprig rosemary sprigs
- sea salt and freshly ground black pepper

Directions:
1. Supply your smoker with wood pellets and follow the start-up procedure. Preheat the grill, with the lid closed, to High heat.
2. Stuff the cavity of the fish with chopped garlic. Sprinkle the fish with sea salt, pepper, rosemary, and lemon.
3. Grill fish directly on the grill grate. Cook for 20-25 minutes. Serve. Enjoy!

Lemon Scallops Wrapped In Bacon

Servings: 4
Cooking Time: 20 Minutes

Ingredients:
- 3 Tbsp Lemon, Juice
- Pepper
- 12 Scallop

Directions:
1. Start your grill on smoke with the lid open until a fire is established in the burn pot (3-7 minutes).

2. Supply your smoker with wood pellets and follow the start-up procedure. Preheat the grill, with the lid closed, to 400° F.Cut the bacon rashers in half, wrap each half around a scallop and use a toothpick to keep it in place.
3. Next drizzle the lemon juice over the scallops, and then place them on a baking tray.
4. Place in the grill, and grill for about 15-20 minutes, or until the bacon is crisp, remove from the grill, then serve.

Grilled Salmon

Servings: 4
Cooking Time: 25 Minutes

Ingredients:
- 1 (2-pound) half salmon fillet
- 3 tablespoons mayonnaise
- 1 batch Dill Seafood Rub

Directions:
1. Supply your smoker with wood pellets and follow the start-up procedure. Preheat the grill, with the lid closed, to 325°F.
2. Using your hands, rub the salmon fillet all over with the mayonnaise and sprinkle it with the rub.
3. Place the salmon directly on the grill grate, skin-side down, and grill until its internal temperature reaches 145°F. Remove the salmon from the grill and serve immediately.

Grilled Crab Legs With Herb Butter

Servings: 2
Cooking Time: 15 Minutes

Ingredients:
- 12 Tablespoon butter
- 3 Tablespoon Fresh Herbs (Parsley, Chives, Tarragon), finely chopped
- 4 Pound King Crab Legs or Dungeness Crab Leg Clusters
- 3 Whole Lemons, cut into wedges

Directions:
1. Supply your smoker with wood pellets and follow the start-up procedure. Preheat the grill, with the lid closed, to 375° F.
2. Place the butter, garlic, herbs, and a pinch of salt into a small cast iron sauce pan. Place on grill for 5 minutes to melt. Remove from grill and stir. Grill: 375 °F
3. If using king crab legs, split down the center and pour herb butter over meat reserving a quarter for serving. If using crab clusters, toss clusters with herb butter in a large mixing bowl reserving a quarter for serving.
4. Place crab legs directly on the grill grate, meat side up. Grill for 5 to 10 minutes or until hot and beginning to develop a little char on the shell. Grill: 375 °F
5. Serve crab legs with lemon wedges and reserved herb butter. Enjoy!

Mezcal Shrimp With Salsa De Molcajete

Servings: 4
Cooking Time: 14 Minutes

Ingredients:

- 18 to 24 jumbo shrimp, about 1½lb (680g) total, peeled and deveined
- ⅓ cup mezcal
- juice of ½ lime
- 2 tbsp extra virgin olive oil
- 2 tsp coarse salt
- 1 tsp ground cumin
- lime wedges
- for the salsa
- 2 Roma tomatoes
- 2 tomatillos, husked and washed
- 2 garlic cloves, peeled and impaled on a toothpick
- 1 jalapeño or serrano pepper
- 1 small white onion, halved
- ½ tsp coarse salt, plus more
- juice of ½ lime
- ¼ cup loosely packed fresh cilantro leaves

Directions:
1. Supply your smoker with wood pellets and follow the start-up procedure. Preheat the grill, with the lid closed, to 450° F.
2. In a large bowl, combine the shrimp, mezcal, lime juice, olive oil, salt, and ground cumin. Toss with your hands to mix thoroughly. Set aside for 15 minutes and then toss once more.
3. Begin to make the salsa by placing the tomatoes, tomatillos, garlic, jalapeño, and onion on the grate. Grill until they begin to char, about 3 minutes for the garlic and about 6 to 8 minutes for the other vegetables, turning as needed. Transfer the vegetables to a rimmed sheet pan. Remove the skewers from the garlic. Let everything cool. Coarsely chop the vegetables and leave them in separate piles.
4. Place the garlic in the molcajete and add the salt. Mash the garlic to a purée using the temolote.

Add the onion and grind it into the garlic paste. Stir in the jalapeño (deseeded for a milder salsa), tomatoes, and tomatillos. Stir in the lime juice and cilantro leaves. Taste, adding salt. (If you don't own a molcajete or temolote, prepare the salsa using a small food processor.)

5. Drain the shrimp and discard the marinade. Thread the shrimp on wood or bamboo skewers. Place the shrimp on the grate and grill until they're white and opaque, about 4 to 6 minutes, tossing with tongs.

6. Transfer the shrimp to a platter. Serve with the salsa and lime wedges.

Coconut Shrimp Jalapeño Poppers

Servings: 6
Cooking Time: 55 Minutes

Ingredients:
- 8 Whole shrimp, peeled and deveined
- 1/2 Teaspoon Chicken Rub, plus more as needed
- olive oil
- 6 Whole jalapeños
- 8 Ounce cream cheese, softened
- 2 Tablespoon fresh chopped cilantro
- 1/2 Cup unsweetened coconut flakes
- 12 Slices bacon

Directions:
1. Supply your smoker with wood pellets and follow the start-up procedure. Preheat the grill, with the lid closed, to 425° F.
2. Rinse and season the shrimp with the Traeger Chicken Rub.
3. Drizzle the shrimp with olive oil and cook on the Traeger for about 5 minutes per side, or until the shrimp is opaque. Grill: 425 °F
4. Remove the shrimp and let cool.

5. Reduce Traeger temperature to 350°F. Grill: 350 °F
6. Meanwhile, get those poppers going. Cut the jalapeños in half then remove the stems and seeds.
7. Chop the shrimp. Mix together the softened cream cheese, chopped shrimp, 1/2 teaspoon Traeger Chicken Rub and 2 tablespoons chopped cilantro.
8. Load a generous amount of the filling in each pepper half. Top with a sprinkle of coconut.
9. Wrap each stuffed pepper with a slice of bacon and place on a foil-lined baking sheet.
10. Cook the peppers on the Traeger for about 45 minutes, or until the bacon fat has rendered and the cream cheese is golden. Enjoy! Grill: 350 °F

Lobster Tail

Servings: 2
Cooking Time: 25 Minutes

Ingredients:
- 2 lobster tails
- Salt
- Freshly ground black pepper
- 1 batch Lemon Butter Mop for Seafood

Directions:
1. Supply your smoker with wood pellets and follow the start-up procedure. Preheat the grill, with the lid closed, to 375°F.
2. Using kitchen shears, slit the top of the lobster shells, through the center, nearly to the tail. Once cut, expose as much meat as you can through the cut shell.
3. Season the lobster tails all over with salt and pepper.
4. Place the tails directly on the grill grate and grill until their internal temperature reaches 145°F. Remove the lobster from the grill and serve with the mop on the side for dipping.

Cold-smoked Salmon Gravlax

Servings: 6

Cooking Time: 30 Minutes

Ingredients:

- 1 Cup kosher salt
- 1 Cup sugar
- 1 Tablespoon freshly ground black pepper
- 2 Pound Sushi-Grad Salmon Fillet, Skin-on, Pin Bones Removed
- 2 Bunch Dill Weed, fresh
- capers, drained
- red onion, sliced
- cream cheese
- lemons

Directions:

1. In a bowl stir together the salt, sugar and black pepper until thoroughly combined. On a work surface, turn salmon skin side up and sprinkle about half of salt mixture all over and rub in.

2. Arrange half the dill on the bottom of a baking dish large enough to hold the salmon. Set salmon skin side down on bed of dill.

3. Rub remaining salt mixture all over top and sides of salmon, then top with remaining dill. Cover with plastic, then top with a weight on a smaller baking dish or a plate with cans of beans on top, then place in refrigerator and allow to cure for 2 days.

4. Remove salmon from refrigerator, rinse under cold water and pat dry with paper towels. Allow to sit at room temperature on the counter for 1 hour

5. Supply your smoker with wood pellets and follow the start-up procedure. Preheat the grill, with the lid closed, to 180° F. Place salmon onto a baking pan. Fill another baking pan with ice and place baking pan with salmon over ice. Place onto grill and smoke for 30 minutes.

6. Remove from grill and slice thin. Serve with capers, red onion, dill, cream cheese, and lemon. Enjoy!

Flavour Fire Spiced Shrimp

Servings: 2

Cooking Time: 8 Minutes

Ingredients:

- 1 pound of extra large raw whole wild shrimp
- 1 tablespoon vegetable oil
- 1 tablespoon chili powder
- 1 teaspoon garlic powder
- 1/2 teaspoon onion powder
- 1/2 teaspoon cayenne pepper
- 1/4 teaspoon paprika
- 1/4 teaspoon dried oregano
- Pinch of Kosher salt

Directions:

1. Supply your smoker with wood pellets and follow the start-up procedure. Preheat the grill, with the lid closed, to High heat.

2. While grill is preheating, remove the shrimp shells, leaving the heads.

3. Butterfly shrimp by using a knife to cut each shrimp down the middle, from the head down to the tail.

4. Remove the vein, rinse off the shrimp and lightly dry off with paper towels.

5. Place the shrimp in a large bowl, sprinkle with all the seasonings and the oil.

6. Mix together, ensuring the mixture evenly covers each shrimp.

7. Using a skewer, impale the whole body of a shrimp, from head to tail. (Wrap them in aluminum foil if using wooden skewers).

8. Place the whole shrimp on the grill and cook for 3-4 minutes on each side (Or until shells turns pink and the shrimp is opaque).

9. Serve with your favorite sauce or condiment.

Teriyaki Smoked Honey Tilapia

Servings: 4

Cooking Time: 120 Minutes

Ingredients:

- 4 tilapia fillets
- 1 cup teriyaki sauce
- 2/3 cup honey
- 1 tbsp sriracha sauce
- Green onions (optional)

Directions:

1. In a large bowl, make the marinade by mixing together the teriyaki sauce, honey,and sriracha. Make sure honey is dissolved and well blended.

2. Place the tilapia fillets in the marinade. Turn the fillets so they are completely coated. Cover with a plastic wrap and marinate in the fridge for about 2 hours.

3. Supply your smoker with wood pellets and follow the start-up procedure. Preheat the grill, with the lid closed, to 275° F.

4. Remove the tilapia fillets from the marinade and transfer them to the grill. Smoke the fillets until they reach an internal temperature of 145°F, about 2 hours.

5. Sprinkle with green onions if desired.

Florentine Shrimp Al Cartoccio

Servings: 4

Cooking Time: 13 Minutes

Ingredients:

- 6 tbsp unsalted butter, melted
- ½ cup heavy whipping cream
- ½ cup grated Parmesan cheese
- 2 garlic cloves, peeled and minced
- 1 cup thinly sliced button mushrooms, cleaned and destemmed
- 1 cup baby spinach leaves
- 2 tbsp chopped sun-dried, oil-packed tomatoes
- ½ tsp dried oregano
- ½ tsp dried basil
- ½ tsp crushed red pepper flakes, plus more
- ½ tsp coarse salt
- ½ tsp freshly ground black pepper
- 20 to 24 jumbo shrimp, about 1lb (450g) total, peeled and deveined
- sprigs of fresh rosemary, basil, thyme, or oregano

Directions:

1. Supply your smoker with wood pellets and follow the start-up procedure. Preheat the grill, with the lid closed, to 400° F.

2. In a large bowl, combine the butter and whipping cream. Stir in the Parmesan, garlic, mushrooms, spinach, tomatoes, oregano, basil, red pepper flakes, and salt and pepper. Add the shrimp and stir gently to coat.

3. Place four 12-inch (30.5cm) sheets of wide heavy-duty aluminum foil on a workspace and pull up the sides. Divide the shrimp mixture evenly between the sheets of foil. Roll and crimp the top and sides of the foil to create sealed packages.

4. Place the packets seam side up on the grate and grill until the shrimp are cooked through, about 10 to 13 minutes. (You can carefully open one package to check on the shrimp.)

5. Transfer the packets to plates. Carefully open the packets to avoid any steam. Scatter fresh herbs over the shrimp before serving.

Honey-soy Garlic Salmon

Servings: 4

Cooking Time: 6 Minutes

Ingredients:

- 1 Tsp Chili Paste
- Chives, Chopped
- 2 Grate Garlic, Cloves
- 2 Tbsp Minced Ginger, Fresh
- 1 Tsp Honey
- 2 Tbsp Lemon, Juice
- 4 Salmon, Fillets (Skin Removed)
- 1 Tsp Sesame Oil
- 2 Tbsp Soy Sauce, Low Sodium

Directions:

1. Supply your smoker with wood pellets and follow the start-up procedure. Preheat the grill, with the lid closed, to 400° F.

2. Take the salmon and place it in a large resealable plastic bag, and then top with all remaining ingredients, except the chives. Seal the plastic bag and toss evenly to coat the salmon. Marinade in the refrigerator for 20 minutes.

3. After the salmon has been marinading for 20 minutes, place salmon on a flat pan or right on the grates and grill for about 3 minutes, and then flip and grill on the second side for about 3 minutes. Turn off the Grill, remove the pan from grill, plate, garnish with chives, and enjoy!

Alder Smoked Scallops With Citrus & Garlic Butter Sauce

Servings: 4

Cooking Time: 35 Minutes

Ingredients:

- 2 Pound large dry sea scallops
- kosher salt
- freshly ground black pepper
- 8 Tablespoon salted butter, melted
- 1 Clove garlic, minced
- 1 Small orange
- 1/4 Teaspoon Worcestershire sauce
- 1 1/2 Teaspoon fresh chopped parsley or tarragon
- flat-leaf parsley, for serving

Directions:

1. Wash the scallops under cold running water and thoroughly pat dry on paper towels. Remove any tags of abductor muscle tissue you find on the sides of the scallops.

2. Arrange the scallops on a baking sheet fitted with a cooling rack, and season with salt and pepper.

3. Supply your smoker with wood pellets and follow the start-up procedure. Preheat the grill, with the lid closed, to 165° F.

4. Place the baking sheet with the scallops on the grill grate and smoke for 20 minutes.

5. While your scallops are smoking, make your sauce. Melt the butter in a small saucepan over medium-low heat. Add a pinch of salt, garlic, Worcestershire sauce, zest and juice from half of the orange, and parsley. Simmer for 5 minutes. Keep warm.

6. Remove the baking sheet with the scallops from the grill and set aside. Increase the temperature to 400°F and preheat, lid closed. Optional: Place an oyster bed or oyster pan in the grill to preheat. These heavy iron pans are a great way to sear the scallops. Grill: 400 °F

7. Return the baking sheet with the scallops to the grill, brush with the butter sauce, reserving some for serving. Roast until just opaque and tender, 10 to 15 minutes. The time will depend

on how thick the scallops are. Do not overcook. If you are using an oyster pan, brush each compartment lightly with olive oil to prevent sticking. Spoon butter sauce on each of the scallops, reserving some for serving.

8. Serve the scallops hot with a little more orange zest, fresh parsley and the the warm citrus and garlic butter sauce. Enjoy!

Spicy Lime Shrimp

Servings: 4
Cooking Time: 10 Minutes

Ingredients:

- 2 Tsp Chili Paste
- 1/2 Tsp Cumin
- 2 Cloves Garlic, Minced
- 1 Large Lime, Juiced
- 1/4 Tsp Paprika, Powder
- 1/4 Tsp Red Flakes Pepper
- 1/2 Tsp Salt

Directions:

1. In a bowl, whisk together the lime juice, olive oil, garlic, chili powder, cumin, paprika, salt, pepper, and red pepper flakes.

2. Then pour it into a resealable bag, add the shrimp, toss the coat, let it marinate for 30 minutes.

3. Supply your smoker with wood pellets and follow the start-up procedure. Preheat the grill, with the lid closed, to 400° F.

4. Next place the shrimp on skewers, place on the grill, and grill each side for about two minutes until it's done. One finished, remove the shrimp from the grill and enjoy!

Cajun Catfish

Servings: 6

Cooking Time: 15 Minutes

Ingredients:

- 2½ pounds catfish fillets
- 2 tablespoons olive oil
- 1 batch Cajun Rub

Directions:

1. Supply your smoker with wood pellets and follow the start-up procedure. Preheat the grill, with the lid closed, to 300°F.

2. Coat the catfish fillets all over with olive oil and season with the rub. Using your hands, work the rub into the flesh.

3. Place the fillets directly on the grill grate and smoke until their internal temperature reaches 145°F. Remove the catfish from the grill and serve immediately

Garlic Grilled Shrimp Skewers

Servings: 3
Cooking Time: 6 Minutes

Ingredients:

- 1 pound large shrimp
- 1/4 cup olive oil
- 1/4 cup fresh cilantro, finely chopped
- 1/4 cup fresh parsley, finely chopped
- 4 cloves garlic, minced
- 1 tablespoon lemon juice
- 1/2 teaspoon salt
- 1/4 teaspoon black pepper
- Pinch cayenne pepper, adjust to spice preference

Directions:

1. Add the olive oil, herbs, and spices to a small mixing bowl and whisk together.

2. Place the shrimp in a bowl and pour 3/4 of the marinade on top of the shrimp. Mix together gently to coat the shrimp evenly.

3. Cover the bowl and marinate the shrimp for 30 minutes to an hour.

4. Thread the shrimp on the skewers and make sure to get all the good garlic and herbs from the bowl and spread on to the shrimp.

5. Supply your smoker with wood pellets and follow the start-up procedure. Preheat the grill, with the lid closed, to medium high heat.

6. Once the grill is hot, arrange the shrimp skewers on the grill and cook for 2-3 minutes per side, or until they turn pink and opaque.

7. Remove the shrimp skewers to a plate and spoon the remaining marinade on top before serving.

Baked Steelhead

Servings: 4
Cooking Time: 20 Minutes

Ingredients:

- 1 steelhead fillet
- 16-oz bottle Italian dressing
- 3 Tablespoon unsalted butter
- Blackened Saskatchewan Rub
- 1/2 shallot, minced
- 2 Clove garlic, minced
- 1 lemon

Directions:

1. Supply your smoker with wood pellets and follow the start-up procedure. Preheat the grill, with the lid closed, to 350° F.

2. Put butter in a small cast iron pan and place inside Traeger while preheating to soften. Pour Italian dressing over fillet to evenly coat.

3. Shake Traeger Blackened Saskatchewan rub evenly in a thin layer to cover dressing. Mince shallot and garlic.

4. Remove butter from pre-heated grill, careful as the cast iron will be hot. Stir in shallots and garlic.

5. Spread a nice thick layer of mixture on the top-middle of the fillet. Cut lemon into thin slices and place on top of butter mix.

6. Place steelhead on the grill and cook for 20 to 30 minutes, until fish is flaky, being careful not to over cook.

7. Remove fillet from the grill. Enjoy!

Thai-style Swordfish Steaks With Peanut Sauce

Servings: 4
Cooking Time: 8 Minutes

Ingredients:

- 4 center-cut swordfish steaks, each about 6oz (170g) and 1 inch (2.5cm) thick
- Peanut Sauce
- lime wedges
- for the marinade
- 1/2 cup light Thai-style unsweetened coconut milk
- 2 garlic cloves, peeled and smashed with a chef's knife
- juice and zest of 1 lime
- 1-inch (2.5cm) piece of fresh ginger, peeled and roughly chopped
- 1/2 Thai bird's eye chili pepper or serrano pepper, deseeded and thinly sliced, plus more
- 2 tbsp fresh cilantro leaves, coarsely chopped
- 1 tbsp Asian fish sauce
- 1 tbsp light soy sauce or liquid aminos

- 1 tbsp light brown sugar or low-carb substitute
- 1 tsp ground coriander
- ½ tsp ground turmeric

Directions:

1. In a medium bowl, make the marinade by whisking together the ingredients. Whisk until the brown sugar dissolves.

2. Place the swordfish steaks in a single layer in a nonreactive baking dish and pour the marinade over them, turning the steaks to coat thoroughly. Refrigerate for 1 hour.

3. Supply your smoker with wood pellets and follow the start-up procedure. Preheat the grill, with the lid closed, to 450° F.

4. Remove the swordfish from the marinade and scrape off any solids. (Discard the marinade.) Place the steaks on the grate and grill until the fish easily flakes when pressed with a fork, about 3 to 4 minutes per side, turning with a thin-bladed spatula.

5. Transfer the swordfish steaks to a platter. Serve with the peanut sauce and lime wedges.

Charleston Crab Cakes With Remoulade

Servings: 4
Cooking Time: 45 Minutes

Ingredients:

- 1¼ cups mayonnaise
- ¼ cup yellow mustard
- 2 tablespoons sweet pickle relish, with its juices
- 1 tablespoon smoked paprika
- 2 teaspoons Cajun seasoning
- 2 teaspoons prepared horseradish
- 1 teaspoon hot sauce
- 1 garlic clove, finely minced
- 2 pounds fresh lump crabmeat, picked clean
- 20 butter crackers (such as Ritz brand), crushed
- 2 tablespoons Dijon mustard
- 1 cup mayonnaise
- 2 tablespoons freshly squeezed lemon juice
- 1 tablespoon salted butter, melted
- 1 tablespoon Worcestershire sauce
- 1 tablespoon Old Bay seasoning
- 2 teaspoons chopped fresh parsley
- 1 teaspoon ground mustard
- 2 eggs, beaten
- ¼ cup extra-virgin olive oil, divided

Directions:

1. For the remoulade:

2. In a small bowl, combine the mayonnaise, mustard, pickle relish, paprika, Cajun seasoning, horseradish, hot sauce, and garlic.

3. Refrigerate until ready to serve.

4. For the crab cakes:

5. Supply your smoker with wood pellets and follow the start-up procedure. Preheat, with the lid closed, to 375°F.

6. Spread the crabmeat on a foil-lined baking sheet and place over indirect heat on the grill, with the lid closed, for 30 minutes.

7. Remove from the heat and let cool for 15 minutes.

8. While the crab cools, combine the crushed crackers, Dijon mustard, mayonnaise, lemon juice, melted butter, Worcestershire sauce, Old Bay, parsley, ground mustard, and eggs until well incorporated.

9. Fold in the smoked crabmeat, then shape the mixture into 8 (1-inch-thick) crab cakes.

10. In a large skillet or cast-iron pan on the grill, heat 2 tablespoons of olive oil. Add half of the crab cakes, close the lid, and smoke for 4 to 5 minutes on each side, or until crispy and golden brown.

11. Remove the crab cakes from the pan and transfer to a wire rack to drain. Pat them to remove any excess oil.

12. Repeat steps 6 and 7 with the remaining oil and crab cakes.

13. Serve the crab cakes with the remoulade.

Lemon Shrimp Scampi

Servings: 3
Cooking Time: 10 Minutes

Ingredients:
- 2 Tsp Blackened Sriracha Rub Seasoning
- 1/2 Cup Butter, Cubed, Divided
- 1/2 Tsp Chili Pepper Flakes
- 3 Garlic Cloves, Minced
- To Taste, Lemon Wedges, For Serving
- 1 Lemon, Juice & Zest
- Linguine, Cooked
- 3 Tbsp Parsley, Chopped
- 1 1/2 Lbs Shrimp, Peeled & Deveined
- Toasted Baguette, For Serving

Directions:
1. Supply your smoker with wood pellets and follow the start-up procedure. Preheat the grill, with the lid closed, to medium-high heat. If using a gas or charcoal grill, set it up for medium-high heat.

2. Add half of the butter to the griddle, then sauté the garlic, Blackened Sriracha, and chili flakes for 1 minute, until fragrant.

3. Add the shrimp, turning occasionally for 2 minutes, until opaque.

4. Add the remaining butter, parsley, lemon zest and juice. Toss the shrimp to coat in lemon butter, then remove from the griddle, and transfer to a serving bowl.

5. Serve immediately, with fresh lemon wedges, and toasted baguette. Serve over linguine, spaghetti or zucchini noodles, if desired.

Grilled Blackened Saskatchewan Salmon

Servings: 4
Cooking Time: 30 Minutes

Ingredients:
- 1 salmon fillets
- zesty Italian dressing
- Blackened Saskatchewan Rub
- lemon wedges

Directions:
1. Brush salmon with Italian dressing and season with Traeger Blackened Saskatchewan Rub.

2. Supply your smoker with wood pellets and follow the start-up procedure. Preheat the grill, with the lid closed, to 325° F.

3. Place salmon on the grill and cook for 20 to 30 minutes, until it reaches an internal temperature of 145°F and flakes easily. Remove salmon from grill. Serve with lemon wedges. Enjoy! Grill: 325 °F Probe: 145 °F

Smoked Sugar Halibut

Servings: 8
Cooking Time: 120 Minutes

Ingredients:
- 1/4 cup granulated sugar
- 1/4 cup brown sugar
- 1/2 cup kosher salt

- 1 tsp ground coriander
- 2 lbs fresh halibut

Directions:

1. In a small bowl, mix the sugars, salt,and coriander together. Season the halibut on all sides.

2. Wrap the halibut in plastic wrap, place on a rimmed sheet pan,and brine in the fridge for 3 hours.

3. Remove the plastic wrap and rinse the fish. Pat it dry. Set it on a drying rack over a sheet pan for 1-2 hours in the fridge.

4. Supply your smoker with wood pellets and follow the start-up procedure. Preheat the grill, with the lid closed, to 200° F. Smoke the fish for 2 hours or until its internal temperature reaches 140 °F.

5. Serve your preferred sauce with the fish.

Peper Fish Tacos

Servings: 12

Cooking Time: 10 Minutes

Ingredients:

- 1 Tsp Black Pepper
- 1/4 Tsp Cayenne Pepper
- 1 1/2 Lbs Cod Fish
- 1/2 Tsp Cumin
- 1 Tsp Garlic Powder
- 1 Tsp Oregano
- 1 1/2 Tsp Paprika, Smoked
- 1/2 Tsp Salt

Directions:

1. Supply your smoker with wood pellets and follow the start-up procedure. Preheat the grill, with the lid closed, to 350° F.

2. Mix together paprika, garlic powder, oregano, cumin, cayenne, salt and pepper. Sprinkle over cod.

3. Place the cod on your preheated for about 5 minutes per side. Toast tortillas over heat, if desired.

4. Break the cod into pieces, smash the avocado, slice the tomatoes in half and place evenly among the tortillas. Top with red onion, lettuce, jalapenos, sour cream, and cilantro. Spritz with lime juice and enjoy!

Smoked Crab Legs

Servings: 4

Cooking Time: 30 Minutes

Ingredients:

- 4 Whole crab legs
- 4 Tablespoon butter, melted
- 1/2 Cup Texas Spicy BBQ Sauce
- salt and pepper
- 1 Tablespoon Fin & Feather Rub

Directions:

1. Supply your smoker with wood pellets and follow the start-up procedure. Preheat the grill, with the lid closed, to 250° F.

2. Place the crab legs directly on the grill grate and smoke for 20 minutes. Grill: 250 °F

3. While the crab is smoking, make the sauce. In a medium bowl, combine melted butter, Traeger Texas Spicy BBQ sauce, salt, pepper and Traeger Fin & Feather Rub.

4. After 20 minutes of cooking, brush the crab legs with the BBQ sauce mixture. Continue to cook for another 10 minutes reserving the remaining sauce to serve. Remove crab legs from the grill, and serve with melted butter and BBQ sauce mixture. Enjoy!

Sweet Mandarin Salmon

Servings: 2

Cooking Time: 10 Minutes

Ingredients:

- 1 Whole lime juice
- 1 Teaspoon sesame oil
- 1 1/2 Cup Mandarin Orange Sauce
- 1 1/2 Tablespoon soy sauce
- 2 Tablespoon cilantro, finely chopped
- Freshly cracked black pepper
- 1 Whole (4 oz) wild salmon fillets

Directions:

1. Supply your smoker with wood pellets and follow the start-up procedure. Preheat the grill, with the lid closed, to 375° F.

2. For the glaze, combine Mandarin orange sauce, lime juice, sesame oil, soy sauce, cilantro and fresh cracked black pepper. Mix together.

3. Cut the salmon into 4 fillets. Brush with glaze and place directly on the grill grate, skin side down.

4. Cook until salmon reaches an internal temperature of 155 degrees F (about 15-20 minutes). Half way through cook time, brush salmon again with the glaze.

5. Remove the salmon from the grill and serve with remaining glaze if desired. Enjoy!

Spiced Smoked Swordfish

Servings: 4

Cooking Time: 60 Minutes

Ingredients:

- 4 swordfish fillets (about 4 ounces each)
- For the brine:
- 1 gallon water
- ½ cup kosher salt
- ½ cup brown sugar
- For the rub:
- 1 tablespoon olive oil
- 1 tablespoon kosher salt
- 1 tablespoon coarse ground black pepper
- 1 tablespoon garlic powder
- 1 tablespoon onion powder

Directions:

1. Make the brine by mixing the water, salt,and sugar in a large pot and stir. Add swordfish fillets to the bowl and refrigerate overnight in the mixture.

2. Supply your smoker with wood pellets and follow the start-up procedure. Preheat the grill, with the lid closed, to 225° F.

3. Remove the fillets from the brine, rinse,and blot dry.

4. Brush a coat of olive oil on each fillet and mix salt, pepper, garlic powder,and onion powder in a small bowl for the rub. Apply the rub liberally to each fillet.

5. Put the fillets skin-side down on the smoker and cook for about 1 hour or until the internal temperature in the thickest part of the fillets reaches 145 °F.

6. Enjoy.

Spicy Shrimp Skewers

Servings: 4

Cooking Time: 6 Minutes

Ingredients:

- 2 Pound shrimp, peeled and deveined
- 6 Thai chiles
- 6 Clove garlic
- 2 Tablespoon Winemaker's Napa Valley Rub
- 1 1/2 Teaspoon sugar
- 1 1/2 Tablespoon white vinegar

- 3 Tablespoon olive oil

Directions:

1. If using bamboo skewers, place them in cold water to soak for 1 hour before grilling.

2. Place shrimp in a bowl and set aside. Combine all remaining ingredients in a blender and blend until a coarse-textured paste is reached. Note: if a milder flavor is preferred, feel free to adjust amount of chiles to taste.

3. Add chile-garlic mixture to the shrimp and place in fridge to marinate for at least 30 minutes.

4. Remove from fridge and thread shrimp onto bamboo or metal skewers.

5. Supply your smoker with wood pellets and follow the start-up procedure. Preheat the grill, with the lid closed, to 450° F.

6. Place shrimp on grill and cook for 2 to 3 minutes per side or until shrimp are pink and firm to touch. Enjoy! Grill: 450 °F

Vodka Brined Smoked Wild Salmon

Servings: 4
Cooking Time: 60 Minutes

Ingredients:
- 1 Cup brown sugar
- 1 Tablespoon black pepper
- 1/2 Cup coarse salt
- 1 Cup vodka
- 1 (1-1/2 to 2 lb) wild caught salmon
- 1 lemon wedges
- capers

Directions:

1. In a small bowl, whisk together brown sugar, pepper, salt and vodka.

2. Place the salmon in a large resealable bag. Pour in marinade and massage into the salmon. Refrigerate for 2 to 4 hours.

3. Remove from bag, rinse and dry with paper towels.

4. Supply your smoker with wood pellets and follow the start-up procedure. Preheat the grill, with the lid closed, to 180° F.

5. Smoke the salmon, skin-side down for 30 minutes.

6. Increase grill temperature to 225°F and continue to cook salmon for an additional 45 to 60 minutes or until the internal temperature in the thickest part of the fish reaches 140°F or the fish flakes easily when pressed with a finger or fork. Grill: 225 °F Probe: 140 °F

7. Serve with lemons and capers. Enjoy!

Grilled Fresh Fish

Servings: 2
Cooking Time: 15 Minutes

Ingredients:
- 1 Whole fillet of firm white fish: sea bass, halibut or cod
- Fin & Feather Rub
- 2 Whole lemons

Directions:

1. Supply your smoker with wood pellets and follow the start-up procedure. Preheat the grill, with the lid closed, to 325° F.

2. Season fish with Traeger Fin & Feather Rub and let sit for 30 minutes. Slice lemons in half.

3. Place the fish and the lemons (cut side down) directly on the grill grates. Cook for 10 to 15 minutes until the fish is flaky and is at least 145°F in the thickest part of fish. Be careful not to over cook.

4. Serve with the grilled lemons. Enjoy!

Baked Whole Fish In Sea Salt

Servings: 4

Cooking Time: 30 Minutes

Ingredients:

- 3 Pound Whole Branzino, (1.5 each)
- 10 Sprig thyme sprigs
- 1 Medium lemon, thinly sliced
- 5 Cup sea salt
- 10 Whole egg white
- olive oil
- 1 Whole lemon juice

Directions:

1. Supply your smoker with wood pellets and follow the start-up procedure. Preheat the grill, with the lid closed, to High heat.

2. Clip the fins and remove the gills from the fish. Stuff cavity with thyme and lemon slices. Whip the egg whites to soft peaks and fold in the sea salt.

3. Place directly on the grill grate and bake for 30 minutes or until a thermometer poked through the salt crust and into the flesh of the fish registers an internal temperature of 135-140 degrees F. Remove fish from the grill and let stand 10 minutes.

4. Using a wooden spoon, strike the crust to crack it open and brush remaining salt from the surface of the fish.

5. Remove the skin and drizzle fish with good olive oil and a squeeze of lemon. Enjoy!

Smoke-roasted Halibut With Mixed Herb Vinaigrette

Servings: 4

Cooking Time: 12 Minutes

Ingredients:

- 4 halibut fillets, each about 6 to 8oz (170 to 225g)
- for the vinaigrette
- 2 tbsp white wine vinegar or sherry vinegar, plus more
- ¼ tsp coarse salt, plus more
- ¼ tsp freshly ground black pepper, plus more
- ½ cup extra virgin olive oil
- 2 tbsp minced fresh herbs, such as dill, flat-leaf parsley, or oregano
- for serving
- 4 cups loosely packed baby arugula, spinach, or other mixed greens
- 1 lemon, cut lengthwise into 4 wedges

Directions:

1. Supply your smoker with wood pellets and follow the start-up procedure. Preheat the grill, with the lid closed, to 400° F.

2. In a small bowl, make the vinaigrette by whisking together the vinegar, and salt and pepper. Whisk until the salt dissolves. Continue to whisk while slowly adding the olive oil. Whisk until the vinaigrette is emulsified. Stir in the herbs. Taste, adding vinegar or salt and pepper to taste. Pour 1/3 of the vinaigrette into a separate container. Reserve the remainder.

3. Place the fillets on a rimmed sheet pan. Lightly brush both sides with the smaller portion of vinaigrette. (Dividing the vinaigrette into two containers prevents cross-contamination.) Lightly season with salt and pepper.

4. Place the fillets on the grate at an angle to the bars. Grill until the edges begin to look opaque, about 4 to 6 minutes. Gently turn and grill until the fish is cooked through, about 4 to 6 minutes more. (A fillet will break into clean flakes when pressed with a fork when it's done.)

5. Remove the fish from the grill. Place the greens in a large bowl and toss them with 2 to 3 tablespoons of the reserved vinaigrette (you want the greens lightly coated) and divide between 4 plates. Place a fillet on the greens on each plate. Drizzle a bit more of the vinaigrette over the top. Serve with lemon wedges.

Garlic Bacon Wrapped Shrimp

Servings: 4
Cooking Time: 11 Minutes

Ingredients:
- 8 Bacon, Strip
- 1/4 Cup Butter Style Shortening (Melted)
- 1 Clove Garlic, Minced
- 1 Tsp Lemon, Juice
- Pepper
- Salt
- 16 (Peeled And Veined) Shrimp, Jumbo

Directions:
1. Supply your smoker with wood pellets and follow the start-up procedure. Preheat the grill, with the lid closed, to 450° F.
2. Take one slice of bacon, and wrap it around each piece of shrimp, and lock it in place with a wooden toothpick.
3. Place the shortening into a mixing bowl and whisk in the garlic and lemon juice. Brush each shrimp with the sauce on both sides.
4. Place on the grill, and barbecue for 11 minutes.
5. Turn the grill off, remove the shrimp, serve and enjoy!

Tequila & Lime Shrimp With Smoked Tomato Sauce

Servings: 4
Cooking Time: 6 Minutes

Ingredients:
- 24 to 28 jumbo shrimp, about 2lb (1kg) total, peeled and deveined
- 1 lime, quartered
- Smoked Tomato Sauce
- for the marinade
- ½ cup tequila or mezcal
- juice and zest of 1 lime
- 2 garlic cloves, peeled and roughly chopped
- ½ cup freshly squeezed orange juice
- ¼ cup extra virgin olive oil
- 2 tsp agave, light brown sugar, or low-carb substitute
- 2 tsp Mexican hot sauce, plus more
- 1½ tsp coarse salt
- 1 tsp baking soda
- 1 tsp chili powder
- ½ tsp ground cumin

Directions:
1. In a medium bowl, make the marinade by whisking together the ingredients. Whisk until the salt dissolves. Taste for seasoning, adding more hot sauce if desired.
2. Place the shrimp in a resealable plastic bag and pour the marinade over them, turning the bag several times to coat thoroughly. Refrigerate for 30 minutes.
3. Supply your smoker with wood pellets and follow the start-up procedure. Preheat the grill, with the lid closed, to 450° F.
4. Drain the shrimp and discard the marinade. Pat the shrimp dry with paper towels. Thread the shrimp on 4 bamboo skewers (preferably flat ones). Make sure all the shrimp face the same direction. Finish each skewer with a lime wedge.

5. Place the skewers on the grate and grill until the shrimp are white and opaque, about 2 to 3 minutes per side, turning once. (Don't overcook.)
6. Remove the shrimp from the grill. Serve immediately with the warm tomato sauce.

Dijon-smoked Halibut

Servings: 6
Cooking Time: 120 Minutes

Ingredients:

* 4 (6-ounce) halibut steaks
* ¼ cup extra-virgin olive oil
* 2 teaspoons kosher salt
* 1 teaspoon freshly ground black pepper
* ½ cup mayonnaise
* ½ cup sweet pickle relish
* ¼ cup finely chopped sweet onion
* ¼ cup chopped roasted red pepper
* ¼ cup finely chopped tomato
* ¼ cup finely chopped cucumber
* 2 tablespoons Dijon mustard
* 1 teaspoon minced garlic

Directions:

1. Rub the halibut steaks with the olive oil and season on both sides with the salt and pepper. Transfer to a plate, cover with plastic wrap, and refrigerate for 4 hours.
2. Supply your smoker with wood pellets and follow the start-up procedure. Preheat, with the lid closed, to 200°F.
3. Remove the halibut from the refrigerator and rub with the mayonnaise.
4. Put the fish directly on the grill grate, close the lid, and smoke for 2 hours, or until opaque and an instant-read thermometer inserted in the fish reads 140°F.

5. While the fish is smoking, combine the pickle relish, onion, roasted red pepper, tomato, cucumber, Dijon mustard, and garlic in a medium bowl. Refrigerate the mustard relish until ready to serve.
6. Serve the halibut steaks hot with the mustard relish.

Summer Paella

Servings: 6
Cooking Time: 45 Minutes

Ingredients:

* 6 tablespoons extra-virgin olive oil, divided, plus more for drizzling
* 2 green or red bell peppers, cored, seeded, and diced
* 2 medium onions, diced
* 2 garlic cloves, slivered
* 1 (29-ounce) can tomato purée
* 1½ pounds chicken thighs
* Kosher salt
* 1½ pounds tail-on shrimp, peeled and deveined
* 1 cup dried thinly sliced chorizo sausage
* 1 tablespoon smoked paprika
* 1½ teaspoons saffron threads
* 2 quarts chicken broth
* 3½ cups white rice
* 2 (7½-ounce) cans chipotle chiles in adobo sauce
* 1½ pounds fresh clams, soaked in cold water for 15 to 20 minutes2 tablespoons chopped fresh parsley
* 2 lemons, cut into wedges, for serving

Directions:

1. Make the sofrito: On the stove top, in a saucepan over medium-low heat, combine ¼ cup

of olive oil, the bell peppers, onions, and garlic, and cook for 5 minutes, or until the onions are translucent.

2. Stir in the tomato purée, reduce the heat to low, and simmer, stirring frequently, until most of the liquid has evaporated, about 30 minutes. Set aside. (Note: The sofrito can be made in advance and refrigerated.)

3. Supply your smoker with wood pellets and follow the start-up procedure. Preheat, with the lid closed, to 450°F.

4. Heat a large paella pan on the smoker and add the remaining 2 tablespoons of olive oil.

5. Add the chicken thighs, season lightly with salt, and brown for 6 to 10 minutes, then push to the outer edge of the pan.

6. Add the shrimp, season with salt, close the lid, and smoke for 3 minutes.

7. Add the sofrito, chorizo, paprika, and saffron, and stir together.

8. In a separate bowl, combine the chicken broth, uncooked rice, and 1 tablespoon of salt, stirring until well combined.

9. Add the broth-rice mixture to the paella pan, spreading it evenly over the other ingredients.

10. Close the lid and smoke for 5 minutes, then add the chipotle chiles and clams on top of the rice.

11. Close the lid and continue to smoke the paella for about 30 minutes, or until all of the liquid is absorbed.

12. Remove the pan from the grill, cover tightly with aluminum foil, and let rest off the heat for 5 minutes.

13. Drizzle with olive oil, sprinkle with the fresh parsley, and serve with the lemon wedges.

Seared Bluefin Tuna Steaks

Servings: 2
Cooking Time: 5 Minutes

Ingredients:
- 3 Whole Tuna, steak
- olive oil
- salt and pepper
- soy sauce
- Sriracha

Directions:
1. Lightly baste both sides of tuna steaks in olive oil; sprinkle sea salt and ground pepper on each side.

2. Supply your smoker with wood pellets and follow the start-up procedure. Preheat the grill, with the lid closed, to High heat.

3. Grill tuna steaks on each side for 2 to 2-1/2 minutes.

4. Remove tuna from grill and allow to cool slightly.

5. Cut into 1/2 - 3/4" pieces. Serve with a mixture of Soy Sauce and Sriracha. Enjoy!"

Delicious Smoked Trout

Servings: 8
Cooking Time: 120 Minutes

Ingredients:
- 6 rainbow trout fillets
- Brine:
- 2 Tablespoons kosher salt
- 2 Tablespoons brown sugar
- 4 cups cool water

Directions:
1. For the brine, dissolve the kosher salt and brown sugar in water.

2. Place the trout fillets in the brine, skin side up, and brine the fillets for 15 minutes.

3. Supply your smoker with wood pellets and follow the start-up procedure. Preheat the grill, with the lid closed, to 180° F.

4. Remove the trout from the brine and transfer it to the grill grates.

5. Smoke the trout for 1.5 to 2 hours with the lid closed, depending on the thickness of your fillets.

6. Smoke until the trout reaches an internal temperature of 145 ˚F, or until the trout flakes easily.

7. Remove the trout from the smoker and serve warm, or let it cool completely and serve chilled with your favorite accouterments.

Smoked Mango Shrimp

Servings: 4
Cooking Time: 5 Minutes

Ingredients:
- 2 Tablespoon Olive Oil
- 1 Pound Raw Tail-On, Thawed And Deveined Shrimp, Uncooked

Directions:
1. Supply your smoker with wood pellets and follow the start-up procedure. Preheat the grill, with the lid closed, to 425° F. Rinse shrimp off in sink with cold water. Place in bowl and season generously with Mango Magic seasoning and olive oil. Toss well in bowl.

2. Thread several shrimp onto a skewer, so that they are all just touching each other. Repeat with other skewers and remaining shrimp.

3. Grill shrimp for 2 - 3 minutes on each side, or until pink and opaque all the way through. Remove from grill and serve immediately.

Barbecued Shrimp

Servings: 4
Cooking Time: 10 Minutes

Ingredients:
- 1 pound peeled and deveined shrimp, with tails on
- 2 tablespoons olive oil
- 1 batch Dill Seafood Rub

Directions:
1. Soak wooden skewers in water for 30 minutes.

2. Supply your smoker with wood pellets and follow the start-up procedure. Preheat the grill, with the lid closed, to 375°F.

3. Thread 4 or 5 shrimp per skewer.

4. Coat the shrimp all over with olive oil and season each side of the skewers with the rub.

5. Place the skewers directly on the grill grate and grill the shrimp for 5 minutes per side. Remove the skewers from the grill and serve immediately.

PORK RECIPES

Pig On A Stick With Buffalo Glaze

Servings: 12

Cooking Time: 75 Minutes

Ingredients:

- 4lb (1.8kg) pork shanks, each about 4 to 6oz (110 to 170g), trimmed and thawed if frozen
- 1½ cups sugar-free dark-colored soda, sugar-free root beer, or no-sugar-added apple juice
- for the brine (optional)
- 1 gallon (3.8 liters) distilled water
- ¾ cup kosher salt
- 5 tsp pink curing salt #1
- for the glaze (optional)
- ½ cup unsalted butter
- 1 cup hot sauce
- 2 tsp granulated garlic
- 1 tsp Worcestershire sauce

Directions:

1. In a stockpot on the stovetop over medium-high heat, make the brine by combining the ingredients and bringing the mixture to a boil. Stir until the salts dissolve. Remove the pot from the stovetop and let the brine cool to room temperature.

2. Add the pork shanks to the brine. Cover and refrigerate for 2 days.

3. Supply your smoker with wood pellets and follow the start-up procedure. Preheat the grill, with the lid closed, to 180° F.

4. Drain the pork shanks and discard the brine. (If you didn't brine the pork shanks, season them on all sides with your favorite barbecue rub.) Place the pork on the grate and smoke for 3 hours. Transfer the shanks to an aluminum roasting pan.

5. Raise the temperature to 275°F (135°C).

6. Add the soda to the pan and cover tightly with aluminum foil. Place the pan on the grate and braise the meat until it's tender but still attached to the bone, about 2 to 3 hours. Be careful when removing the foil because steam will escape. Remove the pan from the grill and set aside.

7. Raise the temperature to 325°F (163°C).

8. In a saucepan on the stovetop over medium heat, make the buffalo glaze by melting the butter. Stir in the remaining ingredients. Let the sauce simmer for 5 minutes to allow the flavors to blend.

9. Dip the pork shanks into the glaze and then transfer them to an aluminum foil roasting pan. Cover tightly with aluminum foil. Place the pan on the grate and cook the shanks until hot, about 30 minutes.

10. Remove the pan from the grill. Serve the pork with plenty of napkins.

Grilled Mac And Cheese Quesadillas

Servings: 4

Cooking Time: 75 Minutes

Ingredients:

- 1/2 Lb Bacon, Sliced And Halved
- 3 Tbsp Butter
- 1 Cup Cheddar Cheese, Shredded
- 1 Cup Cheddar Jack Cheese, Shredded
- 4 Oz Cream Cheese
- 2 Tbsp Flour
- 4 Flour Tortillas

- 1 1/2 Tsp Hickory Bacon Seasoning
- 8 Oz Macaroni, Cooked Al Dente
- 1 Tsp Mustard Powder
- 1/2 Cup Parmesan Cheese, Grated
- 1 2/3 Cups Whole Milk

Directions:

1. Fire up your   Platinum Series KC Combo and with the lid open, set your temperature to SMOKE mode.

2. Supply your smoker with wood pellets and follow the start-up procedure. Preheat the grill, with the lid open, to 225° F. If using a gas or charcoal grill, set it up for low, indirect heat.

3. Set a cast iron skillet on the grill. Melt the butter then whisk in flour until smooth. Cook for 1 minute, then whisk in Hickory Bacon and mustard powder.

4. Pour in milk and bring to a boil, whisking constantly. When sauce begins to thicken, whisk in the cream cheese until smooth, then add cheddar and parmesan and stir until melted

5. Add the pasta to the cheese sauce. Close the lid, and smoke for 1 hour.

6. Fire up your   griddle to medium-low flame, and cook bacon, turning occasionally, until desired crispness is reached, about 3 to 5 minutes.

7. Set bacon aside, then place 4 tortillas on the griddle. Sprinkle cheddar jack cheese on top of the tortilla, a heaping scoop of smoked mac 'n cheese on one side, topped with bacon.

8. Fold over the tortilla and press down gently with a spatula. Remove from the griddle, rest for 2 minutes, then cut into wedges, and serve warm with an extra side of smoked mac 'n cheese.

Bacon Grilled Cheese Sandwich

Servings: 4

Cooking Time: 10 Minutes

Ingredients:

- mayonnaise
- 8 Slices Texas toast
- 16 Slices cheddar cheese
- 1 Pound applewood smoked bacon slices, cooked
- butter，softened

Directions:

1. Supply your smoker with wood pellets and follow the start-up procedure. Preheat the grill, with the lid closed, to 350° F.

2. Spread a little bit of mayonnaise on each piece of bread.

3. Place 1 piece of cheddar cheese on bread slice then top with a couple slices of bacon. Add another slice of cheese then top with the other piece of bread. Spread softened butter on the exterior of the top piece of bread.

4. When the grill is hot, place the grilled cheese directly on a cleaned, oiled grill grate buttered side down. Spread softened butter on the exterior of the top slice. Grill: 350 °F

5. Cook the grilled cheese on the first side for 5 to 7 minutes until grill marks develop and the cheese has begun to melt. Flip the sandwich and repeat on the other side. Grill: 350 °F

6. Remove from the grill when the cheese is melted and the exterior is lightly toasted. Enjoy!

Jamaican Jerk Pork Chops

Servings: 4

Cooking Time: 720 Minutes

Ingredients:

- 4 thick pork rib or loin chops, each about 12oz (340g) and 1 inch (2.5cm) thick
- for the marinade

- ½ to 1 Scotch bonnet or habanero pepper, destemmed, deseeded, and coarsely chopped, plus more
- 2 scallions, trimmed, white and green parts coarsely chopped
- 1 garlic clove, peeled and coarsely chopped
- juice of 1 lime
- 2 tbsp vegetable oil
- 2 tbsp distilled water
- 1 tbsp light soy sauce
- 2 tsp coarsely chopped fresh thyme leaves
- 2 tsp peeled and minced fresh ginger
- 2 tsp dark brown sugar or low-carb substitute, plus more
- 1 tsp coarse salt, plus more
- ½ tsp freshly ground black pepper
- ½ tsp ground allspice
- ½ tsp ground nutmeg
- ½ tsp ground cinnamon

Directions:

1. In a blender, make the jerk marinade by combining the ingredients. Blend until fairly smooth. Taste for seasoning, adding more Scotch bonnet, brown sugar, or salt. Place the pork chops in a resealable plastic bag and pour the marinade over them, turning and massaging the bag to thoroughly coat the meat. Refrigerate for 2 to 4 hours.

2. Supply your smoker with wood pellets and follow the start-up procedure. Preheat the grill, with the lid closed, to 425° F.

3. Remove the pork from the marinade and scrape off the excess. (Discard the marinade.) Grill the chops until the internal temperature reaches 145°F (63°C), about 6 to 8 minutes per side.

4. Transfer the chops to a platter. Let rest for 2 minutes before serving.

Jalapeño-bacon Pork Tenderloin

Servings: 4-6
Cooking Time: 150 Minutes

Ingredients:

- ¼ cup yellow mustard
- 2 (1-pound) pork tenderloins
- ¼ cup Pork Rub
- 8 ounces cream cheese, softened
- 1 cup grated Cheddar cheese
- 1 tablespoon unsalted butter, melted
- 1 tablespoon minced garlic
- 2 jalapeño peppers, seeded and diced
- 1½ pounds bacon

Directions:

1. Slather the mustard all over the pork tenderloins, then sprinkle generously with the dry rub to coat the meat.

2. Supply your smoker with wood pellets and follow the start-up procedure. Preheat, with the lid closed, to 225°F.

3. Place the tenderloins directly on the grill, close the lid, and smoke for 2 hours.

4. Remove the pork from the grill and increase the temperature to 375°F.

5. In a small bowl, combine the cream cheese, Cheddar cheese, melted butter, garlic, and jalapeños.

6. Starting from the top, slice deeply along the center of each tenderloin end to end, creating a cavity.

7. Spread half of the cream cheese mixture in the cavity of one tenderloin. Repeat with the remaining mixture and the other piece of meat.

8. Securely wrap one tenderloin with half of the bacon. Repeat with the remaining bacon and the other piece of meat.

9. Transfer the bacon-wrapped tenderloins to the grill, close the lid, and smoke for about 30 minutes, or until a meat thermometer inserted in the thickest part of the meat reads 160°F and the bacon is browned and cooked through.

10. Let the tenderloins rest for 5 to 10 minutes before slicing and serving.

Smoked Pig Shots

Servings: 8
Cooking Time: 45 Minutes

Ingredients:

- 1 (8 oz) block cream cheese, softened
- 2 Large green chile peppers, diced
- 1 Cup shredded cheese
- 1 Tablespoon chile powder
- 2 Tablespoon Meat Church Honey Hog BBQ Rub
- 1 Pound Sausage, Smoked
- 1 Pound thick-cut bacon

Directions:

1. Supply your smoker with wood pellets and follow the start-up procedure. Preheat the grill, with the lid closed, to 350° F.

2. Mix cream cheese, chiles, shredded cheese, chili powder and Honey Hog BBQ Rub thoroughly in a mixing bowl. Set aside.

3. Slice sausage into 1/2 inch slices. Cut bacon strips in half. Wrap bacon around the sausage, creating a bowl and secure with a toothpick.

4. Fill the bowl with the cream cheese mixture. Top with more Honey Hog BBQ Rub.

5. Place the pig shots on the Traeger until the bacon is crispy and golden brown, about 45 to 60 minutes. Grill: 350 °F

6. Remove the pig shots from the grill and cool for 10 minutes, the cream cheese may still be hot. Enjoy!

Beer Braised Garlic Bbq Pork Butt

Servings: 6-8
Cooking Time: 300 Minutes

Ingredients:

- One 12Oz Bottle Dark Beer
- 1/2 Cup Brown Sugar
- 2 Tablespoons Granulated Garlic
- 4 Tablespoons Honey
- 1 Cup Ketchup
- 1 Tablespoon Olive Oil
- Pulled Pork Rub
- 1 Pork Butt, Boneless
- 2 Tablespoons Worcestershire Sauce
- 4 Tablespoons Yellow Mustard

Directions:

1. Generously season the pork butt with Pulled Pork Rub, making sure to rub the seasoning in on all surfaces of roast. Place the pork onto a roasting rack inside a 9x13 pan.

2. Pour about half a bottle of dark beer into the bottom of the pan and save the remaining amount of beer, you'll need this later.

3. Supply your smoker with wood pellets and follow the start-up procedure. Preheat the grill, with the lid open, to high heat. If you're using a gas or charcoal, set it up for high direct heat. Place the pan in the center of the grill and grill for 30 minutes until the pork roast is dark in color and charred in some spots.

4. Remove the pork from the grill and decrease the temperature of the grill to 325°F. Set aside and began to make the BBQ sauce.

5. In a medium sized bowl, add ketchup, brown sugar, yellow mustard, honey, Worcestershire, granulated garlic, half bottle of dark beer, and finally 1 tbsp of Pulled Pork Rub. Mix together thoroughly.

6. Take the sauce and pour it over the roast, cover with aluminum foil.

7. Cook the roast for 4 - 6 hours or until the meat is falling apart tender and the bone easily comes away from the meat and reaches an internal temperature of 200°F. Remove the pork from the grill and allow it to rest for 10-15 minutes.

8. Shred the pork with meat claws or forks, discarding any fat or gristle. Toss the shredded pork with the barbecue sauce and serve immediately.

Cocoa-crusted Pork Tenderloin

Servings: 4
Cooking Time: 25 Minutes

Ingredients:

- 1 pork tenderloin
- 1/2 Teaspoon Fennel, ground
- 2 Teaspoon unsweetened cocoa powder
- 1 Teaspoon smoked paprika
- 1/2 Teaspoon kosher salt
- 1/2 Teaspoon black pepper
- 1 Tablespoon extra-virgin olive oil
- 3 green onions, thinly sliced

Directions:

1. With a paring knife, remove the silver skin and connective tissue from the loin. In a small mixing bowl, combine the remaining ingredients, making paste. Rub the paste on the pork loin, and refrigerate for 30 minutes.

2. Supply your smoker with wood pellets and follow the start-up procedure. Preheat the grill, with the lid closed, to 450° F.

3. Place the loin on the front of the grill and sear it on all sides. After it has been seared, reduce the temperature to 350°F and move the pork to the center of the grill. Grill: 350 °F

4. Continue to cook for 10- 15 minutes, or until it has reached an internal meat temp of 145°F for medium to medium well. Probe: 145 °F

5. Once it has cooked, remove it from the grill and let rest for at least 8 to 10 minutes before slicing. Garnish with green onions. Enjoy!

Grilled Lasagna With Cold-smoked Mozzarella

Servings: 8-12
Cooking Time: 70 Minutes

Ingredients:

- 15 Oz. Ricotta Cheese
- 3 Cups Cold-Smoked Mozzarella, Grated Divided
- 2 Eggs
- 6 Garlic Cloves, Chopped
- 1 Tsp Garlic Powder
- 1 Cup Grated Parmesan Cheese, Divided
- 1 Lb. Italian Sausage
- 1 Tbsp Italian Seasoning
- 1 Pkg. "No-Bake" Lasagna Noodles
- 48 Oz. Marinara Sauce
- 1 Lb. Mozzarella Block
- 1 Tbsp Olive Oil
- 1 Tbsp Chopped Oregano
- ¼ Cup Italian Parsley, Chopped
- 1 Yellow Onion, Chopped

Directions:

1. In a glass bowl, mix together the eggs, Italian seasoning, garlic powder, ricotta cheese, ½ cup parmesan cheese, and 1 cup of smoked mozzarella, and 2 tablespoons of parsley. Cover and refrigerate for 1 hour.

2. Supply your smoker with wood pellets and follow the start-up procedure. Preheat the grill, with the lid open, to 400° F. If using a gas or charcoal grill, set it up for medium-high heat. Place a cast iron skillet on the grill grates and allow to preheat.

3. Heat olive oil in skillet, then add Italian sausage and cook for 5 minutes, then add in onion and garlic, and cook an additional 3 minutes. Remove from heat and stir in 1 tablespoon of parsley and dried oregano. Set aside and reduce grill temperature to 350° F.

4. To assemble, begin by covering the bottom of a 9x13 pan with 1 cup of sauce. For the first layer, place a single layer of uncooked noodles over the sauce, followed by ⅓ of the ricotta cheese mixture, half of the Italian sausage, 1 cup of mozzarella cheese, and 1 cup of sauce. Repeat for layer two with a single layer of uncooked lasagna noodles, ⅓ of the ricotta cheese mixture, and 1 ½ cups of sauce. Repeat for layer three with a layer of uncooked lasagna noodles, remaining ricotta mixture, remaining Italian sausage, 1 cup of sauce. For the final layer, add a layer of uncooked lasagna noodles, remaining sauce, and remaining 1 cup mozzarella plus ½ cup parmesan.

5. Transfer lasagna to grill and cook, covered with foil, for 35 minutes. Remove foil and continue cooking for 10 minutes, sprinkle with additional parmesan and parsley, if desired.

Remove from grill and let stand 15 minutes before serving.

Smoke-roasted Beer-braised Brats

Servings: 8
Cooking Time: 65 Minutes

Ingredients:

- 8 Wisconsin-style bratwursts
- low-carb beer (enough to cover the brats)
- 2 tbsp unsalted butter
- 2 large sweet onions, peeled and sliced crosswise
- 2 garlic cloves, peeled and smashed with a chef's knife
- 8 brat buns (optional)
- coarse ground mustard or German-style mustard

Directions:

1. Supply your smoker with wood pellets and follow the start-up procedure. Preheat the grill, with the lid closed, to 325° F.

2. Place the brats on the grate at a diagonal to the bars. (Don't pierce the brats or the juices will run out.) Grill until the skin is nicely browned, about 40 to 45 minutes.

3. In a Dutch oven on the stovetop over medium-high heat, bring the beer, butter, onions, and garlic to a boil. Transfer the Dutch oven to the grill.

4. Use tongs to transfer the brats to the Dutch oven and let them steep for at least 20 minutes. The brats will stay at serving temperature—160°F (71°C)—for 1 hour or more.

5. Remove the Dutch oven from the grill and serve the brats on buns (if using) with mustard.

Double Smoked Apple Spiral Ham

Servings: 12

Cooking Time: 150 Minutes

Ingredients:

- 1 10 lb ham spiral cut
- 1 cup apple jelly
- 1 cup raspberry chipotle BBQ sauce

Directions:

1. Supply your smoker with wood pellets and follow the start-up procedure. Preheat the grill, with the lid closed, to 275° F.

2. Remove ham from all packaging and transfer to a chicken tray, cut-side-down. Then place on a cooking tray and transfer to the smoker. Close the lid and cook for 2 hours.

3. Heat up saucepan over medium heat. Add apple jelly and stir well, until it reaches a liquid consistency.

4. Add raspberry chipotle. Stir in and bring glaze to a simmer. Leave saucepan on warm heat until ham is ready.

5. After two hours, transfer ham to a shallow aluminum pan. Apply the glaze to ham generously using a basting brush. Make sure all cracks on ham surfaceare glazed.

6. Still in a shallow pan, put ham back in smoker. Close the lid and leave to smoke for over 30 minutes.

7. Remove ham from smoker and transfer to a cutting board. Leave to rest for 10 minutes.

8. Cut along the outer seam of the ham, allowing the slices to fall away.

Baked Maple And Brown Sugar Bacon

Servings: 4

Cooking Time: 60 Minutes

Ingredients:

- 1 Pound cold bacon
- 1/2 Cup pure maple syrup, warmed
- 1/2 Cup brown sugar, plus more as needed

Directions:

1. Supply your smoker with wood pellets and follow the start-up procedure. Preheat the grill, with the lid closed, to 300° F.

2. Line a rimmed baking sheet with foil and place a wire rack on top. Lay bacon strips in a single layer on the wire rack.

3. Using a pastry brush, brush each strip of bacon on both sides with the warmed maple syrup, then sprinkle brown sugar evenly on both sides.

4. Put the baking sheet in the grill and cook bacon for 60-75 minutes, or until bacon browns and appears to be crisping. Grill: 300 °F

5. Allow the bacon to cool slightly before eating. Enjoy!

Roasted Ham With Apricot Sauce

Servings: 8

Cooking Time: 120 Minutes

Ingredients:

- 1 (8-10 lb) Snake River Farms Kurobuta Whole Bone-In Ham
- 1 Bottle Apricot BBQ Sauce
- 1/4 Cup horseradish
- 2 Tablespoon Dijon mustard

Directions:

1. Supply your smoker with wood pellets and follow the start-up procedure. Preheat the grill, with the lid closed, to 325° F.

2. Place ham in a large roasting pan lined with aluminum foil. Place pan on grill and cook for 90 minutes. Grill: 325 °F

3. For the Glaze: In a saucepan over medium heat, combine the Traeger Apricot BBQ Sauce, horseradish and mustard. Set aside and keep warm.

4. After 90 minutes, brush the ham with the glaze. Continue to cook for another 30 minutes or until a thermometer inserted into the thickest part of the ham reaches an internal temperatures of 135°F. Grill: 325 °F Probe: 135 °F

5. Remove ham from grill and rest for 20 minutes before slicing.

6. Serve with remaining glaze if desired. Enjoy!

Hanging St. Louis-style Grilled Ribs

Servings: 4
Cooking Time: 270 Minutes

Ingredients:
- 1 1/3 Cup Apple Juice
- 1 2/3 Cup BBQ Sauce, Divided
- Pulled Pork Rub
- 4 Half Racks Spare Ribs, St. Louis Style

Directions:
1. Supply your smoker with wood pellets and follow the start-up procedure. Preheat the grill, with the lid open, to 250° F. If using a gas or charcoal grill, set it up for low, indirect heat.

2. Using a sharp knife, remove the back membrane from the rib racks and pat dry with paper towel. Cut rib racks in half, then season generously with Pulled Pork Rub.

3. Insert a hanging hook under the top rib, then transfer racks to the smoking cabinet. Smoke for 2 ½ hours.

4. Remove ribs from the smoking cabinet and set on heavy duty foil. Mix together ⅔ cup BBQ sauce and ⅓ cup apple juice, then brush thinned BBQ sauce on both sides of ribs. Pour ¼ cup of apple juice around each of the ribs. Fold over foil, then transfer to the grill, meat side down. Increase temperature to 300° F and continue cooking for an additional 2 hours.

5. Remove ribs from the grill, baste with BBQ, then return to the grill and cook for another 10 to 15 minutes. Allow to rest for 15 minutes, then slice and serve hot.

Smoked Porchetta With Italian Salsa Verde

Servings: 8-12
Cooking Time: 180 Minutes

Ingredients:
- 3 Tablespoon dried fennel seed
- 2 Tablespoon red pepper flakes
- 2 Tablespoon sage, minced
- 1 Tablespoon rosemary, minced
- 3 Clove garlic, minced
- As Needed lemon zest
- As Needed orange zest
- To Taste salt and pepper
- 6 Pound Pork Belly, skin on
- As Needed salt and pepper
- 1 Whole shallot, thinly sliced
- 6 Tablespoon parsley, minced
- 2 Tablespoon freshly minced chives
- 1 Tablespoon Oregano, fresh
- 3 Tablespoon white wine vinegar
- 1/2 Teaspoon kosher salt

- 3/4 Cup olive oil
- 1/2 Teaspoon Dijon mustard
- As Needed fresh lemon juice

Directions:

1. Prepare herb mixture: In a medium bowl, mix together fennel seeds, red pepper flakes, sage, rosemary, garlic, citrus zest, salt and pepper.

2. Place pork belly skin side up on a clean work surface and score in a crosshatch pattern. Flip the pork belly over and season flesh side with salt, pepper and half of the herb mixture.

3. Place trimmed pork loin in the center of the belly and rub with remaining herb mixture. Season with salt and pepper.

4. Roll the pork belly around the loin to form a cylindrical shape and tie tightly with kitchen twine at 1" intervals.

5. Season the outside with salt and pepper and transfer to refrigerator, uncovered and let air dry overnight.

6. When ready to cook, start the smoker grill and set to Smoke.

7. Fit a rimmed baking sheet with a rack and place the pork on the rack seam side down.

8. Place the pan directly on the grill grate and smoke for 1 hour.

9. Increase the grill temperature to 325 degrees F and roast until the internal temperature of the meat reaches 135 degrees, about 2 1/2 hours. If the exterior begins to burn before the desired internal temperature is reached, tent with foil.

10. Remove from grill and let stand 30 minutes before slicing.

11. To make the Italian salsa verde: Combine shallot, parsley, chives, vinegar, oregano and salt in a medium bowl. Whisk in olive oil then stir in mustard and lemon juice.

12. Drizzle slices with Italian salsa verde and enjoy!

Championship Ribs With Kansas City Style

Servings: 4
Cooking Time: 210 Minutes

Ingredients:
- Apple Juice
- 2 Racks Baby Back Rib
- 2 Cups Brown Sugar
- 24 Oz Dijon Mustard
- 4 Tbsp Sweet Rib Rub
- Spray Bottle

Directions:

1. Pour Dijon Mustard into a mixing bowl. Mix in brown sugar until mustard taste diminishes and a sweet taste takes over.

2. Generally, you will use a half bag of brown sugar for 2 bottles and the whole bag for 4 bottles. The key is for the tangy mustard taste to turn sweet.

3. When this mix is brushed on the ribs the mix of pork flavor and this glaze will produce a sweet and sassy result. The easiest way to mix is with an electric mixer but a whisk will do nicely. This will become very thick and sticky.

4. Supply your smoker with wood pellets and follow the start-up procedure. Preheat the grill, with the lid open, to 275° F.

5. Place ribs, back side down, on the cooking grid. Note: If you are doing multiple slabs, I suggest you use a rib rack. Most Rib Racks will hold 6 slabs. This will allow ribs to cook evenly. The rib rack allows for more slabs since ribs will sit in rack on their edge. Try to put meatier side up.

6. Spray ribs thoroughly with apple juice every 30-40 minutes. Apple Juice not only helps to keep meat moist and juicy while cooking, the acidity also helps to break down the muscles, thus tenderizing as well. I have had people tell me they prefer Pineapple juice or a mixture of apple and pineapple. Personally, I can't tell the difference, but you can experiment for yourself if you want to. The result will be same.

7. Note: How to tell when ribs are done? It is hard to measure temp of a rib with a meat thermometer due to the meat between the bones being so tight. You can get a false reading if the thermometer is touching a bone. Take your tongs and pick up slab in the middle. If the rib folds over and is limp and the meat just begins to pull away from the bone, they are done.

8. Remove ribs from grill and place in a pan (long enough for ribs to fit)

9. Glaze both sides of ribs with a light coat of the sassy glaze. This is a flavor enhancer, not a cover up. Just a light coat is plenty. If you really like the glaze there will generally always be some left over, and you can add to your desire while on the plate.

10. Wrap ribs in foil and let stand for 15 minutes

11. Serve (you can serve in slab form and let each guest cut his own or I like to cut ribs and serve as single bones.

12. Enjoy!

Smoked Spare Ribs

Servings: 4-8
Cooking Time: 360 Minutes

Ingredients:
- 2 (2- or 3-pound) racks spare ribs
- 2 tablespoons yellow mustard
- 1 batch Sweet Brown Sugar Rub
- ¼ cup The Ultimate BBQ Sauce

Directions:

1. Supply your smoker with wood pellets and follow the start-up procedure. Preheat the grill, with the lid closed, to 225°F.

2. Remove the membrane from the backside of the ribs. This can be done by cutting just through the membrane in an X pattern and working a paper towel between the membrane and the ribs to pull it off.

3. Coat the ribs on both sides with mustard and season with the rub. Using your hands, work the rub into the meat.

4. Place the ribs directly on the grill grate and smoke until their internal temperature reaches between 190°F and 200°F.

5. Baste both sides of the ribs with barbecue sauce.

6. Increase the grill's temperature to 300°F and continue to cook the ribs for 15 minutes more.

7. Remove the racks from the grill, cut them into individual ribs, and serve immediately.

Traeger Cajun Broil

Servings: 8
Cooking Time: 60 Minutes

Ingredients:
- 2 Tablespoon olive oil
- 2 Pound red potatoes
- Old Bay Seasoning
- 6 Corn Ears, each cut into thirds
- 2 Pound smoked kielbasa sausage
- 3 Pound large shrimp with tails, deveined
- 2 Tablespoon butter

Directions:

1. Supply your smoker with wood pellets and follow the start-up procedure. Preheat the grill, with the lid closed, to 450° F.

2. Drizzle potatoes with half of the olive oil and lightly season with Old Bay seasoning. Place directly on the grill grate. Roast 20 minutes or until tender. Grill: 450 ˚F

3. Drizzle corn with remaining olive oil and lightly season with Old Bay seasoning. Place corn and kielbasa directly on the grill grate next to the potatoes. Roast 15 minutes. Grill: 450 ˚F

4. Season shrimp with Old Bay seasoning. Place shrimp directly on grill grate next to the rest of the items and cook for 10 minutes, or until bright pink and cooked through. Grill: 450 ˚F

5. Remove everything from the grill and transfer to a large bowl. Add butter and season with more Old Bay seasoning to taste. Toss to coat and serve immediately. Enjoy!

Smoked Pork Tomato Tamales

Servings: 6-8

Cooking Time: 60 Minutes

Ingredients:

- 1 Boneless, Netted Pork Roast
- 1 Cup, Fresh Cilantro, Chopped
- 3 Cloves Garlic, Peeled
- 20 Dried Cornhusks
- 1 Tbsp Lime Juice
- ¼ Cup Olive Oil
- 1 Onion, Quartered
- 4 - 6 Cups Prepared Masa Harina Tamale Dough
- 3 – 4 Serrano Peppers, Deseeded
- 1 Tbsp Sweet Heat Rub
- 1 Lb. Tomatillos, Husked And Washed

Directions:

1. Began by soaking the corn husks in a pan filled with water. Soak for 2 – 4 hours, or if needed, overnight.

2. Unwrap the tomatillos from their shell and place all of them into a grill basket followed by a few Serranos, deseeded, garlic cloves and 1 onion cut into quarters.

3. Supply your smoker with wood pellets and follow the start-up procedure. Preheat the grill, with the lid open, to 400° F. If you're using a gas or charcoal grill, set it up for medium low heat, and use smoke chips to fill your grill with smoke for 15 minutes. Place the grill basket filled with your vegetables and roast them over an open flame on your smoker until vegetables have become charred.

4. Place tomatillos, peppers, garlic and onions in a bowl, cover with plastic wrap, and let stand until cool enough to handle, 10 to 15 minutes.

5. Season the pork roast generously with Sweet Heat Rub and grill at 350°F for 1 hour until the roast has a nice crust on the outside.

6. While the pork roast is cooking, add a handful of cilantro, charred vegetables, 1 tbsp of Sweet Heat Rub, 1 tbsp lime juice, and ¼ cup of olive oil to a food processor. Pulse in food processor until mixture is consistent. Set aside

7. After the pork roast has been grilled for an hour, turn heat down to 275°F. Put roast in pan with about a cup of water, cover with aluminum foil and cook for another 4 hours or until the roast can be shredded. Pour chile verde sauce over shredded pork and toss to combine.

8. To being assembling tamales, place a corn husk on a work surface. Place 2-3 tablespoons of tamale dough on larger end of husk and spread into a rectangle, about ¼" thick, leaving a small

border along the edge. Place large tablespoon of chili and pork filling on top of dough. Fold over sides of husk so dough surrounds filling, then fold bottom of husk up and secure closed by tying a thin strip of husk around tamale.

9. To cook tamales, place them in a large metal colander over a large stockpot filled with water. Cover and let steam for 1 hour. After the tamales have been steamed, take them off and grill them at 350°F for about 10-20 minutes until corn husks have charred marks.

Honey Glazed Pork Chops

Servings: 6
Cooking Time: 16 Minutes

Ingredients:
- 4-6 Pork Chop
- 1/2 Cup of Honey
- 4 Tablespoons Soy Sauce
- 2 Tablespoons Olive Oil
- 2 Garlic Cloves, pressed
- Salt & Pepper

Directions:
1. Supply your smoker with wood pellets and follow the start-up procedure. Preheat the grill, with the lid closed, to 350° F.
2. Mix together the honey, soy sauce, and garlic in a small dish.
3. Brush the olive oil over the pork chops and sprinkle with salt and pepper.
4. Place the pork chops on the grill and brush the honey mixture over the top side.
5. When you flip the pork chops over, brush the second side with the honey mixture.
6. Grill for about 8 minutes on each side or until a thermometer inserted reads 170 degrees. Brush

a final layer of the honey glaze over the pork chops before serving. Enjoy!

Traeger Smoked Sausage

Servings: 4
Cooking Time: 120 Minutes

Ingredients:
- 3 Pound ground pork
- 1/2 Tablespoon ground mustard
- 1 Tablespoon onion powder
- 1 Tablespoon garlic powder
- 1/2 Teaspoon pink curing salt
- 1 Tablespoon salt
- 4 Teaspoon black pepper
- 1/2 Cup ice water
- Hog casings, soaked and rinsed in cold water

Directions:
1. In a medium bowl, combine the meat and seasonings, mix well.
2. Add ice water to meat and mix with hands working quickly until everything is incorporated.
3. Place mixture in a sausage stuffer and follow manufacturers Directions:for operating. Use caution not to overstuff or the casing might burst.
4. Once all the meat is stuffed, determine your desired link length and pinch and twist a couple of times or tie it off. Repeat for each link.
5. Supply your smoker with wood pellets and follow the start-up procedure. Preheat the grill, with the lid closed, to 225° F.
6. Place links directly on the grill grate and cook for 1 to 2 hours or until the internal temperature registers 155°F. Let sausage rest a few minutes before slicing. Enjoy! Grill: 225 °F Probe: 155 °F

Lynchburg Bacon

Servings: 4
Cooking Time: 20 Minutes

Ingredients:

- 1 Pound country-style bacon
- 1 Cup Tennessee whiskey, such as Jack Daniel's or apple juice
- 1 Tablespoon Pork & Poultry Rub
- 3/4 Cup all-purpose flour
- 1/3 Cup brown sugar
- 1 Teaspoon freshly ground black pepper

Directions:

1. Separate the bacon slices and place them into a large resealable bag.
2. Stir the Traeger Pork & Poultry Rub into the whiskey (or apple juice). Pour the whiskey over the bacon, massaging the bag to coat all the slices.
3. Set aside for at least 30 minutes.
4. On a piece of wax paper, sift together the flour, brown sugar and black pepper. Transfer to a second resealable bag.
5. Drain the bacon and add to the flour mixture a few slices at a time.
6. Shake the bag to coat each piece evenly, then arrange in a single layer on a baking pan.
7. Supply your smoker with wood pellets and follow the start-up procedure. Preheat the grill, with the lid closed, to 375° F.
8. Bake the bacon until it is golden brown and crisp, about 20 to 25 minutes. Enjoy! Grill: 375 °F

Bbq Pulled Pork Grilled Cheese Sandwich

Servings: 8
Cooking Time: 540 Minutes

Ingredients:

- 1 Pork Butt, bone-in, 8-10 lbs.
- 2 Tablespoon Pork & Poultry Rub
- 1 1/2 Cup apple juice
- 4 Tablespoon brown sugar
- 1 Tablespoon salt
- Sweet & Heat BBQ Sauce
- 16 Pieces White Bread
- cheddar cheese
- butter, softened

Directions:

1. Trim pork butt of all excess fat leaving 1/4-inch of the fat cap attached.
2. Combine 2 Tbsp Traeger Pork & Poultry Rub, apple juice, brown sugar and salt in a small bowl stirring until most of the sugar and salt are dissolved.
3. Inject the pork butt every square inch or so with the apple juice mixture. Season the exterior of the pork butt with remaining rub.
4. Supply your smoker with wood pellets and follow the start-up procedure. Preheat the grill, with the lid closed, to 250° F.
5. Place pork butt directly on the grill grate and cook for about 6 hours or until the internal temperature reaches 160 degrees F. Remove pork butt from grill and wrap in two layers of foil. Pour in 1/2 cup of apple juice. Secure tin foil tightly to contain the apple juice. Grill: 250 °F Probe: 160 °F
6. Increase temperature to 275 degrees F and return to grill in a pan large enough to hold the pork butt in case of leaks. Cook an additional 3 hours or until internal temperature reaches 205 degrees F. Grill: 275 °F Probe: 205 °F
7. Remove from the grill and discard the bone. Shred the pork removing any excess fat or

tendons. Season with additional Traeger Pork & Poultry Rub and salt if needed. Add Traeger Sweet & Heat BBQ Sauce and mix to combine. Set pork aside.

8. For the grilled cheese sandwiches: Butter two pieces of bread and place one in a pan warmed over medium heat, butter side down. Place a slice of cheddar cheese on top of the bread and top with pulled pork. Place another slice of cheese on top of pork and finish with the other slice of bread, butter side up.

9. Cook on first side 5-7 minutes until bread is lightly browned. Flip and cook for another 5-7 minutes. Remove from heat and slice in half. Enjoy!

First-timer's Pulled Pork

Servings: 8
Cooking Time: 540 Minutes

Ingredients:

*   1 bone-in pork shoulder, about 5 to 7lb (2.3 to 3.2kg)
*   coarse salt
*   freshly ground black pepper
*   1½ cups low-carb beer or sugar-free dark-colored soda
*   for the sauce
*   1½ cups apple cider vinegar
*   ½ cup distilled water
*   2 tbsp ketchup
*   1½ tbsp granulated brown sugar or low-carb substitute
*   1 tsp coarse salt, plus more
*   1 tsp freshly ground black pepper
*   ½ to 1 tsp crushed red pepper flakes

Directions:

1. Supply your smoker with wood pellets and follow the start-up procedure. Preheat the grill, with the lid closed, to 250° F.

2. In a medium saucepan on the stovetop over medium-high, make the vinegar sauce by bringing the ingredients to a boil. Whisk to dissolve the sugar and salt. Let the sauce cool to room temperature and then transfer to a jar with a tight-fitting lid. Set aside.

3. Season the pork shoulder on all sides with salt and pepper. Place the pork on the grate and smoke until the bone releases easily from the meat and the internal temperature reaches 200°F (93°C), about 7 to 9 hours. Wrap the pork tightly in a large piece of heavy-duty aluminum foil and let rest in an insulated cooler for up to 1 hour.

4. Carefully remove the pork from the foil and reserve the juices. Wear heatproof gloves to pull the pork into chunks. Discard the bone and any large lumps of fat. Pull the meat into shreds and transfer to a clean aluminum foil roasting pan. Moisten with some of the reserved juices. Taste, adding more salt and pepper. Serve with the vinegar sauce.

Honey Pork Belly Burnt Ends

Servings: 4
Cooking Time: 270 Minutes

Ingredients:

*   2/3 Cup Bbq Sauce
*   2 Tbsp Butter, Melted
*   2 Tbsp Honey
*   2 Tbsp Olive Oil
*   Blackened Sriracha Rub
*   3 Lbs Pork Belly, Skin Removed

Directions:

1. Supply your smoker with wood pellets and follow the start-up procedure. Preheat the grill, with the lid open, to 225° F. If using a gas or charcoal grill, set it up for low, indirect heat.

2. Cut pork belly into 2-inch cubes and place into a large mixing bowl.

3. Drizzle olive oil over pork belly, then generously season with Blackened Sriracha.

4. Transfer seasoned pork belly to a wire rack and place on the grill grate. Cook for 3 hours.

5. Remove the pork belly from the wire rack and transfer into a foil-lined aluminum pan or disposable foil pan.

6. Whisk together BBQ sauce, melted butter, and honey, then pour mixture over pork.

7. Toss to coat, then cover the pan with aluminum foil and return to the grill rack.

8. Cook for another 1 to 1 ½ hours, until the internal temperature reaches 200° F.

9. Remove the foil, transfer pork belly to a cast iron skillet and place in the center of the grill.

10. Open the sear slide and continue cooking for another 5 to 7 minutes, turning halfway, to crisp up the pork.

11. Remove pork belly from the grill, and serve warm.

Egg Sausage Casserole

Servings: 12

Cooking Time: 60 Minutes

Ingredients:
- 12 sausage links
- 30 oz hash browns, thawed
- 1 1/2 c. marble jack cheese, shredded
- 1/2 tsp pepper
- 12 large eggs
- 1 tsp salt
- 1/2 c. yellow onion, chopped
- 1 c. milk

Directions:

1. Supply your smoker with wood pellets and follow the start-up procedure. Preheat the grill, with the lid closed, to 350° F.

2. Grill sausage links on the preheated grill for 10-15 minutes or until heated through.

3. Remove the sausage links from grill and cut them into 1-inch pieces.

4. Spray a 9" ×13" tin pan with non-stick spray. Spread out hash browns on bottom of pan. Top with sausage pieces.

5. Combine eggs, salt, pepper, 1 c. cheese, onions, and milk in a bowl. Pour the mixture over sausage and hash browns. Then top with the remaining 1/2 c. of cheese.

6. Transfer the tin pan to the grill grate, and grill at 350 °F for 45 minutes or until the middle is set.

Wet-rubbed St. Louis Ribs

Servings: 2

Cooking Time: 240 Minutes

Ingredients:
- 1/2 Cup brown sugar
- 1 Tablespoon ground cumin
- 1 Tablespoon ancho chile powder
- 1 Tablespoon smoked paprika
- 1 Tablespoon garlic salt
- 3 Tablespoon balsamic vinegar
- 1 Rack St. Louis-style ribs
- 2 Cup apple juice

Directions:

1. In a bowl, combine all ingredients except ribs. Place wet rub on both sides of ribs; let sit for at least 10 minutes.

2. Supply your smoker with wood pellets and follow the start-up procedure. Preheat the grill, with the lid closed, to 180° F.

3. Turn temperature to 250°F; transfer the ribs into a foil pan, or wrap in tinfoil. Pour apple juice in the foil. Place foiled ribs back on grill. Cook for 2 hours. Remove from grill and let rest 10 minutes. Enjoy! Grill: 250 °F

Grilled Pork Tacos Al Pastor

Servings: 8
Cooking Time: 15 Minutes

Ingredients:

- 2 Tsp Annatto Powder
- Cilantro, Chopped
- Corn Tortillas
- 2 Tsp Cumin
- 1 Tsp Granulated Garlic
- 2 Tbsp Guajillo Chili Powder
- Jalapeno Pepper, Minced
- Lime, Wedges
- 1 Tsp Oregano, Dried
- 1/2 Tsp Pepper
- 1/2 Cup Pineapple, Juice
- 1/2 Pineapple, Skinned & Cored
- 2 Lbs Pork Shoulder, Boneless, Sliced Thin
- 1 1/2 Tsp Salt
- 2 Tbsp Tomato Paste
- 2 Tbsp Vegetable Oil
- 1/4 Cup White Vinegar
- Yellow Onion, Chopped

Directions:

1. Prepare marinade: In a mixing bowl, whisk together pineapple juice, vinegar, oil, tomato paste, chili powder, annatto, cumin, granulated garlic, oregano, salt, and pepper. Set aside.

2. Slice pork shoulder into thin slices (around ¼" thick), then place in a resealable plastic bag. Pour marinade over pork, seal bag, and turn to coat. Refrigerate overnight.

3. Supply your smoker with wood pellets and follow the start-up procedure. Preheat the grill, with the lid open, to 450° F. If using a gas or charcoal grill, set it up for high heat.

4. Remove the pork from the marinade and set on the grill. Grill over high heat for 3 to 5 minutes, turning frequently. Transfer to a cutting board to rest for 10 minutes, then slice thin.

5. Grill pineapple for 3 minutes, turning once. Set aside on a cutting board, and chop once cooled.

6. Assemble tacos: tortillas, pork, pineapple, jalapeño, onion, and cilantro. Serve warm with fresh lime wedges.

Grilled Bratwurst With Apple Slaw

Servings: 2
Cooking Time: 20 Minutes

Ingredients:

- 2 Whole Granny Smith Apples, Unpeeled
- 1/2 Small Red Onion, peeled
- 1/2 Cup mayonnaise
- 1/2 Tablespoon apple cider vinegar
- 1/4 Cup spicy brown mustard
- 1 Teaspoon Veggie Rub
- 1 Stick butter, melted
- 6 Whole bratwurst
- 6 Whole buns

Directions:

1. Supply your smoker with wood pellets and follow the start-up procedure. Preheat the grill, with the lid closed, to 350° F. For the apple slaw:

Grate unpeeled Granny Smith apples and red onion into a large bowl. Toss with mayonnaise, apple cider vinegar, spicy brown mustard, Traeger Veggie Rub and melted butter.

2. Place brats directly on the grill grate and cook for 10 minutes per side, or when an instant read thermometer inserted into the thickest part of the meat registers 160 degrees F. Grill: 350 ℉ Probe: 160 ℉

3. Remove from grill, place in bun and top with apple slaw. Enjoy!

Bacon Weave Smoked Country Sausage

Servings: 4
Cooking Time: 120 Minutes

Ingredients:
- Pound Sausage, Uncooked
- Pork & Poultry Rub
- 8 Slices bacon

Directions:
1. Using your hands, form sausage into a loaf-shape. Season lightly with Traeger Pork and Poultry Shake.

2. Supply your smoker with wood pellets and follow the start-up procedure. Preheat the grill, with the lid closed, to 180° F.

3. Put the sausage loaf directly on the grill grate and smoke for 1-1/2 hours.

4. While sausage is smoking, assemble the bacon weave on a piece of wax paper. First, lay out 4 pieces of bacon so they are touching each other on the wax paper. Next, lay the 5th piece of bacon so it crosses the others. Tuck every other slice under the 5th piece of bacon. Find the two pieces of bacon that were under the 5th piece of bacon and fold them back on top of themselves.

5. Lay down the 6th piece of bacon and unfold the two that were laid back. Continue folding the bacon back that was most recently under the last piece of bacon, two pieces at a time, laying the next piece of bacon on top until your weave is complete. Set aside. After your sausage has smoked for 1-1/2 hours, take it off the grill and increase the heat of your Traeger, lid closed to 350℉ and preheat. Grill: 350 ℉

6. While the grill is heating, wrap your sausage loaf in the bacon weave. Lay the middle of the weave directly on top of the sausage loaf and press the bacon all around the sausage.

7. Flip the sausage and bacon over to finish the weave on the bottom of the sausage. Alternate the bacon ends across the bottom and tuck the ends around each other.

8. Put your sausage back on the grill and cook for 25-30 minutes until the internal temperature of the sausage reaches 160℉. Enjoy! Probe: 160 ℉

Smoked Sausage & Potatoes

Servings: 4
Cooking Time: 50 Minutes

Ingredients:
- 2 Pound Hot Sausage Links
- 2 Pound fingerling potatoes
- 1 Tablespoon fresh thyme
- 4 Tablespoon butter

Directions:
1. Supply your smoker with wood pellets and follow the start-up procedure. Preheat the grill, with the lid closed, to 375° F.

2. Put your sausage links on the grill to get some color. This should take about 3 minutes on each side. Grill: 375 ℉

3. While sausage is cooking, cut the potatoes into bite size pieces all about the same size so they cook evenly. Chop the thyme and butter, then combine all the ingredients into a Traeger cast iron skillet.

4. Pull your sausage off the grill, slice into bite size pieces and add to your cast iron.

5. Turn grill down to 275℉ and put the cast iron in the grill for 45 minutes to an hour or until the potatoes are fully cooked. Grill: 275 ℉

6. After 45 minutes, use a butter knife to test your potatoes by cutting into one to see if its done. To speed up cook time you can cover cast iron will a lid or foil. Serve. Enjoy!

Hawaiian Pulled Pork

Servings: 8-10
Cooking Time: 640 Minutes

Ingredients:

- 2 Cups Aloe Leaf Juice
- 1 Tsp Coriander, Ground
- 2 Tsp Cracked Pepper
- 1 Tsp Cumin
- Dash Of Salt
- 4-6 Garlic, Cloves
- 1 (3-Inch) Ginger, Fresh
- 1-2 Limes
- 4 Cups No Sodium Added Chicken Bone Broth
- ¼ Cup Olive Oil
- 4 Tsp Paprika
- 6-8 Lbs Pork Shoulder/Butt
- 1/2 Sweet Onion
- 2 Packets Truvia To Sweeten Above Aloe Juice
- 2 Tbs Or 2 Tbs Swerve Brown Sugar Truvia – Honey Substitute

Directions:

1. Supply your smoker with wood pellets and follow the start-up procedure. Preheat the grill, with the lid closed, to 300° F. Make sure your flame broiler is closed, you want to use indirect heat for this recipe.

2. Add all spices into a bowl (salt, paprika, cumin, coriander, pepper, onion powder if needed). Set bowl aside.

3. Grate the ginger into a separate bowl (wet ingredients bowl).

4. Mince or smash the garlic cloves into the same bowl.

5. Dice onion and add it to the ginger and garlic (if no onion sub onion powder).

6. Juice 1-2 limes and add to the "wet" ingredients bowl.

7. Add 4 cups chicken bone broth.

8. Add two cups aloe leaf juice w/lemon and add two packets Truvia to sweeten.

9. Add 1-2 tbsp Truvia honey substitute. Mix and set bowl aside.

10. Add the oil to your Cast Iron and coat the bottom and sides. Place the pork in the cast iron roasting pan.

11. Take your dry rub and coat the pork.

12. Pour the wet ingredients around the pork, into the Cast Iron Roasting Pan.

13. Cover the roasting pan with the lid and set it on your grill.

14. Check the pork every couple hours (basting if you prefer). When internal temperature reaches 195℉ (after around 6 – 8 hours of cook time), it should easily start to pull apart. Don't pull apart the whole shoulder yet.

15. Remove the Roasting Pan from the grill and set aside to allow it to rest for 1 hour. Remove the lid to help speed cooling.

16. Once cooled, shred the pork into a separate bowl, removing the fat as you go.

17. If you want to add some of the marinade to the pork for additional flavor, make sure you skim the fat off the top first and discard.

18. Viola! Pair with fresh grilled veggies, delicious fruit or make tacos or salads! So many options for this type of protein.

Grilled German Sausage With A Smoky Traeger Twist

Servings: 8
Cooking Time: 120 Minutes

Ingredients:

- 2 Tablespoon Jacobsen Salt Co. Pure Kosher Sea Salt
- 1 Teaspoon The Sausage Maker Instacure #1
- 1 Tablespoon ground nutmeg
- 2 Teaspoon ground mace
- 1 Teaspoon ground ginger
- 4 Pound ground pork, 80% lean
- 1 Pound ground veal or ground beef
- 2 Large eggs
- 1 Cup nonfat dry milk powder

Directions:

1. Combine salt, Instacure #1, nutmeg, mace and ginger in a large pitcher or small bowl. Add the milk and eggs. Beat until well combined. Pour the egg mixture over the ground meat and mix gently. Using your hands, mix in the milk powder until evenly distributed.

2. Form the meat into sausage links, roughly 4 to 6 inches in length.

3. Supply your smoker with wood pellets and follow the start-up procedure. Preheat the grill, with the lid closed, to 225° F.

4. Smoke for approximately 2 hours, or until the internal temperature reaches 175°F. Serve immediately or refrigerate until ready to serve. Enjoy! Grill: 225 °F Probe: 175 °F

Bbq Sweet & Smoky Ribs

Servings: 6
Cooking Time: 300 Minutes

Ingredients:

- 2 Rack Pork, Spare Ribs Trimmed
- 6 Cup apple juice
- 2 Tablespoon Big Game Rub
- 2 Cup 'Que BBQ Sauce
- 1/4 Cup brown sugar

Directions:

1. If your butcher has not already done so, remove the thin papery membrane from the bone-side of the ribs by working the tip of a butter knife underneath the membrane over a middle bone. Use paper towels to get a firm grip, then tear the membrane off.

2. Lay the ribs in a baking dish. Pour the apple juice over ribs, using as much apple juice as needed to submerge the meaty side of the ribs. Turn to coat.

3. Cover and refrigerate ribs for 4 to 6 hours or overnight. Remove the ribs from the apple juice; reserve juice.

4. Sprinkle ribs on all sides with Traeger Big Game Rub.

5. Supply your smoker with wood pellets and follow the start-up procedure. Preheat the grill, with the lid closed, to 225° F.

6. Transfer the apple juice to a saucepan and place in a corner of the grill, the juice will keep the cooking environment moist.

7. Arrange the ribs bone side down, directly on the grill grate. Cook for 4 to 5 hours, or until a skewer or paring knife inserted between the bones goes in easily.

8. Check the internal temperature of the ribs, the desired temperature is 202°F. If not at temperature, cook for an additional 30 minutes or until temperature is reached.

9. Meanwhile, combine the BBQ sauce and brown sugar in a small saucepan. Generously brush the ribs on all sides with the BBQ sauce the last hour of cooking

10. Using a sharp knife, cut the slabs into individual ribs. Serve. Enjoy!

Spiced Smoked Pork Carnitas

Servings: 12
Cooking Time: 360 Minutes

Ingredients:
- 1 Pork Butt/Shoulder Roast (3-5 lb)
- 1 Tablespoon Ground Cumin
- 1 1/2 Teaspoons Chili Powder
- 1 1/2 Teaspoon Salt
- 1 Teaspoon Cayenne Pepper
- 1 Teaspoon Garlic Powder
- 1/2 Teaspoon Ground Cloves
- 1/2 Cup Vegetable Oil

Directions:
1. Supply your smoker with wood pellets and follow the start-up procedure. Preheat the grill, with the lid closed, to 225° F.

2. Cut pork into 1 inch-thick strips and place into a disposable aluminum foil pan.

3. Sprinkle cumin, chili powder, salt, cayenne pepper, garlic powder, and cloves on the pork stripes. Drizzle on the vegetable oil. Using tongs, toss until pork strips are well coated.

4. Cover the pan with a piece of aluminum foil and place it on the grill grate. Smoke it at 225 °F for 4 hours.

5. After 4 hours, take the pan out and remove the aluminum foil. Then return to the smoker and cook approximately 2 more hours until pork is tender and easily shreds with a fork.

Rub-injected Pork Shoulder

Servings: 8-12
Cooking Time: 1200 Minutes

Ingredients:
- 1 (6- to 8-pound) bone-in pork shoulder
- 2 cups Tea Injectable made with Pork Rub
- 2 tablespoons yellow mustard
- 1 batch Pork Rub

Directions:
1. Supply your smoker with wood pellets and follow the start-up procedure. Preheat the grill, with the lid closed, to 225°F.

2. Inject the pork shoulder throughout with the tea injectable.

3. Coat the pork shoulder all over with mustard and season it with the rub. Using your hands, work the rub into the meat.

4. Place the shoulder directly on the grill grate and smoke until its internal temperature reaches 160°F and a dark bark has formed on the exterior.

5. Pull the shoulder from the grill and wrap it completely in aluminum foil or butcher paper.

6. Increase the grill's temperature to 350°F.

7. Return the pork shoulder to the grill and cook until its internal temperature reaches 195°F.

8. Pull the shoulder from the grill and place it in a cooler. Cover the cooler and let the pork rest for 1 or 2 hours.

9. Remove the pork shoulder from the cooler and unwrap it. Remove the shoulder bone and pull the pork apart using just your fingers. Serve immediately.

Old-fashioned Roasted Glazed Ham

Servings: 8
Cooking Time: 60 Minutes

Ingredients:
- 1 (10 lb) fully cooked bone-in spiral cut ham
- 1 Cup pineapple juice
- 1/2 Cup brown sugar
- 1 cinnamon stick
- 14 whole cloves
- 1 Whole Pineapple, fresh
- 10 Cherries, fresh, sweet

Directions:
1. Supply your smoker with wood pellets and follow the start-up procedure. Preheat the grill, with the lid closed, to 325° F.

2. Rinse ham under cold water and pat dry with paper towel.

3. In a saucepan combine pineapple juice, brown sugar, cinnamon stick and four cloves. Bring to a boil. Reduce heat to medium low and simmer for about 15 minutes or until pineapple juice is reduced by half, thick and syrupy.

4. Brush half of the glaze onto the ham and into the folds of the cut slices. Reserve the other half of the glaze for later.

5. Cut pineapple in desired sized pieces, about 2 inch squares, then place on ham with a cherry and a clove to pin in place, repeating all over ham.

6. Put ham in a deep baking dish with fat side up. Place on the Traeger and cook for about 1-¼ hours. Grill: 325 °F

7. Carefully remove from Traeger and brush remaining glaze onto ham.

8. Return ham to Traeger and continue cooking for another 15 to 20 minutes, until internal temperature of ham reaches 160°F. Grill: 325 °F Probe: 160 °F

9. Allow ham to rest for 15 – 20 minutes before serving. Enjoy!

Grilled Bbq Pork Chops

Servings: 6
Cooking Time: 12 Minutes

Ingredients:
- 6 Thick-Cut Pork Chops
- Generous amounts BBQ rub

Directions:
1. Supply your smoker with wood pellets and follow the start-up procedure. Preheat the grill, with the lid closed, to 450° F. Place seasoned pork chops on grill. Cook 6 minutes per side, or until internal temps reach 145 °F.

2. Remove from heat and let sit for 5-10 minutes before serving.

Whiskey- & Cider-brined Pork Shoulder

Servings: 8
Cooking Time: 540 Minutes

Ingredients:
- 1 bone-in pork shoulder, about 5 to 7lb (2.3 to 3.2kg)
- fresh coarsely ground black pepper
- granulated garlic

- 1 cup apple juice or apple cider
- low-carb barbecue sauce, warmed
- hamburger buns (optional)
- for the brine
- 1 gallon (3.8 liters) cold distilled water
- 1 cup coarse salt
- 1¼ cup whiskey, divided
- ½ cup light brown sugar or low-carb substitute

Directions:

1. In a large saucepot on the stovetop over medium-high heat, make the brine by bringing the water, salt, 1 cup of whiskey, and brown sugar to a boil. Stir with a long-handled wooden spoon until the salt and sugar dissolve. Let the brine cool to room temperature. Cover and cool completely in the refrigerator.

2. Submerge the pork in the brine. If it floats, place a resealable bag of ice on top. Refrigerate for 24 hours.

3. Supply your smoker with wood pellets and follow the start-up procedure. Preheat the grill, with the lid closed, to 250° F.

4. Remove the pork shoulder from the brine and pat dry with paper towels. (Discard the brine.) Season the pork with pepper and granulated garlic. Place the pork on the grate and smoke until the internal temperature reaches 165°F (74°C), about 5 hours.

5. Transfer the pork to an aluminum foil roasting pan and add the apple juice and the remaining ¼ cup of whiskey. Cover tightly with aluminum foil. Place the pan on the grate and cook the pork until the bone releases easily from the meat and the internal temperature reaches 200°F (93°C), about 3 hours more. (Be careful when lifting a corner of the foil to check on the roast because steam will escape.)

6. Remove the pan from the grill and let the pork rest for 20 minutes. Reserve the juices.

7. Wearing heatproof gloves, pull the pork into chunks. Discard the bone or any large lumps of fat. Pull the meat into shreds and transfer to a clean aluminum foil roasting pan. Moisten with the barbecue sauce or serve the sauce on the side. Stir in some of the drippings—not too much because you don't want the pork to be swimming in its juices. Serve on buns (if using).

VEGETABLES RECIPES

Roasted Asparagus

Servings: 4

Cooking Time: 30 Minutes

Ingredients:

- 1 Bunch asparagus
- 2 Tablespoon olive oil, plus more as needed
- Veggie Rub

Directions:

1. Coat asparagus with olive oil and Veggie Rub, stirring to coat all pieces.
2. Supply your smoker with wood pellets and follow the start-up procedure. Preheat the grill, with the lid closed, to 350° F.
3. Place asparagus directly on the grill grate for 15-20 minutes.
4. Remove from grill and enjoy!

Roasted Red Pepper White Bean Dip

Servings: 4

Cooking Time: 40 Minutes

Ingredients:

- 4 Whole garlic
- 4 Tablespoon extra-virgin olive oil
- 2 Bell Pepper, Red
- 3 Tablespoon Dill Weed, fresh
- 3 Tablespoon chopped flat-leaf parsley
- 2 Can cannellini beans, mashed
- 4 Teaspoon lemon juice
- 1 1/2 Teaspoon salt

Directions:

1. Roasting the garlic and red peppers:

2. Supply your smoker with wood pellets and follow the start-up procedure. Preheat the grill, with the lid closed, to 400° F.

3. Peel away the outside layers of the garlic husk. Cut off the top of the garlic bulb, exposing each of the individual cloves. Drizzle olive oil over the top of the head of garlic and rub it in. Wrap the garlic in foil, completely covering it. Put the head of garlic and the two red peppers (washed and dried) on the Traeger.

4. Roast the garlic for 25-30 minutes and the peppers for about 40 minutes. Rotate the peppers a quarter-turn every 10 minutes until the exterior is blistered and blackened. Grill: 400 °F

5. Pull the peppers off the grill and put them in a bowl. Cover the bowl with plastic wrap and leave them for 15 minutes. The steam will loosen the skins so that they slip off like a drumstick covered in barbecue sauce.

6. Peel off the pepper skin. Cut off the stems and scrape out the seeds and they're ready to use.

7. As for the garlic, let it cool and then pull out the individual cloves as needed.

8. The dip:

9. In a blender put the roasted red peppers, 4 cloves of roasted garlic, dill, parsley, drained and rinsed beans, olive oil, lemon juice and salt.

10. Blend until the dip is smooth and creamy. You may need to scrape down the sides of the blender a couple of times. If it's having difficulty blending or looks too thick add more olive oil or lemon juice. (Add more lemon juice if it tastes like it needs more acid or brightness.) Enjoy!

Baked Winter Squash Au Gratin

Servings: 8

Cooking Time: 45 Minutes

Ingredients:

- 2 Cup heavy cream
- salt and pepper
- 3 Cup shredded Gruyere cheese
- 4 Clove garlic, diced
- 2 Tablespoon butter
- 3 yellow potatoes, peeled and cubed
- 1 butternut squash seeded, peeled and cubed
- 1 acorn squash seeded, peeled and cubed

Directions:

1. Supply your smoker with wood pellets and follow the start-up procedure. Preheat the grill, with the lid closed, to 375° F.

2. In a medium saucepan, cook the cream, stirring constantly, until it comes to a low boil. Add salt, pepper, garlic and shredded Gruyere cheese. Stir until cheese is melted.

3. Grease a 9x13 inch baking dish with 2 tablespoons of butter. In a large mixing bowl, combine potatoes, butternut and acorn squash. Stir in the cheese sauce. Place mixture in the prepared baking dish and place in grill.

4. Cook for 45 minutes or until potatoes and squash are fork tender. Remove from grill and let cool for 10 minutes before serving. Enjoy! Grill: 375 °F

Grilled Asparagus And Hollandaise Sauce

Servings: 4

Cooking Time: 10 Minutes

Ingredients:

- 1 Pound asparagus
- 2 Teaspoon red pepper flakes
- 2 Tablespoon olive oil
- salt and pepper
- 4 egg yolk
- 1 Tablespoon lemon juice
- 1/2 Cup butter, melted
- cayenne pepper
- salt

Directions:

1. Supply your smoker with wood pellets and follow the start-up procedure. Preheat the grill, with the lid closed, to 375° F.

2. In a large bowl, mix asparagus with olive oil, red pepper flakes and salt. Arrange asparagus on a cooking sheet and take to the grill. Cook for approximately 10 to 15 minutes. Grill: 375 °F

3. In an aluminum bowl, whisk the egg yolks well. Add the lemon juice and whisk until creamy.

4. Place bowl over a double boiler, over low heat, making sure that it does not touches the water.

5. While whisking, add the melted butter slowly. Whisk until it doubles the volume. Take off the heat, still whisking and add the cayenne pepper and salt.

6. Arrange asparagus over a serving plater. Pour hollandaise sauce over asparagus and serve. Enjoy!

Double-smoked Cheese Potatoes

Servings: 12

Cooking Time: 35 Minutes

Ingredients:

- 4 large baking potatoes (12 to 14 ounces each—preferably organic)
- 1 1/2 tablespoons bacon fat or butter, melted, or extra virgin olive oil
- Coarse salt (sea or kosher) and freshly ground black pepper

- 4 strips artisanal bacon (like Nueske's), cut crosswise into 1/4-inch slivers
- 6 tablespoons (3/4 stick) cold unsalted butter, thinly sliced
- 2 scallions, trimmed, white and green parts finely chopped (about 4 tablespoons)
- 2 cups coarsely grated smoked or regular white cheddar cheese (about 8 ounces)
- 1/2 cup sour cream
- Spanish smoked paprika (pimentón) or sweet paprika, for sprinkling

Directions:

1. Supply your smoker with wood pellets and follow the start-up procedure. Preheat the grill, with the lid closed, to 400° F.Add enough wood for 1 hour of smoking as specified by the manufacturer.

2. Scrub the potatoes on all sides with a vegetable brush. Rinse well under cold running water and blot dry with paper towels. Prick each potato several times with a fork (this keeps the spud from exploding and facilitates the smoke absorption). Brush or rub the potato on all sides with the bacon fat and season generously with salt and pepper.

3. Place the potatoes on the smoker rack. Smoke until the skins are crisp and the potatoes are tender in the center (they'll be easy to pierce with a slender metal skewer), about 1 hour.

4. Meanwhile, place the bacon in a cold skillet and fry over medium heat until browned and crisp, 3 to 4 minutes. Drain off the bacon fat (save the fat for future potatoes).

5. Transfer the potatoes to a cutting board and let cool slightly. Cut each potato in half lengthwise. Using a spoon, scrape out most of the potato flesh, leaving a 1/4-inch-thick shell. (It's easier to scoop the potatoes when warm.) Cut the potato flesh into 1/2-inch dice and place in a bowl.

6. Add the bacon, 4 tablespoons of the butter, the scallions, and cheese to the potato flesh and gently stir to mix. Stir in the sour cream and salt and pepper to taste; the mixture should be highly seasoned. Stir as little and as gently as possible so as to leave some texture to the potatoes.

7. Spoon the potato mixture back into the potato shells, mounding it in the center. Top each potato half with a thin slice of the remaining butter and sprinkle with paprika. The potatoes can be prepared up to 24 hours ahead to this stage, covered, and refrigerated.

8. Just before serving, preheat your smoker to 400 °F. Add enough wood for 30 minutes of smoking. Place the potatoes in a shallow aluminum foil pan and re-smoke them until browned and bubbling, 15 to 20 minutes.

Baked Artichoke Parmesan Mushrooms

Servings: 8
Cooking Time: 30 Minutes

Ingredients:

- 8 Cremini Mushroom Caps
- 6 1/2 Ounce artichoke hearts
- 1/3 Cup Parmesan cheese, grated
- 1/4 Cup mayonnaise
- 1/2 Teaspoon garlic salt
- your favorite hot sauce
- paprika

Directions:

1. Clean the mushrooms with a damp paper towel. Remove the stems and discard or save for another use.

2. Using a small spoon, scoop out the inside (gills, etc.). Combine the artichoke hearts, parmesan, mayonnaise, garlic salt, and hot sauce and mix well.

3. Mound the filling in the mushroom caps. Dust the tops with paprika.

4. Arrange the mushrooms in an oven-safe baking dish.

5. Supply your smoker with wood pellets and follow the start-up procedure. Preheat the grill, with the lid closed, to 350° F.

6. Bake the mushrooms (uncovered) until the filling is bubbling and just beginning to brown, about 25 to 30 minutes. Serve immediately. Grill: 350 °F

7. For a simple variation, stuff the mushrooms with your favorite bulk sausage and bake on your Traeger as directed above. Enjoy!

Smoked Pico De Gallo

Servings: 4
Cooking Time: 30 Minutes

Ingredients:

- 3 Cup diced Roma tomatoes
- 1 jalapeño, diced
- 1/2 red onion, diced
- 1/2 Bunch cilantro, finely chopped
- 2 lime, juiced
- salt
- olive oil

Directions:

1. Supply your smoker with wood pellets and follow the start-up procedure. Preheat the grill, with the lid closed, to 180° F.

2. Place the diced tomatoes on a small sheet pan spreading them into a thin layer. Place the sheet pan directly on the grill and smoke for 30 minutes. Grill: 180 °F

3. When the tomatoes are finished, toss all ingredients in a medium bowl and finish with lime juice, salt and olive oil to taste. Serve and enjoy!

Baked Loaded Tater Tots

Servings: 6
Cooking Time: 35 Minutes

Ingredients:

- 2 Pound frozen tater tots
- 1 Can Black Beans
- 1 1/2 Cup leftover chili
- 1 Cup leftover queso
- 1 red onion, finely diced
- 1/2 Cup chopped cilantro
- 1/2 Cup sour cream
- 1 jalapeños, sliced

Directions:

1. Supply your smoker with wood pellets and follow the start-up procedure. Preheat the grill, with the lid closed, to 375° F.

2. Spread frozen tots out on a sheet tray and place directly on the grill grate.

3. Cook for 20 to 25 minutes or until tots are crispy. Grill: 375 °F

4. Top with warmed chili, queso and beans. Place back on the grill for 15 minutes. Grill: 375 °F

5. Remove from grill and top with red onion, cilantro, sour cream and jalapeño. Enjoy!

Roasted Tomatoes With Hot Pepper Sauce

Servings: 4

Cooking Time: 60 Minutes

Ingredients:

- 2 Pound fresh Roma tomatoes
- 3 Tablespoon parsley, chopped
- 2 Tablespoon garlic, chopped
- salt and pepper
- 1/2 Cup extra-virgin olive oil
- 1 Pound Spaghetti
- Hot peppers

Directions:

1. Supply your smoker with wood pellets and follow the start-up procedure. Preheat the grill, with the lid closed, to 400° F.

2. Wash tomatoes and cut them in half, lengthwise. Place them in a baking dish cut side up.

3. Sprinkle with chopped parsley, garlic, add salt and black pepper and pour 1/4 cup (100 mL)of olive oil over them.

4. Place on pre-heated grill and bake for 1 1/2 hours. Tomatoes will shrink and the skins will be partly blackened. Grill: 400 ˚F

5. Remove tomatoes from baking dish and place in a food processor leaving the cooked oil, and puree them.

6. Drop pasta into boiling salted water and cook until tender. Drain and toss immediately with the pureed tomatoes.

7. Add the remaining 1/4 cup (60mL) of raw olive oil and crumbled hot red pepper to taste. Toss and serve. Enjoy!

Roasted Garlic Herb Fries

Servings: 4

Cooking Time: 45 Minutes

Ingredients:

- 4 Whole russet potatoes
- 1 Teaspoon salt
- 2 Tablespoon avocado oil
- 1 Teaspoon fresh chopped rosemary
- 1 Teaspoon fresh chopped thyme
- 2 Clove garlic, minced
- 2 Teaspoon flake salt
- 1 Teaspoon chopped parsley, for garnish

Directions:

1. Supply your smoker with wood pellets and follow the start-up procedure. Preheat the grill, with the lid closed, to 425° F.

2. Chop potatoes into fries, (a mandolin works great for this) and place directly into an ice water bath with 1 teaspoon salt for 15 to 30 minutes.

3. Combine oil, rosemary, thyme and garlic in a big bowl. Remove potatoes from ice water and dry thoroughly with paper towels.

4. Toss potatoes in the oil mixture and place them on 2 to 3 parchment-lined baking sheets in a single layer. Sprinkle the flake salt over the fries.

5. Place baking sheets on the grill and roast for 30 minutes, flip the fries, then cook for an additional 15 minutes until golden and crispy. Dust with parsley. Grill: 425 ˚F

6. Serve with your favorite dipping sauce, side dish or as a nacho base.

Carolina Baked Beans

Servings: 12-15

Cooking Time: 180 Minutes

Ingredients:

- 3 (28-ounce) cans baked beans (I like Bush's brand)
- 1 large onion, finely chopped
- 1 cup The Ultimate BBQ Sauce
- ½ cup light brown sugar
- ¼ cup Worcestershire sauce
- 3 tablespoons yellow mustard
- Nonstick cooking spray or butter, for greasing
- 1 large bell pepper, cut into thin rings
- ½ pound thick-cut bacon, partially cooked and cut into quarters

Directions:

1. Supply your smoker with wood pellets and follow the start-up procedure. Preheat, with the lid closed, to 300°F.

2. In a large mixing bowl, stir together the beans, onion, barbecue sauce, brown sugar, Worcestershire sauce, and mustard until well combined

3. Coat a 9-by-13-inch aluminum pan with cooking spray or butter.

4. Pour the beans into the pan and top with the bell pepper rings and bacon pieces, pressing them down slightly into the sauce.

5. Place a layer of heavy-duty foil on the grill grate to catch drips, and place the pan on top of the foil. Close the lid and cook for 2 hours 30 minutes to 3 hours, or until the beans are hot, thick, and bubbly.

6. Let the beans rest for 5 minutes before serving.

Grilled Cabbage Steaks With Warm Bacon Vinaigrette

Servings: 4

Cooking Time: 10 Minutes

Ingredients:

- 3 Strips thick-cut lean bacon, cut into 1/4 inch strips
- 1 Large shallot, minced
- 2 Tablespoon sherry vinegar
- 1 Tablespoon whole grain mustard
- 1 Teaspoon chopped thyme
- 2 Tablespoon olive oil, plus more as needed
- 1 Head green cabbage, cut into 3/4 inch thick slices (about 6 steaks)
- salt and pepper

Directions:

1. Supply your smoker with wood pellets and follow the start-up procedure. Preheat the grill, with the lid closed, to 450° F.

2. For the Vinaigrette: In a large skillet, cook the bacon in 2 tablespoons olive oil over medium-high heat until browned and crisp. Remove bacon from heat and stir in the shallot, vinegar, mustard and thyme then set aside.

3. Brush cabbage steaks with olive oil and season with salt and pepper. Place cabbage steaks directly on grill grate and grill for 5 minutes per side. Grill: 450 °F

4. Remove cabbage steaks from grill and drizzle with bacon vinaigrette. Enjoy!

Smoked Beet-pickled Eggs

Servings: 4
Cooking Time: 30 Minutes

Ingredients:

- 6 Eggs, hard boiled
- 1 Red Beets, scrubbed and trimmed
- 1 Cup apple cider vinegar
- 1 Cup Beet, juice
- 1/4 Onion, Sliced
- 1/3 Cup granulated sugar
- 3 Cardamom
- 1 star anise

Directions:

1. Supply your smoker with wood pellets and follow the start-up procedure. Preheat the grill, with the lid closed, to 275° F.

2. Place the peeled hard boiled eggs directly on the grill and smoke for 30 minutes. Grill: 275 °F

3. Put the smoked eggs in a quart size glass jar with the cooked/chopped beets in the bottom.

4. In a medium sauce pan, add the vinegar, beet juice, onion, sugar, cardamom and anise.

5. Bring to a boil and cook, uncovered, until sugar has dissolved and the onions are translucent (about 5 minutes).

6. Remove from the heat and let cool for a few minutes.

7. Pour the vinegar and onions mixture over the eggs and beets in the jar, covering the eggs completely.

8. Securely close with the jar lid. Refrigerate up to a month. Enjoy!

Roasted Sweet Potato Steak Fries

Servings: 4
Cooking Time: 40 Minutes

Ingredients:

- 3 Whole sweet potatoes
- 4 Tablespoon extra-virgin olive oil
- salt and pepper
- 2 Tablespoon fresh chopped rosemary

Directions:

1. Supply your smoker with wood pellets and follow the start-up procedure. Preheat the grill, with the lid closed, to 450° F.

2. Cut sweet potatoes into wedges and toss with olive oil, salt, pepper and rosemary. Spread on a parchment lined baking sheet and put in the grill. Cook for 15 minutes then flip and continue to cook until lightly browned and cooked through, about 40 to 45 minutes total. Grill: 450 °F

3. Serve with your favorite dipping sauce. Enjoy! Grill: 450 °F

Smoked Macaroni Salad

Servings: 4
Cooking Time: 20 Minutes

Ingredients:

- 1 Pound macaroni, uncooked
- 1/2 Small red onion, diced
- 1 green bell pepper, diced
- 1/2 Cup shredded carrot
- 1 Cup mayonnaise
- 3 Tablespoon white wine vinegar
- 2 Tablespoon sugar
- salt
- black pepper

Directions:

1. Bring a large stock pot of salted water to a boil over medium heat and cook pasta according to package directions. Make sure to cook to al dente, strain, and rinse under cold water.

2. Supply your smoker with wood pellets and follow the start-up procedure. Preheat the grill, with the lid closed, to 225° F.

3. Spread cooked pasta out on a sheet tray and place sheet tray directly on the grill grate. Smoke for 20 minutes, remove from heat, and transfer directly to the refrigerator to cool. Grill: 225 ℉

4. While the pasta is cooling mix the dressing. Place all ingredients in a medium bowl and whisk to combine.

5. When pasta is cool combine chopped veggies, smoked pasta and dressing in a large bowl.

6. Cover with plastic wrap and place in the fridge for 20 minutes before serving. Enjoy!

Roasted Vegetable Napoleon

Servings: 4

Cooking Time: 30 Minutes

Ingredients:

- 2 Whole sweet potatoes
- 2 Whole zucchini
- 2 Whole Squash
- 1 Whole red onion
- 2 Whole Bell Pepper, Red
- salt and pepper

Directions:

1. Supply your smoker with wood pellets and follow the start-up procedure. Preheat the grill, with the lid closed, to High heat.

2. Salt and pepper all vegetables and grill them on both sides. Begin with the peppers and onions as they will take a little longer to cook. Grill: 450 ℉

Roasted Jalapeno Cheddar Deviled Eggs

Servings: 6

Cooking Time: 30 Minutes

Ingredients:

- 7 Eggs, hard boiled
- 3 Tablespoon mayonnaise
- 1 Teaspoon brown mustard
- 1 Teaspoon apple cider vinegar
- 1 Dash hot sauce
- 1 jalapeño pepper, seeded and minced
- salt and pepper
- 1/2 Cup shredded cheddar cheese
- paprika

Directions:

1. Supply your smoker with wood pellets and follow the start-up procedure. Preheat the grill, with the lid closed, to 180° F.

2. Place your eggs directly on the grill grate and smoke for 30 minutes.

3. Remove from the grill and allow the eggs to cool. Smoking the eggs will give them a slightly yellowed color, but an intense smoky flavor. If a classic white egg is your preference, then skip this step.

4. Slice the eggs lengthwise and scoop the egg yolks directly into a gallon zip top bag.

5. Add the mayo, mustard, vinegar, hot sauce, roasted jalapeños and salt and pepper to the bag.

6. Zip the bag closed and, using your hands, knead all of the ingredients together in the bag until completely smooth.

7. Squeeze the yolk mixture into one corner of the bag and then cut the corner off. Pipe the yolk mixture into the whites.

8. Sprinkle with the finely shredded cheddar or paprika and chill until you are ready to serve. Enjoy!

Christmas Brussel Sprouts

Servings: 6
Cooking Time: 50 Minutes

Ingredients:

- 1/2 Pound thick-cut bacon
- 1 Medium onion, diced
- 2 Pound fresh Brussels sprouts
- 2 Tablespoon olive oil
- salt and pepper

Directions:

1. Supply your smoker with wood pellets and follow the start-up procedure. Preheat the grill, with the lid closed, to 350° F.
2. Place bacon directly on grill grate and cook for 15-20 minutes, or until lightly browned. Remove from grill and set aside on paper towel lined plate.
3. Slice onion in half and then slice into 1/4 inch moons and add to large mixing bowl. Slice brussels sprouts in half lengthwise and add to bowl.
4. Cut reserved bacon into 1/2 inch pieces and add to bowl. Drizzle with olive oil and sprinkle with salt and pepper. Toss to coat and pour into baking pan.
5. Turn the temperature on grill to 375 and place baking pan on grill. Roast for 30 minutes mixing halfway through cooking. Grill: 375 °F

Smoked Mushrooms

Servings: 4
Cooking Time: 45 Minutes

Ingredients:

- Pound Mushrooms, fresh
- 1/2 Cup apple cider vinegar
- 1/2 Cup soy sauce
- 1 Teaspoon Blackened Saskatchewan Rub

Directions:

1. Clean mushrooms and place in a large Ziploc bag. Add apple cider vinegar, soy sauce and rub.
2. Mix well and allow to marinate in the refrigerator for at least 2 hours.
3. Supply your smoker with wood pellets and follow the start-up procedure. Preheat the grill, with the lid closed, to 350° F.
4. Place cast iron skillet inside grill for 20 minutes to warm up.
5. Add the mushrooms and marinade slowly into the cast iron skillet.
6. Cook uncovered for 15 minutes, then cover the skillet and cook another 30 minutes until mushrooms are tender. Grill: 350 °F
7. Remove skillet from grill and let mushrooms cool down for 5 minutes before serving. Enjoy!

Roasted Jalapeño Poppers

Servings: 2
Cooking Time: 30 Minutes

Ingredients:

- 8 Slices Bacon, Center Cut
- 2 Cup cream cheese
- 2 Ounce Cheese, sharp cheddar
- 1/2 Cup green onions, minced
- 2 Teaspoon fresh squeezed lime juice
- 4 Tablespoon Seeded Tomato, Chopped
- 4 Tablespoon cilantro, chopped
- 1/2 Teaspoon kosher salt
- 2 Small garlic clove, minced
- 12 Whole Jalapeños

Directions:

1. Supply your smoker with wood pellets and follow the start-up procedure. Preheat the grill, with the lid closed, to 350° F.

2. Place 2 bacon slices directly on the grill grate and cook 10-15 minutes until cooked through and crispy flipping halfway through. Remove from grill, but leave the grill on. When cool enough to handle, coarsely chop the bacon and reserve. Grill: 350 ℉

3. In the bowl of a stand mixer, combine cream cheese, cheddar cheese, green onions, chopped bacon, lime juice, tomatoes, cilantro, salt and garlic. Mix on medium speed with a paddle until combined. Transfer mixture to a piping bag.

4. Cut the tops off the jalapeños and remove the seeds and ribs with a small paring knife.

5. Pipe the filling into each pepper so that the filling comes up a 1/4" over the top of the pepper. Place the tops back on each pepper.

6. With a rolling pin, flatten out the remaining six slices of bacon until they are 1/8" thick. Cut each slice in half. Wrap 1/2 a bacon slice around each pepper and secure with a toothpick.

7. Place the peppers in the Traeger Jalapeno Popper Tray. Place the tray directly on the grill grate and cook for 30-40 minutes until the peppers are tender, bacon is crispy, and cheese is melted. Enjoy! Grill: 350 ℉

Roasted Artichokes With Garlic Butter

Servings: 2
Cooking Time: 60 Minutes

Ingredients:
- 2 Large artichokes
- 3 Tablespoon olive oil
- sea salt
- 1 Stick unsalted butter
- 2 Clove garlic, chopped
- 2 Tablespoon chives, parsley, tarragon or cilantro
- 1 lemon

Directions:
1. Supply your smoker with wood pellets and follow the start-up procedure. Preheat the grill, with the lid closed, to 375° F.

2. Meanwhile, break off and discard any small outer leaves on the artichokes. Use a knife to slice off the tops of the artichokes, then using scissors, cut off any thorns on the remaining artichoke leaves. Trim the very bottom of the stem, then peel the tough and fibrous outer layer of the stem. Finally, cut artichokes in half and rinse off.

3. Transfer artichokes to a large mixing bowl, drizzle with olive oil and generously sprinkle with sea salt. Toss to coat the artichokes thoroughly. Grill: 375 ℉

4. Add the artichokes to the grill, cut side down, and roast at 375°F until the artichoke bottoms are tender when poked with a fork or knife, about 50 to 60 minutes. Grill: 375 ℉

5. When artichokes are almost done, add butter, chopped garlic and a pinch of sea salt to a small sauce pan and melt slowly over medium-low heat. Once the butter melts all the way and starts to bubble slightly, add the herbs.

6. When the artichokes are done, transfer to a butcher paper lined tray with the cut sides up. Drizzle half the garlic butter and squeeze half of the lemon over the artichokes. Add a small sprinkle of sea salt over the artichokes.

7. Serve with a ramekin of the remaining butter for dipping and extra wedges of lemon. Enjoy! Chef Tip: You can also serve with a ramekin of good mayonnaise mixed with a bit of hot sauce.

Salt Crusted Baked Potatoes

Servings: 4

Cooking Time: 60 Minutes

Ingredients:

- 6 russet potatoes, scrubbed and dried
- 3 Tablespoon canola oil
- 1 Tablespoon kosher salt
- butter
- sour cream
- Chives, fresh
- Bacon Bits
- cheddar cheese

Directions:

1. In a large bowl, coat the potatoes in canola oil and sprinkle heavily with salt.

2. Supply your smoker with wood pellets and follow the start-up procedure. Preheat the grill, with the lid closed, to 450° F.

3. Place the potatoes directly on the grill grate and bake for 30-40 minutes, or until soft in the middle when pricked with a fork. Serve loaded with your favorite toppings. Enjoy! Grill: 450 °F

Baked Sweet Potato Casserole With Marshmallow Fluff

Servings: 6

Cooking Time: 60 Minutes

Ingredients:

- 3 Pound sweet potatoes
- 1/2 Cup milk
- 1 Cup brown sugar
- 3 eggs
- 4 Tablespoon butter
- 1/2 Teaspoon salt
- 3 egg white
- 1 Pinch salt
- 1 Pinch ground cinnamon

Directions:

1. Supply your smoker with wood pellets and follow the start-up procedure. Preheat the grill, with the lid closed, to 375° F.

2. Rinse, dry and pierce the sweet potatoes and place in grill whole. Cook for 45 minutes or until fork tender. Remove from grill and peel. Grill: 375 °F

3. Once peeled, mash the sweet potatoes in a large bowl with the milk, brown sugar, eggs, butter and salt. Place mashed potatoes in a baking dish and cook for 35 minutes. Grill: 375 °F

4. While the potatoes bake, make the fluff. Make a double boiler by bringing a small pot of water to a simmer, then placing the bowl of your stand mixer or another large stainless steel bowl atop the water.

5. Add the 3 egg whites, 2/3 cup brown sugar, a pinch of salt and a pinch of cinnamon to the bowl and whisk continuously until the sugar dissolves and the liquid is warm to the touch.

6. Transfer the bowl from the stovetop to your stand mixer and use the whisk attachment to whip the whites on medium-high speed until it turns glossy with stiff peaks, about 5-8 minutes.

7. Once the casserole has finished baking, use a rubber spatula to cover the sweet potato mixture with the fluff. Use the back of the spatula to create dramatic peaks.

8. Return to the grill for 5-7 minutes, or until the fluff starts to turn golden and the peaks are just shy of burnt. Remove from grill and enjoy!

Smoked Asparagus Soup

Servings: 4
Cooking Time: 40 Minutes

Ingredients:
* Pound Asparagus Spears
* 1 Tablespoon olive oil
* salt and pepper
* 1/2 yellow onion, diced
* 1 Tablespoon butter
* 2 Clove garlic, minced
* 1 1/2 Cup chicken stock
* 1 1/2 Cup cream
* 2 Stalk Raw Asparagus, Shaved

Directions:
1. Supply your smoker with wood pellets and follow the start-up procedure. Preheat the grill, with the lid closed, to 180° F.
2. Drizzle 1 pound of asparagus with olive oil and season with salt and pepper. Place directly on the grill grate and smoke for 20-30 minutes. Taste along the way to assess smoke level pulling earlier if needed. Grill: 180 ℉
3. Place 1 Tbsp butter in a saucepan and melt over medium heat. Add onion and garlic and saute for 2-3 minutes or until onion is translucent.
4. Remove asparagus from the grill and cut into 1" pieces. Place asparagus in the pan with the onions and add stock and cream. Bring to a simmer.
5. Remove from heat and puree using a blender or immersion blender until smooth.
6. Season with salt and pepper and serve. Top with fresh shaved asparagus, sprinkle with salt, pepper, and smoked paprika if desired. Enjoy!

Roasted Olives

Servings: 4

Cooking Time: 45 Minutes

Ingredients:
* 2 Cup mixed olives
* 3 Sprig fresh rosemary
* 2 Clove garlic, minced
* 2 Tablespoon orange zest
* 1/3 Cup extra-virgin olive oil
* 2 Tablespoon orange juice
* 1/2 Teaspoon red pepper flakes

Directions:
1. Combine the olives, rosemary, garlic, orange zest, red pepper flakes, olive oil, and orange juice in a glass oven-safe pie plate or baking dish. Cover with foil.
2. Supply your smoker with wood pellets and follow the start-up procedure. Preheat the grill, with the lid closed, to 300° F.
3. Roast the olives for 45 minutes, stirring once or twice. Serve warm in an attractive bowl. Enjoy! Grill: 300 ℉

Green Bean Casserole

Servings: 6
Cooking Time: 25 Minutes

Ingredients:
* 1/2 Stick butter
* 1 Small onion
* 1/2 Cup sliced button mushrooms
* 4 Can green beans, drained
* 2 Can cream of mushroom soup
* 1 Teaspoon Lawry's Seasoned Salt
* pepper
* 1 Can French's Original Crispy Fried Onions
* 1 Cup grated sharp cheddar cheese

Directions:

1. Supply your smoker with wood pellets and follow the start-up procedure. Preheat the grill, with the lid closed, to 375° F.

2. Melt butter in a cast iron skillet and add onions and mushrooms, stirring occasionally until softened.

3. Add drained green beans and cream of mushroom soup and stir gently to combine.

4. Season with seasoned salt and pepper and sprinkle the top with grated cheddar cheese and fried onions.

5. Bake for 25 minutes. Serve warm, enjoy! Grill: 375 °F

Smoked Bbq Onion Brussels Sprout

Servings: 4
Cooking Time: 110 Minutes

Ingredients:

- 4 strip bacon
- 1 onion minced
- 2 cloves garlic minced
- 1 lb brussels sprouts stems trimmed and cut in half
- 1 tbsp BBQ Spice Blend
- 1/2 cup Apple Habanero Bar-B-Que Sauce (or other BBQ sauce)

Directions:

1. Supply your smoker with wood pellets and follow the start-up procedure. Preheat the grill, with the lid closed, to High heat. Place a cast iron skillet over the highest heat spot and cook the bacon until crisp.

2. Remove the bacon from pan and drain, reserving the bacon fat in the pan.

3. Reduce the heat on your smoker to 250°F.

4. Add the onions, garlic, and brussels to the pan and toss to coat in the bacon drippings. Sprinkle the BBQ spice blend over top.

5. Cover the lid and allow to smoke for 1 to 1 1/2 hours, until the sprouts are fork tender.

6. For the last 20 minutes of smoking, toss the brussels sprouts in half of the barbecue sauce.

7. Remove the sprouts from the smoker.

8. Chop the bacon and add it and the remaining barbecue sauce to the pan of sprouts, tossing to coat.

9. Serve hot.

Blt Pasta Salad

Servings: 6
Cooking Time: 45 Minutes

Ingredients:

- 1 pound thick-cut bacon
- 16 ounces bowtie pasta, cooked according to package directions and drained
- 2 tomatoes, chopped
- ½ cup chopped scallions
- ½ cup Italian dressing
- ½ cup ranch dressing
- 1 tablespoon chopped fresh basil
- 1 teaspoon salt
- 1 teaspoon freshly ground black pepper
- 1 teaspoon garlic powder
- 1 head lettuce, cored and torn

Directions:

1. Supply your smoker with wood pellets and follow the start-up procedure. Preheat, with the lid closed, to 225°F.

2. Arrange the bacon slices on the grill grate, close the lid, and cook for 30 to 45 minutes, flipping after 20 minutes, until crisp.

3. Remove the bacon from the grill and chop.

4. In a large bowl, combine the chopped bacon with the cooked pasta, tomatoes, scallions, Italian dressing, ranch dressing, basil, salt, pepper, and garlic powder. Refrigerate until ready to serve.

5. Toss in the lettuce just before serving to keep it from wilting.

Baked Sweet Potatoes

Servings: 8
Cooking Time: 60 Minutes

Ingredients:
- 1 Cup butter, softened
- 1/4 Cup pure maple syrup
- 1/2 Teaspoon ground cinnamon
- 8 Medium sweet potatoes

Directions:
1. Make the Maple-Cinnamon Butter: In a mixing bowl, combine the butter, maple syrup, and cinnamon and whip with a wooden spoon. (Alternatively, blend the ingredients using a hand-held mixer or a stand mixer.) Transfer to a small bowl, cover, and chill until serving time.

2. Supply your smoker with wood pellets and follow the start-up procedure. Preheat the grill, with the lid closed, to 375° F. Arrange the sweet potatoes on the grill grate and bake until soft, 1 to 1-1/2 hours, depending on the size of the potatoes. Make a slit in the side of each, and squeeze the ends gently to fluff.

3. Serve hot with the Maple-Cinnamon Butter. Enjoy!

Baked Stuffed Avocados

Servings: 6
Cooking Time: 15 Minutes

Ingredients:
- 4 avocados, halved and pit removed

- 8 eggs
- 2 Cup shredded cheddar cheese
- 1/4 Cup cherry tomatoes, halved
- 4 Slices Bacon, cooked & chopped
- salt and pepper
- 1 scallion, thinly sliced

Directions:
1. Supply your smoker with wood pellets and follow the start-up procedure. Preheat the grill, with the lid closed, to 450° F.

2. After removing the pit from the avocado, scoop out a little of the flesh to make enough room to fit 1 egg per half.

3. Fill the bottom of a cast iron pan with kosher salt and nestle the avocado halves into the salt, cut side up. The salt helps to keep them in place while cooking, like ice with oysters.

4. Crack one egg into each half, top with shredded cheddar cheese, cherry tomatoes and bacon. Season with salt and pepper to taste.

5. Place the cast iron pan directly on the grill grate and bake the avocados for 12 to 15 minutes until the cheese is melted and the egg is just set. Grill: 450 ˚F

6. Remove from the grill and let rest 5 to 10 minutes. Top with sliced scallions and enjoy!

Whole Roasted Cauliflower With Garlic Parmesan Butter

Servings: 4
Cooking Time: 45 Minutes

Ingredients:
- 1 Whole head cauliflower
- 1/4 Cup olive oil
- salt and pepper
- 1/2 Cup butter, melted
- 1/4 Cup shredded Parmesan cheese

- 2 Clove garlic, minced
- 1/2 Tablespoon chopped parsley

Directions:

1. Supply your smoker with wood pellets and follow the start-up procedure. Preheat the grill, with the lid closed, to 450° F.

2. Brush the cauliflower with olive oil and season liberally with salt and pepper.

3. Put cauliflower in a cast iron skillet, place directly on the grill grate and cook for 45 minutes until golden brown and the center is tender.

4. While the cauliflower is cooking, combine the melted butter, parmesan, garlic and parsley in a small bowl.

5. During the last 20 minutes of cooking, baste the cauliflower with the melted butter mixture.

6. Remove the cauliflower from the grill and top with extra parmesan and parsley if desired. Enjoy!

Grilled Asparagus And Spinach Salad

Servings: 8
Cooking Time: 10 Minutes

Ingredients:

- 4 Fluid Ounce apple cider vinegar
- 8 Fluid Ounce Honey Bourbon BBQ Sauce
- 2 Bunch asparagus, ends trimmed
- 3 Fluid Ounce extra-virgin olive oil
- 2 Ounce Beef Rub
- 24 Ounce Spinach, fresh
- 4 Ounce candied pecans
- 4 Ounce feta cheese

Directions:

1. Combine apple cider vinegar and Traeger Apricot BBQ Sauce to create salad dressing.

2. Supply your smoker with wood pellets and follow the start-up procedure. Preheat the grill, with the lid closed, to High heat.

3. Toss the asparagus with Olive Oil and the Beef Shake. Put asparagus in the Traeger Grilling Basket and move the basket to the grill grate.

4. Grill for about 10 minutes. Remove the asparagus once it is cooked. Grill: 350 ˚F

5. Place the hot asparagus right on top of the bowl of spinach.

6. Add candied pecans, feta cheese & salad dressing then toss and serve. Enjoy!

Chef Curtis' Famous Chimichurri Sauce

Servings: 4
Cooking Time: 5 Minutes

Ingredients:

- 2 Whole lemon, halved
- 2 Medium flat-leaf Italian parsley, washed and chopped with the majority of stems cut off
- 4 Clove garlic, diced
- 1/4 Cup red wine vinegar
- 1/2 Teaspoon black pepper
- 1/4 Cup extra-virgin olive oil
- 1 Teaspoon salt

Directions:

1. Supply your smoker with wood pellets and follow the start-up procedure. Preheat the grill, with the lid closed, to 450° F.

2. Place lemon halves directly on the grill grate and cook for 5 minutes or until grill marks appear. Grill: 450 ˚F

3. Take lemons off grill and juice. Combine all of the ingredients in a food processor or blender and purée until smooth, or leave slightly chunky for some texture.

4. Add additional olive oil to taste for a milder flavor if preferred. Serve on protein or as a dip. Enjoy!

Roasted Green Beans With Bacon

Servings: 4

Cooking Time: 20 Minutes

Ingredients:

- 1 1/2 Pound green beans, ends trimmed
- 4 Strips bacon, cut into small pieces
- 4 Tablespoon extra-virgin olive oil
- 2 Clove garlic, minced
- 1 Teaspoon kosher salt

Directions:

1. Supply your smoker with wood pellets and follow the start-up procedure. Preheat the grill, with the lid closed, to 350° F.

2. Toss all ingredients together and spread out evenly on a sheet tray.

3. Place the tray directly on the grill grate and roast until the bacon is crispy and beans are lightly browned, about 20 minutes. Enjoy! Grill: 450 ˚F

Grilled Broccoli Rabe

Servings: 4

Cooking Time: 10 Minutes

Ingredients:

- 4 Tablespoon extra-virgin olive oil
- 4 Bunch broccoli rabe or broccolini
- kosher salt
- 1 lemon, halved

Directions:

1. Supply your smoker with wood pellets and follow the start-up procedure. Preheat the grill, with the lid closed, to 450° F.

2. On a platter or in a mixing bowl, drizzle the olive oil over the broccoli rabe. Use your hands to mix thoroughly, coating the vegetables evenly with the oil. Season with sea salt.

3. Place the broccoli rabe in one layer directly on the lowest grill grate. Close the lid and cook for 5 to 10 minutes. You want there to be some color and slight char on the first side. Flip and cook for a few more minutes. Grill: 450 ˚F

4. Transfer the broccoli rabe to a serving platter and squeeze the juice of half a lemon evenly over the top.

5. Serve with more lemon wedges on the side. Enjoy!

Grilled Chili-lime Corn

Servings: 8

Cooking Time: 45 Minutes

Ingredients:

- 12 Corn, ears
- 1 Teaspoon chili powder
- 1/2 Teaspoon onion powder
- 1 Teaspoon Leinenkugel's Summer Shandy Rub
- 2 lime, juiced
- 1 Tablespoon lime zest

Directions:

1. Soak the ears of corn, still in their husk, in water for 4 to 8 hours.

2. Supply your smoker with wood pellets and follow the start-up procedure. Preheat the grill, with the lid closed, to 350° F.

3. Place corn directly on grill grates. Turn corn every 15 minutes for 45 minutes total cooking time. Grill: 350 ˚F

4. Combine chili powder, onion powder, Summer Shandy rub, lime juice, lime zest and butter in an oven safe dish and place in grill for 10 minutes. Remove corn and butter from the grill.

5. Pull corn husk back, but not off and remove corn silk. Using the corn husk as a handle, brush the corn with the melted chili-lime butter. Enjoy!

Baked Kale Chips

Servings: 4

Cooking Time: 20 Minutes

Ingredients:

- 2 Bunch kale, leaves washed and stems removed
- 1 As Needed extra-virgin olive oil
- 1 To Taste sea salt

Directions:

1. Dry the kale leaves well and lay them out on a sheet tray. Drizzle lightly with olive oil and sprinkle with sea salt.

2. Supply your smoker with wood pellets and follow the start-up procedure. Preheat the grill, with the lid closed, to 250° F.

3. Place the sheet tray directly on the grill grate and cook until kale is lightly browned and crispy, about 20 minutes. Enjoy! Grill: 250 °F

Grilled Street Corn

Servings: 6
Cooking Time: 10 Minutes

Ingredients:

- 6 ears corn, husked
- 1 As Needed extra-virgin olive oil
- 1/4 Cup mayonnaise
- 1 Tablespoon ancho or guajillo chile powder
- 1/2 Cup chopped cilantro, plus more for serving
- 1 lime, zested and juiced
- salt
- 1/2 Cup Cotija cheese
- 1 As Needed cilantro, finely chopped

Directions:

1. Supply your smoker with wood pellets and follow the start-up procedure. Preheat the grill, with the lid closed, to 450° F.

2. Brush corn with oil and place on grill, turning occasionally.

3. While corn is on the grill, mix mayonnaise with chile powder, cilantro, lime juice and zest in a bowl. Season with salt.

4. After about 10 minutes corn should be cooked through and slightly charred on the outside. Remove from grill.

5. Top corn with chile mayonnaise then sprinkle on the Cotija cheese and chopped cilantro. Enjoy!

Steak Fries With Horseradish Creme

Servings: 6
Cooking Time: 25 Minutes

Ingredients:

- 5 Potatoes, Baking
- 2 Tablespoon extra-virgin olive oil
- 1 Teaspoon butter
- 3 Clove garlic, crushed
- 1 Teaspoon onion powder
- 2 Teaspoon Jacobsen Salt Co. Pure Kosher Sea Salt
- 1 Teaspoon black pepper

Directions:

1. Wash the potatoes thoroughly, and cut them in eighths, then toss them in the olive oil, butter, crushed garlic, onion powder, salt, and pepper.

2. Supply your smoker with wood pellets and follow the start-up procedure. Preheat the grill, with the lid closed, to 450° F.

3. In order to get great grill marks, line up the wedges on the front of the grill and the back of the grill, turning to get grill marks on all sides.

4. Once they have been seared, move them to the center of the grill and finish cooking about ten more minutes, serve hot with the horseradish mayo. Enjoy!

POULTRY RECIPES

Turkey & Bacon Kebabs With Ranch-style Dressing

Servings: 8
Cooking Time: 25 Minutes

Ingredients:

- 1½lb (680g) skinless turkey tenders or boneless, skinless turkey breasts, cut into 1-inch (2.5cm) chunks
- 8 strips of thick-cut bacon
- 12 fresh bay leaves (optional)
- for the dressing
- 1 cup reduced-fat mayo
- 1 cup light sour cream
- ½ cup buttermilk or whole milk, plus more
- 2 tbsp minced fresh parsley
- 2 tbsp minced fresh chives
- 1 tbsp minced fresh dill
- 2 tsp freshly squeezed lemon juice
- 1 tsp Worcestershire sauce
- 1 tsp garlic salt
- 1 tsp onion powder
- ½ tsp coarse salt, plus more
- ½ tsp freshly ground black pepper, plus more

Directions:

1. In a large bowl, make the dressing by whisking together the mayo, sour cream, and buttermilk until smooth. Whisk in the remaining ingredients. Pour half the mixture into a small bowl. Cover and refrigerate.

2. Add the turkey to the mixture remaining in the bowl and toss to coat thoroughly. If the dressing seems too thick (dip-like), add more buttermilk 1 tablespoon at a time. Cover and refrigerate for 2 to 4 hours.

3. Supply your smoker with wood pellets and follow the start-up procedure. Preheat the grill, with the lid closed, to 375° F.

4. Place the bacon on the grate and cook until some of the fat has rendered and the bacon begins to brown, about 15 minutes. Remove the bacon from the grill to cool. Cut the bacon into 1-inch (2.5cm) squares. Set aside.

5. Drain the tenders and discard any excess dressing. Alternate threading the turkey, bacon pieces, and 3 bay leaves on a bamboo skewer. Repeat the threading with 3 more skewers.

6. Place the kebabs on the grate and grill until the turkey is cooked through, about 4 to 5 minutes per side, turning as needed.

7. Transfer the skewers to a platter. Serve with the reserved dressing.

Easy Rapid-fire Roast Chicken

Servings: 4
Cooking Time: 120 Minutes

Ingredients:

- 1 (4-pound) whole chicken, giblets removed
- Extra-virgin olive oil, for rubbing
- 3 tablespoons Greek seasoning
- Juice of 1 lemon
- Butcher's string

Directions:

1. Supply your smoker with wood pellets and follow the start-up procedure. Preheat, with the lid closed, to 450°F.

2. Rub the bird generously all over with oil, including inside the cavity.

3. Sprinkle the Greek seasoning all over and under the skin of the bird, and squeeze the lemon juice over the breast.

4. Tuck the chicken wings behind the back and tie the legs together with butcher's string or cooking twine.

5. Put the chicken directly on the grill, breast-side up, close the lid, and roast for 1 hour to 1 hour 30 minutes, or until a meat thermometer inserted in the thigh reads 165°F.

6. Let the meat rest for 10 minutes before carving.

Grilled Hand Pulled Chicken

Servings: 4

Cooking Time: 90 Minutes

Ingredients:

- 2 Tablespoons Apple Cider Vinegar
- 1 Clove Garlic, Minced
- Juice Of Half Of A Lemon
- 1 Cup Mayo
- 1 Tablespoon Olive Oil
- ½ Teaspoon Paprika, Powder
- 2 Tablespoons Sugar
- 1, 3-4 Pound Chicken, Giblets Removed And Patted Dry
- 4 Tablespoons Champion Chicken Seasoning

Directions:

1. Supply your smoker with wood pellets and follow the start-up procedure. Preheat the grill, with the lid open, to 350° F.

2. In a large bowl, mix all the ingredients for the sauce together. Divide the sauce between two bowls and set aside.

3. On a clean, flat surface, lay your chicken breast side down. Using the kitchen shears, remove the spine and discard. Open the chicken up and flip the chicken over so that it lays breast side up. Press the breastbone down with the heel of your hand to flatten the chicken.

4. Generously rub the chicken with the olive oil and Champion Chicken. Place on the grill, skin-side up, on the grates. Grill for 1 ½ hours, basting with half the reserved sauce every 20 minutes, until the internal temperature reaches 175°F. Remove the chicken from the grill and cover loosely for 10 minutes.

5. Shred the chicken with forks and discard the skin and bones. Serve the chicken with the remaining white BBQ sauce.

Grilled Honey Chicken Kabobs

Servings: 4

Cooking Time: 14 Minutes

Ingredients:

- 1 pound boneless skinless chicken breasts (cut into 1 inch pieces)
- 1/4 cup olive oil
- 1/3 cup soy sauce
- 1/4 cup honey
- 1 teaspoon minced garlic
- salt and pepper to taste
- 1 red bell pepper (cut into 1 inch pieces)
- 1 yellow bell pepper (cut into 1 inch pieces)
- 2 small zucchini (cut into 1 inch slices)
- 1 red onion (cut into 1 inch pieces)
- 1 tablespoon chopped parsley

Directions:

1. In a large bowl combine the olive oil, soy sauce, honey, garlic and salt and pepper, and whisk.

2. Add the chicken, bell peppers, zucchini and red onion to the bowl, tossing to thoroughly coat.

3. Cover and refrigerate for 1 to 8 hours.

4. Soak wooden skewers in cold water for at least 30 minutes. Supply your smoker with wood pellets and follow the start-up procedure. Preheat the grill, with the lid closed, to high heat.

5. Thread the chicken and vegetables onto the skewers.

6. Cook for 5-7 minutes on each side or until chicken is cooked through.

7. To serve, sprinkle with parsley. Enjoy!

Smoked Turkey Legs

Servings: 4
Cooking Time: 300 Minutes

Ingredients:
- 1 Cup Rub
- 1/2 Cup Morton Tender Quick Home Meat Cure
- 1/2 Cup brown sugar
- 1 Tablespoon crushed allspice berries, optional
- 1 Tablespoon grains de poivre noir entiers
- 2 bay leaves
- 2 Teaspoon liquid smoke
- 4 turkey legs

Directions:

1. In a large stockpot, combine one gallon of warm water, the rub, curing salt, brown sugar, allspice (if using), peppercorns, bay leaves and liquid smoke.

2. Bring to a boil over high heat to dissolve the salt granules. Cool to room temperature. Add 1/2 gallon cold water and 4 cups ice; chill in the refrigerator.

3. Add the turkey legs, making sure they're completely submerged in the brine. After 24 hours, drain the turkey legs and discard the brine.

4. Rinse the brine off the legs with cold water, then dry thoroughly with paper towels. Brush off any clinging solid spices.

5. Supply your smoker with wood pellets and follow the start-up procedure. Preheat the grill, with the lid closed, to 250° F.

6. Lay the turkey legs directly on the grill grate.

7. Smoke for 4-5 hours, or until the internal temperature reaches 165°F on an instant-read meat thermometer. Make sure the probe doesn't touch bone or you'll get a false reading. Grill: 250 °F Probe: 165 °F

8. The turkey legs should be deeply browned. Don't be alarmed if the meat under the skin is pinkish: that's a chemical reaction to the cure and the smoke.

9. Serve immediately. Enjoy!

Smoked Chicken Vermicelli Noodles

Servings: 4 – 6
Cooking Time: 120 Minutes

Ingredients:
- 2 Cup Broccoli
- ¼ Cup Chicken Stock
- 6 - 8 Chicken Thighs, Boneless, Skinless
- 1 Tbsp Chili Flakes
- 1 Tsp Cornstarch
- 4, Chopped Garlic Cloves
- 3 Tbsp Hoisin Sauce, Divided
- Knob Of Fresh Ginger, Grated
- 1, Thin Red Bell Peppers, Sliced
- 1 Tbsp Rice Wine Vinegar
- 8 Scallions, Sliced
- 1 ½ Tbsp Sesame Oil, Divided
- 1 Tbsp, Toasted Sesame Seeds
- 3.5 Oz Shitake Mushrooms, Sliced Thin

- 8 Oz Snow Peas
- 3 Tbsp Soy Sauce
- 2 Tbsp Sweet Chili Sauce
- 3 Tbsp Vegetable Oil
- 1 Lb Vermicelli Noodles, Or Linguini, Cooked And Drained

Directions:

1. In a large bowl, whisk together rice wine vinegar, 1 tablespoon of Hoisin sauce, and 1 tablespoon of sesame oil. Toss chicken to coat and allow to marinate for 1 hour.

2. Supply your smoker with wood pellets and follow the start-up procedure. Preheat the grill, with the lid open, to 225° F. If using a gas or charcoal grill, set it for low, indirect heat. Place chicken directly on the grill grate and smoke for 1 ½ to 2 hours, or until the internal temperature reaches 165° F. Remove it from the smoker, cover with foil, and rest for 10 minutes, then slice thin and set aside.

3. In a glass measuring cup whisk together 2 tablespoons of Hoisin sauce, soy sauce, sweet chili sauce, chicken stock, ½ tablespoon of sesame oil, and cornstarch. Set aside.

4. Preheat griddle to medium flame, then add oil. Working quickly, sauté ginger and garlic for 15 seconds, then add bell pepper and mushrooms and continue cooking for another minute, then add in snow peas and slaw. Toss in cooked pasta, chicken, scallions, and pour sauce over. Cook for one minute until sauce thickens and is well incorporated.

5. Transfer to platter and serve hot. Sprinkle with chili flakes and sesame seeds, if desired.

Bourbon Chicken Waffles

Servings: 8

Cooking Time: 30 Minutes

Ingredients:

- 1 Shot Of Bourbon
- 3 Cups Bread Crumbs
- 4 Horizontally Half Sliced Boneless, Skinless Chicken Breast
- Butter Flavored Cooking Spray
- 3 Eggs
- 1 Tsp Garlic Powder
- 1 Tsp Paprika, Powder
- Red Velvet Cake Mix
- 16 Oz. Reduced Fat Sour Cream
- Sweet Rib Rub
- ¼ Cup Vegetable Oil
- 1 ¼ Cup Water
- 1 Tbsp Worcestershire Sauce

Directions:

1. Supply your smoker with wood pellets and follow the start-up procedure. Preheat the grill, with the lid closed, to 350° F. If you're using a gas or charcoal grill, set up the grill for medium heat.

2. In a large bowl, combine the sour cream, bourbon, Worcestershire sauce, paprika, garlic powder, and Sweet Rib Rub seasoning. Add the chicken, turn the chicken breasts to coat, and cover the bowl. Refrigerate for 4-12 hrs.

3. Remove the chicken from the refrigerator and drain the marinade from the chicken. Mix together 3 cups bread crumbs and 2 tbsp Sweet Rib Rub. Mix the coating together and bread the chicken breasts.

4. Moisten a paper towel with cooking oil and using a pair of tongs, lightly grease the grill rack.

5. Grill or smoke until the internal temperature of the chicken reaches 170°F and the chicken is crispy and golden brown.

6. While the chicken is cooking, mix the eggs, vegetable oil, water, and red velvet cake mix in a bowl with the electric mixer.

7. Add the mix into the waffle iron and cook. Make as many waffles as the mix allows.

8. On a plate, place the cooked chicken on top of the waffles and top with maple syrup or honey.

Flavoured Hibachi Chicken

Servings: 4
Cooking Time: 10 Minutes

Ingredients:

- To Taste, Blackened Sriracha Rub Seasoning
- To Taste, Blackened Sriracha Rub Seasoning (For Vegetables)
- 2 Cups Broccoli Florets, Blanched
- 1 Tbsp Brown Sugar
- 1 Tbsp Butter, Unsalted
- 1 1/2 Lbs Chicken Breast, Boneless, Skinless, Sliced Thin
- 1 Tbsp Cilantro, Chopped
- 3 Garlic Cloves, Minced
- 2 Garlic Cloves, Minced (For Vegetables)
- 1 Tsp Ginger, Grated
- 1 Tsp Ginger, Grated (For Vegetables
- 1/2 Lime, Juiced
- 1/2 Red Bell Pepper, Sliced Thin
- For Serving, Rice Noodles, Cooked
- 2 Scallions, Chopped
- 1 Tbsp Sesame Oil
- 2 Tbsp Sesame Oil, Divided
- 1 Cup Snap Peas, Blanched
- 1/4 Cup Tamari
- For Serving, Toasted Sesame Seeds
- 1 Tbsp Vegetable Oil
- 1 Tbsp Vegetable Oil (For Vegetables)
- For Serving, Yum-Yum Sauce

Directions:

1. Supply your smoker with wood pellets and follow the start-up procedure. Preheat the grill, with the lid open, to medium-high heat. When hot, add 1 tablespoon of sesame oil and vegetable oil. Immediately add the chicken and season with Blackened Sriracha. When the chicken starts to brown, flip it over to brown the other side.

2. Add the garlic, ginger, soy sauce, brown sugar, butter, and the remaining tablespoon of sesame oil and stir. Turn the heat down to medium-low and let the mixture simmer for 3 minutes, until it thickens and adheres to the chicken. Add lime juice, cilantro, and scallions, then remove the mixture from the griddle.

3. After starting the sauce for the chicken, sauté the vegetables: Add sesame oil and vegetable oil to the other side of the griddle. Quickly sauté broccoli, snap peas, and red bell pepper with garlic and ginger. Season with Blackened Sriracha. Remove from the griddle after 2 minutes.

4. Serve hibachi chicken warm with sautéed vegetables, toasted sesame seeds, rice noodles, and Yum-Yum sauce if desired.

Buffalo Wings

Servings: 2-3
Cooking Time: 35 Minutes

Ingredients:

- 1 pound chicken wings
- 1 batch Chicken Rub
- 1 cup Frank's Red-Hot Sauce, Buffalo wing sauce, or similar

Directions:

1. Supply your smoker with wood pellets and follow the start-up procedure. Preheat the grill, with the lid closed, to 300°F.

2. Season the chicken wings with the rub. Using your hands, work the rub into the meat.

3. Place the wings directly on the grill grate and smoke until their internal temperature reaches 160°F.

4. Baste the wings with the sauce and continue to smoke until the wings' internal temperature reaches 170°F.

Grilled Chipotle Chicken Skewers

Servings: 4

Cooking Time: 25 Minutes

Ingredients:

- BBQ Sauce
- 1 cup spicy BBQ sauce
- 3 chipotle peppers
- 1 Tbsp adobo sauce
- Skewers
- Olive oil
- 2 lbs boneless skinless chicken breasts
- 10 thick-cut bacon strips
- 1 large green bell pepper, cut into 3/4 to 1 inch pieces
- 1 medium red onion, peeled and cut into 3/4 to 1 inch pieces
- Bamboo skewers
- Garnish: freshly chopped garnish

Directions:

1. Supply your smoker with wood pellets and follow the start-up procedure. Preheat the grill, with the lid closed.

2. Soak the wooden skewers in water for at least 10 to 15 minutes before skewering to avoid them burning as much.

3. Add all ingredients for the sauce to a blender. Blend until they are combined well.

4. Cut chicken into 3/4-inch bite-sized pieces. Cut bacon into 3/4-inch strips.

5. Thread bacon (folding the bacon in half before skewering), chicken, peppers, and onion onto the skewers, alternating as you go.

6. Arrange the skewers on the grill grate and cook for 10 minutes, turning every few minutes. Baste the skewers with BBQ sauce on all sides. Continue to baste and turn the skewers every minute or so to caramelize.

7. The chicken is cooked through when it reaches an internal temperature of 165 °F. The bacon should be nice and crispy at this point.

8. Remove the skewers from the grill and sprinkle with freshly chopped parsley.

Sweet And Spicy Smoked Wings

Servings: 2-4

Cooking Time: 85 Minutes

Ingredients:

- 1 pound chicken wings
- 1 batch Sweet and Spicy Cinnamon Rub
- 1 cup barbecue sauce

Directions:

1. Supply your smoker with wood pellets and follow the start-up procedure. Preheat the grill, with the lid closed, to 325°F.

2. Season the chicken wings with the rub. Using your hands, work the rub into the meat.

3. Place the wings directly on the grill grate and cook until they reach an internal temperature of 165°F.

4. Transfer the wings into an aluminum pan. Add the barbecue sauce and stir to coat the wings.

5. Reduce the grill's temperature to 250°F and put the pan on the grill. Smoke the wings for 1 hour more, uncovered. Remove the wings from the grill and serve immediately.

Grilled Parmesan Chicken Wings

Servings: 4
Cooking Time: 25 Minutes

Ingredients:
- 4 Tbsp Butter
- 4 Lbs Chicken Wings, Trimmed And Patted Dry
- 4 Garlic Cloves, Chopped
- 2 Tbsp Olive Oil
- 1/2 Cup Parmesan Cheese, Grated
- 2 Tbsp Parsley, Chopped
- Champion Chicken Seasoning

Directions:

1. Lay chicken wings out on a sheet tray, blot with paper towel, then season with Champion Chicken.

2. Supply your smoker with wood pellets and follow the start-up procedure. Preheat the grill, with the lid open, to 400° F. If using a gas or charcoal grill, set it up for medium-high heat.

3. Transfer wings to grill and cook for 20 to 25 minutes, turning every 5 minutes, until lightly browned. Remove wings from the grill and set on a sheet tray. Place in the smoking cabinet to keep warm while preparing the garlic butter.

4. Melt butter and olive oil in a cast iron skillet, then add garlic and simmer until fragrant. Remove from the grill.

5. Transfer chicken wings to a large bowl and pour garlic butter over the wings. Add cheese and parsley, then toss well to coat. Serve warm with additional sprinkling of parmesan cheese.

Grilled Cheesy Chicken

Servings: 4
Cooking Time: 45 Minutes

Ingredients:
- 4 Aged Chedder Cheese, Sliced
- 32 Oz Chicken Broth
- 1 Tsp Extra-Virgin Olive Oil
- Sweet Heat Rub And Grill
- 4 Plump Chicken, Boneless/Skinless

Directions:

1. Supply your smoker with wood pellets and follow the start-up procedure. Preheat the grill, with the lid open, to 350° F.

2. Remove the chicken from the brine. Pat the breasts dry and lightly brush olive oil on both sides of the chicken. Take your knife and slice diagonally across the top of each breast. Sprinkle a lit amount of Sweet Heat Rub and Grill on each side.

3. Barbecue your chicken breasts for 30 minutes. Next, place a slice of cheddar cheese on top of each breast.

4. Heat for another 5-10 minutes or until the cheese has fully melted into the incisions you made earlier. Remove and serve for a tender chicken breast with a spicy kick and hot cheesy center. You'll receive too much credit for a recipe this easy.

Smoked Wings

Servings: 6
Cooking Time: 50 Minutes

Ingredients:
- 24 chicken wings, flats and drumettes separated
- 12 Ounce Italian dressing
- 3 Ounce Chicken Rub
- 5 Ounce 'Que BBQ Sauce
- 3 Ounce chili sauce

Directions:

1. Wash all wings and place into resealable bag. Add Italian dressing to the resealable bag containing the wings. Place in refrigerator and allow to marinate for 6 to 12 hours.

2. Supply your smoker with wood pellets and follow the start-up procedure. Preheat the grill, with the lid closed, to 225° F.

3. Remove wings from marinade and shake off excess marinade. Season all sides of the wings with Traeger Chicken Rub and let sit for 15 minutes before putting wings on the Traeger.

4. In a small bowl, combine the BBQ and chili sauces. Set aside.

5. Cook wings to an internal temperature of 160°F. Remove the wings and toss in chili barbecue sauce. Grill: 225 °F Probe: 160 °F

6. Increase the grill temperature to 375°F and preheat. Once at temperature, place the wings on the Traeger and sear both sides until the internal temperature reaches 165°F. Grill: 375 °F Probe: 165 °F

7. Remove the wings from grill and let rest for 5 minutes. Serve with your favorite side wing dressing or sauce. Enjoy!

Smoked Turkey Breast

Servings: 2-4
Cooking Time: 120 Minutes

Ingredients:
- 1 (3-pound) turkey breast
- Salt
- Freshly ground black pepper
- 1 teaspoon garlic powder

Directions:
1. Supply your smoker with wood pellets and follow the start-up procedure. Preheat the grill, with the lid closed, to 180°F.

2. Season the turkey breast all over with salt, pepper, and garlic powder.

3. Place the breast directly on the grill grate and smoke for 1 hour.

4. Increase the grill's temperature to 350°F and continue to cook until the turkey's internal temperature reaches 170°F. Remove the breast from the grill and serve immediately.

Baked Prosciutto-wrapped Chicken Breast With Spinach And Boursin

Servings: 4
Cooking Time: 60 Minutes

Ingredients:
- 1 Tablespoon olive oil
- 10 Ounce baby spinach leaves, washed and dried
- 2 Whole packs (5.2 oz) Boursin Garlic & Fine Herbs Gournay Cheese
- 2 Pound boneless, skinless chicken breasts
- Pork & Poultry Rub
- 14 Slices prosciutto

Directions:
1. Heat olive oil in a medium sauté pan. Add spinach and sauté until wilted, about 3 to 5 minutes. Transfer to a strainer and squeeze out excess liquid. Place spinach and cheese in a medium bowl. Mix well and set aside.

2. Butterfly each chicken breast and open like a book. Cover with plastic wrap and using a meat mallet, pound out thinly. Season the chicken with Pork & Poultry Rub.

3. Lay a sheet of plastic wrap about 2 feet long down on a flat, clean surface. Lay down slices of prosciutto, slightly overlapping and double-wide.

Place the chicken on top of the prosciutto leaving a 1- 1/2 inch border.

4. Spread the spinach mixture on top of the chicken. Roll it up tightly to create a log. Tie off the ends tightly and transfer to the refrigerator. Refrigerate 2 to 3 hours or overnight.

5. Supply your smoker with wood pellets and follow the start-up procedure. Preheat the grill, with the lid closed, to 300° F.

6. Carefully remove the plastic wrap and place directly on the grill grate. Bake for an hour and a half, or until the internal temperature reaches 162°F to 165°F. Remove from Traeger and let rest for 10 minutes before slicing. Enjoy! Grill: 300 ˚F Probe: 162 ˚F

Beer Can–smoked Chicken

Servings: 3-4
Cooking Time: 160 Minutes

Ingredients:
- 8 tablespoons (1 stick) unsalted butter, melted
- ½ cup apple cider vinegar
- ½ cup Cajun seasoning, divided
- 1 teaspoon garlic powder
- 1 teaspoon onion powder
- 1 (4-pound) whole chicken, giblets removed
- Extra-virgin olive oil, for rubbing
- 1 (12-ounce) can beer
- 1 cup apple juice
- ½ cup extra-virgin olive oil

Directions:
1. In a small bowl, whisk together the butter, vinegar, ¼ cup of Cajun seasoning, garlic powder, and onion powder.

2. Use a meat-injecting syringe to inject the liquid into various spots in the chicken. Inject about half of the mixture into the breasts and the other half throughout the rest of the chicken.

3. Rub the chicken all over with olive oil and apply the remaining ¼ cup of Cajun seasoning, being sure to rub under the skin as well.

4. Drink or discard half the beer and place the opened beer can on a stable surface.

5. Place the bird's cavity on top of the can and position the chicken so it will sit up by itself. Prop the legs forward to make the bird more stable, or buy an inexpensive, specially made stand to hold the beer can and chicken in place.

6. Supply your smoker with wood pellets and follow the start-up procedure. Preheat, with the lid closed, to 250°F.

7. In a clean 12-ounce spray bottle, combine the apple juice and olive oil. Cover and shake the mop sauce well before each use.

8. Carefully put the chicken on the grill. Close the lid and smoke the chicken for 3 to 4 hours, spraying with the mop sauce every hour, until golden brown and a meat thermometer inserted in the thickest part of the thigh reads 165°F. Keep a piece of aluminum foil handy to loosely cover the chicken if the skin begins to brown too quickly.

9. Let the meat rest for 5 minutes before carving.

Applewood-smoked Whole Turkey

Servings: 6-8
Cooking Time: 300 Minutes

Ingredients:
- 1 (10- to 12-pound) turkey, giblets removed
- Extra-virgin olive oil, for rubbing
- ¼ cup poultry seasoning
- 8 tablespoons (1 stick) unsalted butter, melted

- ½ cup apple juice
- 2 teaspoons dried sage
- 2 teaspoons dried thyme

Directions:

1. Supply your smoker with wood pellets and follow the start-up procedure. Preheat, with the lid closed, to 250°F.

2. Rub the turkey with oil and season with the poultry seasoning inside and out, getting under the skin.

3. In a bowl, combine the melted butter, apple juice, sage, and thyme to use for basting.

4. Put the turkey in a roasting pan, place on the grill, close the lid, and grill for 5 to 6 hours, basting every hour, until the skin is brown and crispy, or until a meat thermometer inserted in the thickest part of the thigh reads 165°F.

5. Let the bird rest for 15 to 20 minutes before carving.

Beer Chicken

Servings: 4
Cooking Time: 75 Minutes

Ingredients:
- 1 Beer, Can
- 1 Chicken, Whole
- Lemon Pepper Garlic Seasoning

Directions:

1. Supply your smoker with wood pellets and follow the start-up procedure. Preheat the grill, with the lid open, to 400° F.

2. Season the chicken all over with spices. Open the can of your favorite pop/beer and place the opening of the chicken over the can. Make sure that the chicken can stand upright without falling over. Place on your Grill and barbecue until the internal temperature reaching 165 degrees F (about an hour).

3. Remove from grill, slice and serve hot.

Onion Turkey Burger Sliders

Servings: 5
Cooking Time: 30 Minutes

Ingredients:
- 1 Sweet Onion, Chopped
- 1 Pepper, Anaheim
- Bacon Cheddar Burger Seasoning
- Spinach
- 16 Oz Turkey, Ground

Directions:

1. Supply your smoker with wood pellets and follow the start-up procedure. Preheat the grill, with the lid closed, to 400° F.

2. Put the ground turkey into a bowl and generously add the   Bacon Cheddar Burger seasoning to the mixture.

3. Dice the Anaheim pepper and add it to the bowl as well.

4. Dice about 1/3 of the sweet onion and add it to the bowl.

5. Mix with your hands until the meat looks evenly coated in seasoning and the veggies are evenly mixed.

6. Separate the meat out into 3oz balls, disperse or toss the remnants.

7. Use the   3-in-1 Burger press to create the perfect patty! Place the patties on the grill and cook for 15-20 minutes depending on their thickness. Flip every 5ish minutes.

8. Add the buns to the grill if you'd like them toasted!

9. Remove the turkey sliders (and the buns) from the grill, add spinach, and whatever you think will taste good!

Smoked Chicken Legs

Servings: 6
Cooking Time: 110 Minutes

Ingredients:

- 1/4 Cup Brown Sugar
- 1/2 Tsp Or To Taste Cayenne Pepper
- 6 Chicken, Drumsticks
- 1 Cup Of Your Favorite Cola
- 2 Tbs Competition Chicken Seasoning
- 1 Tbs Honey
- 1/2 Tsp To Taste Hot Sauce
- 1 Cup Ketchup
- 2 Tbs   Hot Wing Sauce

Directions:

1. For the chicken: Supply your smoker with wood pellets and follow the start-up procedure. Preheat the grill, with the lid closed, to 300° F.

2. In a small bowl,Pour hot sauce over legs and toss to coat.

3. Sprinkle legs with Competition Chicken Seasoning and Hot Wing Seasoning.

4. Toss to evenly distribute seasoning.

5. Place legs in Grills Wing Rack or lay on grill.

6. Cook for 1 hour 45 minutes, or until legs reach an internal temperature of 170 degrees.

7. Brush legs with sauce and return to grill for 5-10 minutes to allow sauce to cook onto meat.

8. Serve with extra sauce on the side.Place all ingredients into a small sauce pan and whisk.

9. Bring to a boil then immediately reduce to a simmer, whisking often

10. Allow to simmer for 15 minutes or until sauce is beginning to thicken

11. Remove from heat and allow to cool

12. Pork or Beef, chicken does not have as much intramuscular fats that need to render out to result in tender meat

13. You can cook chicken at a hotter temperature to ensure you get tender, moist chicken every time

14. Use a meat thermometer to know exactly when to pull the chicken off the grill

15. I pull white meat at 165 degrees, and dark meat, such as these legs, at 175 degrees

Apricot Glazed Ham

Servings: 8
Cooking Time: 60 Minutes

Ingredients:

- 1 Cup Apricot Preserves
- 1/2 Cup apricot brandy
- 1/4 Cup honey
- 1/4 Cup brown sugar, firmly packed
- 1/4 Teaspoon ground cloves
- 6 Ounce Apricot Nectar, bottled or ginger ale
- 1 Large ham
- fresh parsley
- apricot, halved

Directions:

1. Supply your smoker with wood pellets and follow the start-up procedure. Preheat the grill, with the lid closed, to 325° F.

2. In a saucepan, stir together the apricot preserves, apricot brandy, honey, brown sugar, cloves, and apricot nectar and simmer over medium heat until the preserves, honey, and brown sugar have melted. Set aside and keep warm.

3. Place ham in large roasting pan lined with aluminum foil. Place pan on grill and cook for 1.5 hours.

4. Open Grill and glaze ham with reserved mixture. Continue cooking for another 30 minutes or until a thermometer is inserted into

the thickest part of the meat and reaches an internal temperatures of 135 degrees F. Probe: 135 ˚F

5. Garnish the platter with the parsley and apricots, if desired. Enjoy!

Chile Chicken Thighs

Servings: 4
Cooking Time: 35 Minutes

Ingredients:

- 2 Tablespoon soy sauce
- 1/4 Cup honey
- 2 Clove garlic, minced
- 1/4 Teaspoon red pepper flakes
- 4 boneless, skinless chicken thighs
- 2 Tablespoon olive oil
- 2 Teaspoon Chicken Rub
- ancho chile powder
- 1/4 Teaspoon coarse ground black pepper

Directions:

1. Supply your smoker with wood pellets and follow the start-up procedure. Preheat the grill, with the lid closed, to 400° F.

2. In a small bowl, combine honey, soy sauce, garlic and red pepper chili flakes; blend well with wire whisk. Set aside.

3. Drizzle the chicken thighs with olive oil and season generously on both sides with the Traeger Chicken Rub and black pepper, then give each thigh a few shakes of ancho chili powder on both sides.

4. Place the seasoned chicken thighs directly on the grill grate and cook for about 15 minutes per side or until the internal temperature registers 165°F on an instant-read thermometer. Grill: 400 ˚F Probe: 165 ˚F

5. Brush with chili-honey glaze. Remove from grill. Serve with additional sauce. Enjoy!

Crust Chicken Pizza

Servings: 4
Cooking Time: 35 Minutes

Ingredients:

- ½ Cup Alfredo Sauce
- 1 Tbsp Butter
- ¾ Lb. Shredded Chicken
- 2 Large Eggs
- 2 + 6 Divided Garlic Clove, Minced
- 1 ½ Cups Heavy Cream
- ¾ Cup Kale
- ¼ Cup Mushroom
- 1 Cup Grated Parmesan Cheese
- Champion Chicken Rub
- 2 Tbsp Red Onion, Diced
- ½ Tsp Salt

Directions:

1. Supply your smoker with wood pellets and follow the start-up procedure. Preheat the grill, with the lid open, to 400° F. If using a gas or charcoal grill, set heat to medium-high heat. Place pizza stone on grill grates and allow to preheat. Line a pizza peel with parchment paper and set aside.

2. In a medium bowl, stir together the shredded chicken, grated Parmesan cheese, minced garlic, and sea salt. Whisk the eggs lightly in a small bowl then add to chicken mixture. Mix until well combined.

3. Spread the chicken crust pizza "dough" onto the parchment paper on the pizza peel, as thinly as possible (about ¼" thick).

4. Using the pizza peel, transfer the parchment to the preheated pizza stone. Grill for 15 to 20

minutes, until firm and golden on the edges. Remove from the grill and let rest for 5-10 minutes.

5. Top pizza crust with alfredo sauce, kale, mushrooms, red onion and additional parmesan cheese. Return to the grill for 10 to 15 minutes, until the cheese is melted. Slice and serve!

Easy Grilled Chicken Shawarma

Servings:
Cooking Time: 16 Minutes

Ingredients:

- 2 lbs to 2 ¼ lb chicken thighs
- Shawarma Marinade
- 2 tablespoons ground cumin
- 2 tablespoons ground coriander
- 8 garlic cloves, minced
- 2 teaspoons kosher salt
- 6 tablespoons olive oil
- 1/4 teaspoon cayenne pepper
- 2 teaspoon turmeric
- 1 teaspoon ground ginger
- 1 teaspoon ground black pepper
- 2 teaspoon allspice

Directions:

1. Supply your smoker with wood pellets and follow the start-up procedure. Preheat the grill, with the lid closed, to medium-high heat. Place all marinade ingredients in a bowl and mix, or pulse in a food processor to make a paste.

2. Rub chicken on all sides with the marinade and let sit 20 minutes.

3. Place the chicken on the grill racks, closing the lid to the BBQ, until all sides have nice grill marks, about 8 minutes each side. Move to the warming rack until cooked all the way through, about 10 minutes.

4. Enjoy the chicken shawarma over Israeli salad, or with rice and veggies, or with pita bread and tzatziki.

Smoked Turkey Jerky

Servings: 6
Cooking Time: 240 Minutes

Ingredients:

- 1/2 Cup soy sauce
- 1/4 Cup water
- 2 Tablespoon honey
- 2 Tablespoon Asian chili garlic sauce
- 2 Tablespoon lime juice
- 1 Tablespoon Morton Tender Quick Home Meat Cure
- 2 Pound (4-5 lb) boneless turkey breast

Directions:

1. In a mixing bowl, combine the soy sauce, water, honey, chili-garlic paste, lime juice, and curing salt, if using. With a sharp knife, slice the turkey into 1/4" thick slices with the grain, which helps it hold together better as it dries. (This is easier if the meat is partially frozen.) Trim any fat, membrane, or connective tissue.

2. Put the turkey slices in a large resealable plastic bag. Pour the marinade mixture over the turkey, and massage the bag so that all the slices get coated with the marinade. Seal the bag and refrigerate for several hours, or overnight.

3. Supply your smoker with wood pellets and follow the start-up procedure. Preheat the grill, with the lid closed, to 180° F.

4. Remove the turkey from the marinade and discard the marinade. Dry the turkey slices between paper towels. Arrange in a single layer directly on the grill grate.

5. Smoke for 2 to 4 hours, or until the jerky is dry but still chewy and somewhat pliant when you bend a piece. Grill: 180 ˚F

6. Transfer to a resealable plastic bag while the jerky's still warm. Let the jerky rest for an hour at room temperature. Squeeze any air from the bag, and refrigerate the jerky. It will keep for several weeks. Enjoy!

Texas Style Black Pepper Turkey

Servings: 6

Cooking Time: 240 Minutes

Ingredients:

- 1/2 Cup Coarse Black Pepper
- 1Lb Butter
- 1/2 Cup Salt, Kosher
- 1 Brined Turkey

Directions:

1. Supply your smoker with wood pellets and follow the start-up procedure. Preheat the grill, with the lid closed, to 300° F.

2. Liberally season Turkey with equal parts kosher salt and coarse black pepper.

3. Cook on grill until Internal temp reaches approximately 145°F or the skin has darkened to your liking.

4. Place turkey in a roasting pan topped with a pound of chopped butter and cover.

5. Return to the grill until internal temp of the thigh and breast reaches 165°F

6. Let rest for 30 minutes, carve and serve.

Big Game Roast Chicken

Servings: 4

Cooking Time: 60 Minutes

Ingredients:

- 1 whole chicken
- Big Game Rub

Directions:

1. Supply your smoker with wood pellets and follow the start-up procedure. Preheat the grill, with the lid closed, to 375° F.

2. Remove the neck and gizzards from the cavity of the bird. Rinse and wipe the outside and inside of the chicken with a paper towel. Tie chicken legs together with butcher twine and tuck wings.

3. Apply an even coat of the Traeger Big Game Rub to the inside and outside of the chicken.

4. Place chicken on the grill grate and cook for 60 minutes. After an hour, check the temperature of the bird in the thickest part of the leg. The temperature needs to be between 165 and 180°F. Check every 15 minutes if not up to temperature. When the leg reaches desired internal temperature, check the temperature of the breast. The breast needs to reach an internal temperature of 165°F before it is done. Grill: 375 ˚F Probe: 165 ˚F

5. Let bird rest for 15 to 20 minutes for slicing. Enjoy!

Grilled Beantown Chicken Wings

Servings: 8

Cooking Time: 50 Minutes

Ingredients:

- 3 Pound chicken wings
- 1/4 Cup vegetable oil
- 1 1/2 Tablespoon Pork & Poultry Rub
- 1 Cup Irish Stout
- 1/2 Cup butter
- 2 Tablespoon apple jelly
- 1 Cup Frank's RedHot Sauce

Directions:

1. Rinse the chicken wings under cold running water and pat dry. With a sharp knife, cut the wings into three pieces through the joints. Discard the wing tips, or save for chicken stock.

2. Transfer the remaining "drumettes" and "flats" to a large a bowl. Add the oil and the Traeger Pork and Poultry shake, and toss with your hands to coat the wings evenly.

3. Make the beer sauce: In a small saucepan, bring the beer to a boil over high heat and reduce by half. Reduce the heat to medium-low and add the butter, stirring until melted. Stir in the apple jelly and the hot sauce. Keep warm.

4. Supply your smoker with wood pellets and follow the start-up procedure. Preheat the grill, with the lid closed, to 350° F.

5. Arrange the wings on the grill grate. Cook for 45 to 50 minutes, or until the chicken is no longer pink at the bone, turning once halfway through. Transfer the wings to a large clean bowl and pour the beer sauce over the wings, tossing to coat. Serve immediately. Grill: 350 ˚F

Smoke-roasted Chicken Thighs

Servings: 12-15
Cooking Time: 120 Minutes

Ingredients:

- 3 pounds chicken thighs
- 2 teaspoons salt
- 2 teaspoons freshly ground black pepper
- 2 teaspoons garlic powder
- 2 teaspoons onion powder
- 2 cups prepared Italian dressing

Directions:

1. Place the chicken thighs in a shallow dish and sprinkle with the salt, pepper, garlic powder, and onion powder, being sure to get under the skin.

2. Cover with the Italian dressing, coating all sides, and refrigerate for 1 hour.

3. Supply your smoker with wood pellets and follow the start-up procedure. Preheat, with the lid closed, to 250°F.

4. Remove the chicken thighs from the marinade and place directly on the grill, skin-side down. Discard the marinade.

5. Close the lid and roast the chicken for 1 hour 30 minutes to 2 hours, or until a meat thermometer inserted in the thickest part of the thighs reads 165°F. Do not turn the thighs during the smoking process.

Marinated Grilled Honey Chicken Wings

Servings: 4-6
Cooking Time: 30 Minutes

Ingredients:

- 1/2 Bottle Beer, Any Brand
- 2 Lbs Chicken Wings, Whole
- 2 Tablespoon Honey
- 1 Tablespoon   Sweet Heat Rub
- 2 Tablespoon Rice Wine Vinegar
- 1/2 Tablesoon Sesame Oil
- 1/4 Cup Soy Sauce
- 1 Tablespoon Sriracha Hot Sauce

Directions:

1. In a large glass or plastic bowl, combine the beer, soy sauce, honey, rice wine vinegar, sriracha, sesame oil and   Sweet Heat Seasoning. Whisk well to combine.

2. Add the chicken wings to the marinade and toss well to combine. Cover with plastic wrap and refrigerate for 2 hours and up to 24 hours.

3. Remove chicken wings from refrigerator, drain marinade and pat dry. Supply your smoker

with wood pellets and follow the start-up procedure. Supply your smoker with wood pellets and follow the start-up procedure. Preheat the grill, with the lid open, to 350° F. Place the wings on a grill pan and grill for 20-25 minutes, or until the wings' internal temperature is 165F. Remove from the grill, serve and enjoy!

Roasted Stuffed Turkey Breast

Servings: 6
Cooking Time: 40 Minutes

Ingredients:

- 1 (4-5 lb) boneless turkey breast
- 5 Slices thick-cut bacon, chopped
- 3/4 Cup assorted mushrooms
- 1 Bunch scallions, chopped
- 1/8 Cup white wine
- 3 Tablespoon panko breadcrumbs
- salt
- black pepper

Directions:

1. Supply your smoker with wood pellets and follow the start-up procedure. Preheat the grill, with the lid closed, to 375° F.

2. Slice the turkey breast horizontally, making sure not to slice all the way through. Lay breast open flat.

3. Cook bacon in a skillet over medium heat until crispy. Remove bacon and set aside. Sauté mushrooms in the bacon grease until browned. Add scallions and cook for an additional two minutes. Add white wine and cook down until no wine remains. Stir in breadcrumbs and bacon, adding salt and pepper to taste.

4. Transfer filling to fridge to cool for 15 to 20 minutes. Once chilled, spread the filling onto the turkey breast, pressing lightly to make sure it adheres. Roll the turkey breast tightly and tie with butcher's twine at about 1 inch intervals. Tuck the ends of the turkey breast under and tie with twine lengthwise.

5. Season the outside of the turkey breast with salt and pepper. Place in grill for 40 minutes. Check the internal temperature, desired temperature is 165°F. Once the finished temperature is reached, remove turkey from the grill and let rest for 10 minutes. Slice and serve. Enjoy! Grill: 375 °F Probe: 165 °F

Wild West Wings

Servings: 4
Cooking Time: 60 Minutes

Ingredients:

- 2 pounds chicken wings
- 2 tablespoons extra-virgin olive oil
- 2 packages ranch dressing mix (such as Hidden Valley brand)
- ¼ cup prepared ranch dressing (optional)

Directions:

1. Supply your smoker with wood pellets and follow the start-up procedure. Preheat, with the lid closed, to 350°F.

2. Place the chicken wings in a large bowl and toss with the olive oil and ranch dressing mix.

3. Arrange the wings directly on the grill, or line the grill with aluminum foil for easy cleanup, close the lid, and smoke for 25 minutes.

4. Flip and smoke for 20 to 35 minutes more, or until a meat thermometer inserted in the thickest part of the wings reads 165°F and the wings are crispy. (Note: The wings will likely be done after 45 minutes, but an extra 10 to 15 minutes makes them crispy without drying the meat.)

5. Serve warm with ranch dressing (if using).

Bbq Chicken Wings With Spicy Honey Glaze

Servings: 4
Cooking Time: 30 Minutes

Ingredients:

- 4 Pound chicken wings
- 6 Ounce Chicken Rub
- 2 Tablespoon corn starch
- 1 Cup honey
- 1 Cup Sriracha
- 1/2 Cup soy sauce
- 2 Tablespoon sesame oil
- 3 Tablespoon unsalted butter
- 2 Tablespoon sesame seeds

Directions:

1. Supply your smoker with wood pellets and follow the start-up procedure. Preheat the grill, with the lid closed, to 375° F.

2. While grill is preheating, dry off chicken wings with a paper towel. Mix the Traeger Chicken rub with the cornstarch and coat both sides of the chicken wings.

3. When the grill is heated, place the wings on the grill for 35 minutes flipping half way through. Grill: 375 ℉

4. While the wings are cooking, mix the honey, Sriracha, soy sauce, sesame seed oil, and unsalted butter and heat on a stove top.

5. After the wings have cooked for 35 minutes, check the temperature. The minimum temperature must reach an internal temperature of 165 degrees F. An internal temperature between 175 to 180 degrees F may yield a better texture. Grill: 375 ℉ Probe: 177 ℉

6. When wings are done, place in large bowl and toss with the warmed sauce.

7. Place wings on platter and sprinkle the sesame seeds. Enjoy!

Roasted Chicken With Wild Rice & Mushrooms

Servings: 2
Cooking Time: 120 Minutes

Ingredients:

- 1 Whole whole chicken
- salt
- pepper
- 2 Tablespoon butter
- 1 Medium onion, chopped
- 4 Strips Bacon, diced
- 1 Cup Rice, wild
- 1 mushrooms, sliced
- salt
- 2 1/4 Cup water
- 2 Tablespoon parsley, chopped

Directions:

1. Supply your smoker with wood pellets and follow the start-up procedure. Preheat the grill, with the lid closed, to 375° F.

2. Season inside and outside of chicken with salt and pepper.

3. In a large saucepan, melt 2 Tbsp butter over medium heat. Add onions and cook until soft, 3-5 minutes. Add bacon to onions and cook, stirring, until bacon and onions are browned. Stir in rice, mushrooms, salt, and pepper.

4. Add 2-1/4 cups of water to mixture and bring to a boil. Reduce heat to low, cover and simmer for 25 minutes, until rice has absorbed liquid. Add fresh parsley and mix.

5. Stuff cavity loosely with rice mixture. Tie chicken legs back with butcher's twine.

6. Place chicken directly on grill grate and roast for 1 hr 15 mins or until an instant-read thermometer inserted into the thickest part of the breast reads 160°F and the thigh 170°F. Grill: 375 °F Probe: 160 °F

7. Remove chicken from grill and allow to rest for 10 minutes.

8. Spoon stuffing out of chicken cavity to a platter and slice chicken. Serve immediately with chicken pieces over rice stuffing. Enjoy!

Garlic Sriracha Buffalo Chicken Wings

Servings: 6-8
Cooking Time: 160 Minutes

Ingredients:

- 1 Cup Buffalo Sauce
- 6 Lbs Chicken Wings
- 2 Tbsp Garlic Powder
- 1 Tsp Pepper
- Divided By 2 Tbsp And ½ Tbsp Sweet Heat Rub
- 1 Tsp Salt
- ⅓ Cup, Divided Sriracha Sauce

Directions:

1. In a non-stick sauce pot, add the remaining Sriracha and buffalo sauce. Stir to combine and set aside.

2. Supply your smoker with wood pellets and follow the start-up procedure. Preheat the grill, with the lid open, to 250° F. If using a gas or charcoal grill, set it to low heat with indirect heat. Place marinated wings directly on grill grate and cook (covered) for 1 hour 15 minutes.

3. Flip wings and baste each piece with Sriracha sauce. Season with additional   Sweet Heat Rub,

cover, and continue to grill for an additional 1 hour 15 minutes.

4. Remove wings from grill and place on sheet tray. Baste with additional sauce, then open Sear Slide and return wings to the grill. Grill for 3-5 minutes, rotating often, until wings begin to char lightly.

5. Transfer wings to a serving tray, baste with remaining sauce and serve!

Smoked Drumsticks

Servings: 2-4
Cooking Time: 25 Minutes

Ingredients:

- 1 pound chicken drumsticks
- 2 tablespoons olive oil
- 1 batch Sweet and Spicy Cinnamon Rub

Directions:

1. Supply your smoker with wood pellets and follow the start-up procedure. Preheat the grill, with the lid closed, to 350°F.

2. Coat the drumsticks all over with olive oil and season with the rub. Using your hands, work the rub into the meat.

3. Place the drumsticks directly on the grill grate and smoke until their internal temperature reaches 170°F. Remove the drumsticks from the grill and serve immediately.

Easy Bbq Chicken Wings

Servings: 4
Cooking Time: 40 Minutes

Ingredients:

- 1 Pack Chicken Wings
- Extra Virgin Olive Oil
- Champion Chicken Seasoning

Directions:

1. Supply your smoker with wood pellets and follow the start-up procedure. Preheat the grill, with the lid closed, to 350° F.

2. Blot the defrosted chicken wings dry with paper towels.

3. Brush oil onto each side of the wings and sprinkle with seasoning.

4. Grill at 350° for 40 minutes or until wings are crispy. Flip halfway through. Serve hot.

BEEF LAMB AND GAME RECIPES

Savory Smoked Beef Short Ribs

Servings: 4
Cooking Time: 360 Minutes

Ingredients:

- 1 Cup Apple Cider Vinegar
- 1 Cup Apple Juice
- 4 Tablespoon Olive Oil
- 4 Tbsp Beef And Brisket Rub
- 2 1/2 Pounds (Or 6 Large) Beef Short Rib(S)

Directions:

1. Supply your smoker with wood pellets and follow the start-up procedure. Preheat the grill, with the lid closed, to 225° F.

2. In a food-safe spray bottle, combine the apple cider vinegar and apple juice. Set aside.

3. Flip the beef short ribs over, bone side up, and pull off the thick membrane. Discard. Flip the short ribs right side up and trim any excess fat from the top. Generously rub down the short ribs with olive oil and Beef and Brisket Rub.

4. Place the beef ribs on the center rack. Smoke for about 2 hours, until the short ribs have developed a crust and are a rich lacquered brown.

5. After 2 hours, remove the beef short ribs from the smoker, place in the heat-proof baking dish, and pour the apple cider vinegar and apple juice into the dish. Cover tightly with foil and smoke for another 1½-2 hours or until the ribs are fall-apart tender and register 200°F. Remove from the smoker and serve immediately.

Korean Style Bbq Prime Ribs

Servings: 5
Cooking Time: 480 Minutes

Ingredients:

- 3 lbs beef short ribs
- 2 tbsp sugar
- 3/4 cup water
- 1 tbsp ground black pepper
- 3 tbsp white vinegar
- 2 tbsp sesame oil
- 3 tbsp soy sauce
- 6 cloves garlic, minced
- 1/3 cup light brown sugar
- 1/2 yellow onion, finely chopped

Directions:

1. Combine soy sauce, water, and vinegar in a bowl. Mix and whisk in brown sugar, white sugar, pepper, sesame oil, garlic, and onion. Whisk until the sugars have completely dissolved

2. Pour marinade into large bowl or baking pan with high sides. Dunk the short ribs in the marinade, coating completely. Cover marinaded short ribs with plastic wrap and refrigerate for 6 to 12 hours3. Preheat pellet grill to 225°F.

3. Remove plastic wrap from ribs and pull ribs out of marinade. Shake off any excess marinade and dispose of the contents left in the bowl.

4. Place ribs on grill and cook for about 6-8 hours, until ribs reach an internal temperature of 203°F. Measure using a probe meat thermometer

5. Once ribs reach temperature, remove from grill and allow to rest for about 20 minutes. Slice, serve, and enjoy!

Smoked Bacon Brisket Flat

Servings: 4
Cooking Time: 480 Minutes

Ingredients:
- 1/2 lbs bacon
- 4 lbs brisket flat, trimmed
- tt lonestar brisket rub

Directions:
1. Supply your smoker with wood pellets and follow the start-up procedure. Preheat the grill, with the lid open, to 250° F. If using a gas or charcoal grill, set it up for low, indirect heat.
2. Place the brisket in a foil-lined aluminum pan. Season the fat side of the brisket with Lonestar Brisket Rub, then flip and season the meat side with additional rub.
3. Transfer the brisket to the grill and smoke for 1 hour.
4. Use tongs to flip the brisket over, so the fat side is up, then drape half the bacon slices over the brisket. Smoke for 2 hours, then remove the browned bacon, and set aside.
5. Lay the remaining raw bacon strips over the brisket, and continue cooking until these new bacon strips are browned and the internal temperature of the brisket reads 202°F, which will likely take an additional 3 to 4 hours cook time.
6. Remove the brisket from the grill, and rest for 1 hour, then slice thin. Serve warm.

Savory Teriyaki Smoked Steak Bites

Servings: 2
Cooking Time: 90 Minutes

Ingredients:
- Sirloin steak
- Teriyaki sauce
- Light brown sugar
- Garlic powder
- Garlic salt
- Soy sauce
- Apple cider vinegar
- Pepper

Directions:
1. Mix all ingredients for the marinade.
2. Trim steak and cut into 2 inches pieces.
3. Place in a zip lock bag and pour marinade over the steak. Squeeze as much air out as possible and tightly seal the bag.
4. Freeze the steak for at least 8 hours or overnight.
5. Supply your smoker with wood pellets and follow the start-up procedure. Preheat the grill, with the lid closed, to 225 °F.
6. Place the steak bites directly on the rack. Discard remaining marinade.
7. Smoke for 1 hour and 30 minutes or until the internal temp is 135-140 degrees F.

Beer Chili Bratwurst

Servings: 4
Cooking Time: 45 Minutes

Ingredients:
- 1 Chopped Chipotle In Adobo
- 3 - 4 Cans Of Beer, Any Brand
- 4 Bratwursts, Raw
- 4 Bratwurst Buns
- ½ Cup Prepared Nacho Cheese Sauce
- 1 Cup Chili, Prepared
- Caramelized Onions
- Sweet Rib Rub

Directions:

1. Supply your smoker with wood pellets and follow the start-up procedure. Preheat the grill, with the lid closed, to 350° F. If you're using charcoal or gas, set the temperature to medium high.

2. Place a pot filled with beer, Sweet Rib Rub, caramelized onions and raw brats. Place on grill and par-boil for 20 minutes.

3. Grill the brats for 7-10 minutes, or until internal temperature of the brats is 160°F. Remove the brats from the grill and allow them to rest for 5 minutes.

4. While the brats rest, place the chili in a sauce pan, and place the sauce pan on the grill. Heat the chili all the way through.

5. In a separate sauce pan, add the nacho cheese to the pan, add adobo chili peppers and a shake of Sweet Rib Rub. Place the saucepan on the grill and heat until warm all the way through.

6. Assemble the brats: place a brat in a bun, then top with a spoonful of chili and a spoonful of nacho cheese. Serve immediately.

Teriyaki Bbq Beef Skewers

Servings: 8
Cooking Time: 8 Minutes

Ingredients:

- 2 Pound Top Round Steak, boneless, cut into 1/4" slices
- 3/4 Cup light brown sugar
- 1/2 Cup soy sauce
- 1/4 Cup Pineapple Juice (optional)
- 1/4 Cup water
- Cup vegetable oil
- 1 Clove Garlic (Large), finely chopped

Directions:

1. Slice the beef into 1-1/2 - 2" wide strips.

2. Whisk brown sugar, soy sauce, pineapple juice, water, vegetable oil, and garlic together.

3. Pour the marinade into a large zip-top bag and drop beef slices into the mixture. Marinate beef in refrigerator for 24 hours.

4. Remove beef from the marinade, shaking to remove any excess liquid. Discard marinade. Thread beef slices in a zig-zag onto the skewers.

5. Supply your smoker with wood pellets and follow the start-up procedure. Preheat the grill, with the lid closed, to 325° F.

6. Cook skewers on preheated grill until the beef is cooked through, about 3 minutes per side. Enjoy! Grill: 325 °F

Spiced Leg Of Lamb Gyros

Servings: 8 – 10
Cooking Time: 180 Minutes

Ingredients:

- 1 Tbsp Black Pepper
- 4 Oz. Cremini Mushrooms
- ¼ Cup Dijon Mustard
- 8, Smashed Garlic Cloves
- 1 Cup + 1 Tbsp Grapeseed Oil, Divided
- 5 Lb, Bone-In Sirloin Leg Of Lamb
- ⅓ Cup Lemon Juice
- ½ Tbsp + 1 Tsp Dried, Divided Oregano
- 8-10 Pita
- Large Wedge Chop Red Onion
- 1 Tbsp Rosemary Leaves, Dried
- ⅔ Cup Scallions, Chopped
- 3 Tbsp, Coarse Sea Salt
- ½ Tbsp Thyme, Dried
- Tzatziki Sauce
- 1 Vine-Ripe Tomato, Chopped

Directions:

1. Fire up your grill and preheat to "Smoke" mode. If using a gas or charcoal grill, set it up for low, indirect heat.

2. In a food processor, combine grapeseed oil, lemon juice, mustard, scallions, garlic, rosemary, thyme, salt and pepper. Process until it forms a thick marinade.

3. Score the fat cap of the lamb, then truss with butcher's twine. Pour two-thirds of the marinade onto the leg of lamb to cover completely. Set remaining marinade aside for vegetables. Wrap the lamb in foil and marinate at room temperature for 1 hour.

4. Place the lamb in the smoking cabinet by hanging truss from S hooks. Insert temperature probe and smoke for 45 minutes. Increase the temperature to 400°F.

5. Supply your smoker with wood pellets and follow the start-up procedure. Preheat the grill, with the lid closed, to 225 to 250° F. (If you're using a grill or vertical smoker, set your temperature to 225°F). Once it has reached this temperature, make sure the upper chimney caps are fully open, and you can lower the grill temp to 300°F. As long as the cabinet doors remain closed this should maintain temperature in the upper cabinet.

6. Smoke the lamb until the internal temperature of the meat reaches 135°F, about 3 hours.

7. While the lamb is cooking, skewer together red onion and mushrooms. Brush with remaining marinade, then transfer to grill with sear slide open, 3 to 5 minutes. In a small bowl combine 1 tbsp of grape seed oil and 1 tsp of oregano and brush lightly over pita breads. Grill pita bread to warm while skewers are on the grill.

8. Remove the leg of lamb from the smoker and loosely cover with aluminum foil. Rest the meat for 30 minutes before slicing.

9. Thinly slice the lamb, and serve in warm pita with grilled mushrooms and onions, and chopped tomatoes, and tzatziki, if desired.

Texas Pepper Beef Ribs

Servings: 16
Cooking Time: 360 Minutes

Ingredients:
- 8 lbs beef ribs (two 4 bone racks of plate ribs)
- 8 tbsp salt, pepper, garlic
- 4 tbsp olive oil

Directions:
1. Supply your smoker with wood pellets and follow the start-up procedure. Preheat the grill, with the lid closed, to 250 °F.

2. Pour two tbsp of olive oil on each rack of ribs and rub into meat on all sides.

3. Season the ribs on all sides using the salt, pepper, and garlic seasoning.

4. Set ribs in the smoker and cook for 3 hours before checking for color. Insert a temperature probe into the thickest part of the ribs.

5. Continue cooking until it reaches an internal temperature of around 170 °F.

6. Wrap ribs tightly with two layers of Peach Butcher Paper. Replace the probe into the ribs.

7. Continue cooking until it reaches an internal temperature of 205 °F(usually takes about 2 hours). Use a toothpick or the probe to check for doneness. Meat should be tender like butter. If meat is still tough, continue to cook until it becomes tender.

8. Once meat is tender, leave ribs wrapped and rest until the temperature lowers to around 160-170 °F(about 1 hour).

9. Slice and serve.

Traeger Smoked Salami

Servings: 8

Cooking Time: 480 Minutes

Ingredients:

- Pound Ground Sirloin
- 1 Tablespoon Morton Tender Quick Home Meat Cure
- Tablespoon Worcestershire sauce
- 1 Tablespoon ground black pepper
- 2 Teaspoon mustard seeds
- 1 Teaspoon red pepper flakes
- 1 Teaspoon black peppercorn
- Teaspoon honey

Directions:

1. Plan ahead! This recipe requires overnight time. In a large glass bowl combine the beef, curing salt, Worcestershire, pepper, mustard, red pepper flakes, and peppercorns. Gently distribute the ingredients through the meat.

2. Cover with plastic wrap and refrigerate for 1 day.

3. After the meat has cured for 1 day, lay two pieces of long plastic wrap on top of each other on your work surface. Overturn the meat directly into the middle of the plastic wrap. Form the meat into a long log shape.

4. Pull the plastic wrap around one side and smooth out the edges of the log. Use even pressure across the length to work out any bubbles. Pull the plastic wrap tightly around the other side and overlap the edges of the wrap to create a tight seal. Roll the sausage forward and back with both hands. Once you have the sausage fairly uniform in width, tightly twist the ends of the plastic wrap. Return to the refrigerator for 1 day.

5. Supply your smoker with wood pellets and follow the start-up procedure. Preheat the grill, with the lid closed, to 180° F.

6. Unwrap the sausage and drizzle with the honey. Place directly on the grill grate, close the lid and smoke for 6-8 hours or until the internal temperature of the sausage reads 170°F with a meat thermometer. Probe: 170 °F

7. Allow the sausage to cool completely before slicing and serving. Enjoy!

Spicy Chopped Brisket Sandwich

Servings: 4

Cooking Time: 10 Minutes

Ingredients:

- 3 Cups Cooked And Chopped Brisket
- Dill Pickle, Slice
- Pickled Jalapeno, Sliced
- 4 Sandwich Buns
- 1 Cup Spicy Barbecue Sauce
- White Onion, Sliced

Directions:

1. Supply your smoker with wood pellets and follow the start-up procedure. Preheat the grill, with the lid closed, to 350° F. If you're using gas or charcoal, prep your grill to cook with medium indirect heat.

2. Add the chopped brisket and spicy barbecue sauce to the aluminum pan and mix well. The brisket should be fully coated with sauce. If 1 cup is not enough, feel free to more sauce ¼ cup at a time.

3. Cover the aluminum pan tightly with foil and place it in the center of the grill. Close the lid and cook the brisket for about 10 minutes or until it's heated all the way through.

4. Remove the brisket from the grill and pile the meat on top of the sandwich buns. Top the brisket sandwich with pickle slices, jalapeno slices, and sliced onions. Serve immediately.

Tater Tot Nachos With Brisket

Servings: 4
Cooking Time: 600 Minutes

Ingredients:

- Your Favorite BBQ Sauce
- 1 12 Lb Brisket
- 1, Skiced Jalapeno Pepper
- ¼ Cup Beef And Brisket Rub
- ¾ Cup Sharp Cheddar Cheese, Shredded
- ⅓ Cup Sour Cream
- 32 Oz. Tater Tots, Frozen

Directions:

1. Supply your smoker with wood pellets and follow the start-up procedure. Preheat the grill, with the lid closed, to 225° F. If using a gas or charcoal grill, set to medium-low heat.

2. While your grill is heating up, trim your brisket of excess fat (you'll want to leave about ¼ of an inch of fat so the meat stays moist during the long cooking process), and season generously with Beef and Brisket Rub. Place your brisket on the grates of the grill, fat side up. Let it smoke for about 8-10 hours, or until the internal temperature reaches 190°F.

3. Let it rest in the cooler for up to an hour so the juices can settle back into the meat. Shred with meat claws and reserve 1 lb.

4. Return grill to 325°F. Place tater tots on the bottom of a large cast-iron skillet and arrange in one layer. Place skillet on preheated grill and cook tater tots until crispy and golden.

5. Top tater tots with reserved brisket, BBQ sauce and cheddar cheese. Return to the grill for 15 minutes or until cheese has melted.

6. Remove from oven and top with sour cream and jalapenos. Serve immediately.

Mesquite Smoked Brisket

Servings: 8-12
Cooking Time: 720 Minutes

Ingredients:

- 1 (12-pound) full packer brisket
- 2 tablespoons yellow mustard (you can also use soy sauce)
- Salt
- Freshly ground black pepper

Directions:

1. Supply your smoker with wood pellets and follow the start-up procedure. Preheat the grill, with the lid closed, to 225°F.

2. Using a boning knife, carefully remove all but about ½ inch of the large layer of fat covering one side of your brisket.

3. Coat the brisket all over with mustard and season it with salt and pepper.

4. Place the brisket directly on the grill grate and smoke until its internal temperature reaches 160°F and the brisket has formed a dark bark.

5. Pull the brisket from the grill and wrap it completely in aluminum foil or butcher paper.

6. Increase the grill's temperature to 350°F and return the wrapped brisket to it. Continue to cook until its internal temperature reaches 190°F.

7. Transfer the wrapped brisket to a cooler, cover the cooler, and let the brisket rest for 1 or 2 hours.

8. Remove the brisket from the cooler and unwrap it.

9. Separate the brisket point from the flat by cutting along the fat layer, and slice the flat. The point can be saved for burnt ends (see Sweet Heat Burnt Ends), or sliced and served as well.

Smoked Corned Beef & Cabbage

Servings: 6
Cooking Time: 300 Minutes

Ingredients:

- 1 (3-5 lb) corned beef brisket
- 1 Quart chicken stock
- 12 Ounce (12 oz) beer, preferably pilsner or lager
- 1/4 Teaspoon garlic salt
- 1/2 Cup (1 stick) butter, cut into slices
- 2 Cup baby carrots
- 1 Pound baby or fingerling potatoes
- 1 Head cabbage, cut into wedges
- 2 Tablespoon fresh chopped dill

Directions:

1. Soak the corned beef in water for about 8 hours, changing water every 2 hours.

2. Supply your smoker with wood pellets and follow the start-up procedure. Preheat the grill, with the lid closed, to 180° F.

3. Remove brisket from water and pat dry. Place directly on the grill grate and smoke for 2 hours. Grill: 180 ˚F

4. Transfer brisket from grill and place in a roasting pan. Increase grill temperature to 325˚F and preheat, lid closed. Grill: 325 ˚F

5. Sprinkle seasoning packet on top of brisket and pour chicken stock and dark beer over the roast.

6. Cover roasting pan with foil and place on the grill. Cook for 2 hours or until beef is fork tender. Grill: 325 ˚F

7. Remove foil and add carrots and potatoes to the roasting pan. Cover meat and vegetables with garlic salt and butter slices. Grill: 325 ˚F

8. Recover with foil and cook for an additional hour or until carrots and potatoes are just tender. Add cabbage, cover and return to grill for 20 minutes more. Grill: 325 ˚F

9. Remove vegetables from the pan to a bowl or serving platter. Slice beef and serve with potatoes, cabbage and carrots. Garnish with fresh dill and thyme if desired. Enjoy!

Wagyu Corned Beef Hash

Servings: 8
Cooking Time: 360 Minutes

Ingredients:

- 2 1/2 Pound Wagyu Corned Beef Roast
- 2 red bell pepper, diced
- 1 green bell pepper, diced
- 2 Pound Southern Hash Brown
- 3 Cup shredded cheddar cheese
- 2 Tablespoon kosher salt
- 2 Tablespoon black pepper
- 7 eggs
- 1/2 Cup whole milk

Directions:

1. Corned Beef: Corned beef needs to be cooked at least one day prior to making the hash.

2. Supply your smoker with wood pellets and follow the start-up procedure. Preheat the grill, with the lid closed, to 275° F.

3. Rinse the corned beef and place on grill. Cook for 4 to 4.5 hours. Wrap in a double layer of heavy duty tin foil and put back on the grill. Grill: 275 °F

4. Cook meat until it reaches an internal temperature of 204 degrees F. This should take 2-3 more hours. Let vent for 2 hours and place in fridge. Refrigerate overnight. Grill: 275 °F Probe: 204 °F

5. Corned Beef Hash: Chop and cook the peppers in cast iron for 20 minutes.

6. When ready to cook, start the Traeger and set the temperature to 350 degrees F and preheat, lid closed, for 10 minutes. Grill: 350 °F

7. Cut the corned beef into bite-sized pieces. Combine the hash browns, corned beef, bell peppers, cheese, salt and pepper. Mix well and place in a 9x13 baking dish.

8. Mix eggs and milk in a separate bowl. Pour over the top of the hash brown mixture.

9. Cover with foil and set on the grill for a 1.5 hours. The internal temperature should reach 165 degrees F. Serve and enjoy! Grill: 350 °F Probe: 165 °F

Flavour Memphis Bbq Beef Brisket

Servings: 10
Cooking Time: 600 Minutes

Ingredients:
- 1 Cup Beef Broth
- 1, 10-12 Pound Brisket
- 1 Bottle Sweet Rib Rub

Directions:
1. Cut away any silver skin or excess fat from the flat muscle and discard. Next, there will be a large, crescent shaped fat section on the flat of the meat.

2. Trim that fat until it is smooth against the meat so that it looks like a seamless transition between the point and flat. Flip the brisket over and trim the fat cap to ¼ inch thick. Slice between the point and the flat and save the flat for later.

3. Generously season the trimmed brisket point on all sides with the Sweet Rib Rub. Allow the brisket to sit for 30 minutes to marinate.

4. Pour the beef broth in the spray bottle and set aside.

5. Supply your smoker with wood pellets and follow the start-up procedure. Preheat the grill, with the lid closed, to 225° F. Place the brisket in the smoker, insert the smoker's attached temperature probe, if you have one, and set the brisket to cook for about 6-8 hours or until the internal temperature reaches 165°F. Spray the brisket with the beef broth every 2 hours to keep it moist.

6. Once the brisket reaches 165°F, remove from the smoker, wrap in peach butcher paper, folding the edges over to form a leakproof seal, and return to the smoker seam-side down for another 3-4 hours, or until the brisket reaches 200°F.

7. Remove the brisket from the smoker and allow it to rest for at least one hour before serving.

Smoked Texas Bbq Brisket

Servings: 8
Cooking Time: 600 Minutes

Ingredients:
- 1 (14-18 lb) whole packer brisket
- Meat Church Holy Cow BBQ Rub
- Meat Church Holy Gospel BBQ Rub

Directions:

1.   Trim any hard fat from all sides of the brisket, being careful not to dig too deep into the meat. Trim the sides of any excess or loose fat. Trim the fat side of the brisket to 1/4 inch thick.

2.   Season all sides evenly with Meat Church Holy Cow Rub. Optionally add a light layer of Meat Church Holy Gospel Rub. Let the brisket sit in the seasoning at room temp for 20 to 30 minutes.

3.   Supply your smoker with wood pellets and follow the start-up procedure. Preheat the grill, with the lid closed, to 275° F.

4.   Place the brisket fat side up on the grill grate. Cook until it reaches an internal temperature of 165°F, about 5 to 6 hours

5.   Remove brisket and wrap tightly in Traeger Butcher Paper.

6.   Place the wrapped brisket back on the grill and cook until it reaches an internal temperature of 204°F, about 3-4 hours. Grill: 275 °F Probe: 204 °F

7.   When the brisket reaches 204°F, remove from grill and let rest for 30 minutes. When ready to eat, unwrap brisket and slice against the grain. Enjoy!

Grilled Double Burgers With Texas Spicy Bbq Sauce

Servings: 4

Cooking Time: 30 Minutes

Ingredients:

- 3 Pound ground beef
- 4 Tablespoon Beef Rub
- 1/2 Pound bacon
- 8 Slices cheddar cheese
- 4 Whole burger buns, for serving
- 1 Cup Texas Spicy BBQ Sauce
- sliced pickles, for serving

Directions:

1.   Form ground beef into eight 1/3 pound patties. Season each patty on both sides with Traeger Beef Rub.

2.   Supply your smoker with wood pellets and follow the start-up procedure. Preheat the grill, with the lid closed, to 350° F.

3.   For the Bacon: Place bacon slices directly on grill grate and cook for 15 to 20 minutes, or until crispy. Grill: 350 °F

4.   Increase the Traeger temperature to 450°F and preheat. Grill: 450 °F

5.   Place burger patties directly on grill grate and cook for 4 minutes on each side, or to desired doneness. Grill: 450 °F

6.   Top each patty with a slice of cheddar cheese and cook, lid closed, until cheese melts.

7.   To serve, spread the Traeger Texas Spicy BBQ Sauce onto each bottom bun and top with the pickles and patty, then repeat with BBQ sauce, pickles, patty, BBQ sauce, and finally the bacon. Top with top bun. Enjoy!

Braised Mediterranean Beef Brisket

Servings: 8

Cooking Time: 720 Minutes

Ingredients:

- 3 Tablespoon dried rosemary
- 2 Tablespoon ground cumin seeds
- 2 Tablespoon Coriander, Dried
- 1 Tablespoon dried oregano
- 2 Teaspoon ground cinnamon
- 1/2 Teaspoon salt
- 8 Pound beef brisket
- 1 Cup beef stock

Directions:

1. For a 6 to 8 lb brisket, plan for 8 to 12 hours of cook time, roughly 90 minutes per pound. A remote probe thermometer is critical to use for brisket.

2. Mix all seasoning together and coat brisket liberally. Wrap in plastic wrap. Let the wrapped brisket sit 12 to 24 hours in the refrigerator. Allow plenty of time for cooking.

3. Supply your smoker with wood pellets and follow the start-up procedure. Preheat the grill, with the lid closed, to 180° F.

4. Place brisket fat side down on the grill grate, insert thermometer probe and smoke for 4 hours.

5. After 4 hours, turn grill up to 250°F and preheat. Grill: 250 °F Probe: 250 °F

6. When internal meat temperature reaches 160°F, remove brisket from the grill and wrap in foil along with beef stock - DO NOT remove thermometer probe.

7. Place foiled brisket back on grill and cook until internal temperature reaches 204°F. Grill: 250 °F Probe: 204 °F

8. Remove brisket and allow it to rest in the foil for at least 30 minutes before slicing. Enjoy!

Lime Carne Asada Tacos

Servings: 4
Cooking Time: 10 Minutes

Ingredients:

* 1/2 Tsp Black Pepper
* 1 Tsp Garlic Powder
* 2 Lime, Juiced
* 1 Tsp Salt
* 1 1/2 Lbs Steak, Skirt
* 8 Tortilla

Directions:

1. Supply your smoker with wood pellets and follow the start-up procedure. Preheat the grill, with the lid closed, to 400° F. Place the steaks on the grill, and grill them for 4-8 minutes, then flip the steaks and grill for an additional 4-8 minutes.

2. Remove steaks from the grill, loosely cover them with foil, and let them sit for 5-10 minutes. Next chop the steaks into pieces and serve with tortillas and any desired toppings.

Zucchini Onion Meatloaf

Servings: 8
Cooking Time: 180 Minutes

Ingredients:

* 3 Pounds Ground Beef
* 1 Pound Italian Sausage
* 1/2 Cup Diced Onion
* 1/2 Cup Diced Green Pepper
* 1 Cup Shredded Fresh Zucchini
* 1 Egg
* 3/4 Cup Ketchup
* 1 Sleeve Crackers, Crushed (Buttery Or Saltine)
* 4 Slices Bread, Cubed
* 1/3 Cup Grated Parmesan Cheese
* 1/4 Teaspoon Each Salt and Pepper to Taste
* Garnish:
* Onion Slices, For Eyes
* 1 Pound Thick Sliced Bacon, for Bandages
* Green Pepper Slices, Nose and Teeth
* Sweet Ketchup Sauce:
* 2 Cups Ketchup
* 1/3 Cup Brown Sugar
* 1 Tablespoon Worcestershire Sauce
* 1/2 Teaspoon Onion Powder
* 1/2 Teaspoon Garlic Powder

Directions:

1. Supply your smoker with wood pellets and follow the start-up procedure. Preheat the grill, with the lid closed, to 350 °F.

2. In a large bowl mix together all ingredients.

3. Place mixture into a 13 x 9 inch baking dish and shape into a skull.

4. Place onion slices on meatloaf where the eyes should beand green pepper slices for teeth.

5. Randomly place bacon slices on meatloaf skull to look like bandages.

6. Bake meatloaf in your grill, covered with foil for 2 hours (drain excess grease if necessary).

7. Remove foil, and continue baking for another hour (drain excess grease if necessary).

8. Meanwhile, in a small saucepan, stir together ketchup, brown sugar, Worcestershire sauce, onion powder,and garlic powder. Put in the grill grate and simmer on low until warm. Baste meatloaf with sauce every 15 minutes during last hour of baking.

9. Serve with remaining sauce.

Chorizo Cheese Stuffed Burgers

Servings: 2
Cooking Time: 45 Minutes

Ingredients:

- 2 Pound ground beef, 80% lean
- 4 Ounce Prime Rib Rub
- 12 Ounce Chorizo
- 2 Slices cheddar cheese
- 4 Whole Brioche Bun
- Tomatoes, sliced
- red onion, sliced
- lettuce, sliced

Directions:

1. Mix 2 lb of 80/20 ground beef in mixing bowl with Traeger Prime Rib Rub.

2. Divide the ground beef into eight 1/4 lb patties. Make one patty the base, lay down 1/4 of a cheese slice, add 3 oz. of chorizo and top with another 1/4 cheese slice. Apply another patty on top and pinch the ends all the way around the burger to seal together the two patties.

3. Repeat until all 4 patties are done.

4. Supply your smoker with wood pellets and follow the start-up procedure. Preheat the grill, with the lid closed, to 325° F.

5. Place burgers on the Traeger for 15 minutes on each side. If desired, top each burger with slice of Cheddar cheese, let melt. Remove from Traeger and let rest for 10 minutes tented with foil.

6. While burgers are resting, brush the brioche buns with melted better and toast for 30-45 seconds on the grill.

7. Remove buns from grill and assemble burger with toppings. Enjoy!

Venison Bbq Burger By Nikki Boxler

Servings: 4
Cooking Time: 12 Minutes

Ingredients:

- 5 Slices bacon
- 1 Pound Venison, ground
- 1/2 Cup 'Que BBQ Sauce
- 1/2 Cup shredded cheddar cheese

Directions:

1. Supply your smoker with wood pellets and follow the start-up procedure. Preheat the grill, with the lid closed, to 350° F.

2. Place bacon slices directly on the grill grate and cook 15 minutes until fat is rendered and

bacon is crispy. Remove from grill and let cool. When bacon is cool, break it into pieces.

3. Combine the venison, barbecue sauce, bacon and cheese into a large bowl. Then mix carefully so that the ingredients are spread evenly.

4. Once mixed, press the ground venison into burger patties.

5. Place patties directly on the grill grate and cook until the internal temperature reaches 165 degrees F, flipping halfway through.

6. Once the burgers are done, pair it with your favorite bun and top with your choice of toppings. I personally don't add a bun or condiments as the burger is so good, you don't need them. Enjoy!

Grilled Lemon Steak Pinwheels

Servings: 4
Cooking Time: 30 Minutes

Ingredients:

- 2 Tablespoons Chophouse Steak Seasoning
- Zest From 2 Lemons
- ¾ Cup Finely Parsley, Chopped
- 1 Pkg Provolone Cheese, Sliced
- 6 Oz Washed Spinach
- 1 Whole 1 ½ Pound Trimmed Hanger, Skirt, Or Steak, Flank

Directions:

1. Cut the steak into two even size pieces. Lay the steak out on a flat work surface and cover with plastic wrap. Using a meat mallet, gently pound the steak until it's at least 4 inches wide and no more than 1/3 inch thick.

2. Season both sides of each steak with Chophouse Seasoning. Lay the provolone cheese first followed by spinach. Beginning at the thinnest end of the steak, roll the steak up around the filling. Repeat with the second steak.

3. Tie a length of butcher's twin around the middle, then one piece around the ends. Cut the rolls in half, then slice the wheels again at the twine. Repeat this process with the second steak.

4. Supply your smoker with wood pellets and follow the start-up procedure. Preheat the grill, with the lid closed, to 400° F.If you're using a gas or charcoal grill, set it up for high heat.

5. Cook the pinwheels cut-side down, flipping once, or until browned on both sides and cooked to your liking, about 10-15 minutes each side for medium rare (135°F). Let the pinwheels rest for 5 minutes before serving.

Smoked Teriyaki Jerky

Servings: 6
Cooking Time: 240 Minutes

Ingredients:

- 1/2 Cup soy sauce
- 1/4 Cup mirin or sweet cooking wine
- 2 Tablespoon sugar
- 3 coins fresh ginger, each ¼ inch thick
- 1 Clove garlic, crushed
- 1/2 Teaspoon onion powder
- 1/2 Teaspoon black pepper
- 2 Pound trimmed beef top or bottom round, sirloin tip, flank steak or wild game

Directions:

1. In a mixing bowl, combine soy sauce, mirin, sugar, ginger, garlic, onion powder and black pepper.

2. With a sharp knife, slice the beef into 1/4 inch thick slices with the grain. This is much easier to do if the meat is partially frozen. Trim off any fat or connective tissue.

3. Put the beef slices in a large resealable plastic bag and pour the marinade over the beef.

Massage the bag so all the slices get coated with the marinade. Seal the bag and refrigerate for several hours or overnight.

4. Supply your smoker with wood pellets and follow the start-up procedure. Preheat the grill, with the lid closed, to 180° F.

5. Remove the beef from the marinade and discard the marinade.

6. Dry the beef slices between paper towels and arrange the meat in a single layer on the grill grate.

7. Smoke on the Traeger for 4 to 5 hours or until the jerky is dry but still pliant when bent. Grill: 180 °F

8. Immediately transfer the jerky to a resealable plastic bag and let it rest for an hour at room temperature.

9. Squeeze the air out of the bag and keep the jerky in the refrigerator. Enjoy!

Lemon Tomahawk Steak

Servings: 2 – 4
Cooking Time: 215 Minutes

Ingredients:
- Apple Corer Or Metal Spoon
- 3 Lbs Gala Apples
- 1 Lemon
- Chop House Steak Rub
- 1 Tbsp Tennessee Apple Butter Rub
- Sugar
- 4 Cups Water

Directions:
1. Supply your smoker with wood pellets and follow the start-up procedure. Preheat the grill, with the lid closed, to 400° F. If using a gas or charcoal grill, set heat to medium-high heat.

2. Core and halve the apples. Place apples skin-side down on a sheet tray and season with Tennessee Apple Butter and set aside.

3. In a cast iron pot, combine the apple cores with the juice and zest from one lemon. Cover the mixture with water, transfer to the grill and bring to a boil. Reduce heat to 225° F. Place the apples directly on the grill grate (skin-side down) and cook for 1 hour.

4. After 1 hour, remove cast iron pot from the grill. Strain liquid, discard cores, return liquid to pot, and whisk in sugar. Cover with lid and return to grill. Allow to simmer for another hour.

5. Add smoked apples to the pot and continue to simmer for 20 minutes. Remove pot from grill and purée apple mixture in a blender. Pour apple purée back into pot and return to grill. Increase heat to 375° F and simmer for 20 minutes. Remove from grill and allow to cool slightly.

6. Reduce heat on grill to 225° F. Season the tomahawk steak with Chop House Steak Rub on both sides. Place the steak on the grill grates, insert a temperature probe, and grill, undisturbed, for 45 minutes, or until the steak reaches an internal temperature of 120°F

7. Remove steak from grill and set aside. Open the Sear Slide on your and increase temperature to 400°F. Return tomahawk to grill and sear over open flames, about 2-3 minutes per side.

8. Pull the steak off the grill and allow it to rest for 10 minutes. Ladle reserved apple butter over steak and serve.

New York Strip Steaks With Blue Cheese Butter

Servings: 4
Cooking Time: 8 Minutes

Ingredients:

* 4 boneless New York strip steaks, each about 12oz (340g) and 1 inch (2.5cm) thick
* coarse salt
* freshly ground black pepper
* for the butter
* 8 tbsp unsalted butter, at room temperature
* 1 garlic clove, peeled and finely minced
* ⅓ cup crumbled blue cheese, mashed with a fork
* 1 tbsp minced chives
* 1 tsp Worcestershire sauce
* ½ tsp fresh coarsely ground black pepper

Directions:

1. Approximately 45 minutes before you're ready to cook, lightly season the steaks on both sides with salt and pepper. Place the steaks on a wire rack on a rimmed sheet pan.
2. Supply your smoker with wood pellets and follow the start-up procedure. Preheat the grill, with the lid closed, to 450° F.
3. In a small bowl, make the blue cheese butter by combining the ingredients. Mix thoroughly. Set aside.
4. Place the steaks on the grate at an angle to the bars. Sear until the internal temperature reaches 130°F (54°C), about 3 to 4 minutes per side, turning once.
5. Transfer the steaks to a platter and immediately top with a spoonful of room temperature blue cheese butter. Tent the steaks with aluminum foil for 2 to 3 minutes to encourage the butter to melt before serving.

Bbq Brisket Breakfast Tacos

Servings: 6
Cooking Time: 30 Minutes

Ingredients:

* 4 Pound leftover beef brisket
* 1/2 Teaspoon extra-virgin olive oil
* 1 green bell pepper, diced
* 1 Yellow Bell Pepper, diced
* 10 eggs
* 1/2 Cup milk
* salt and pepper
* 2 Cup shredded cheddar cheese
* flour tortillas

Directions:

1. Supply your smoker with wood pellets and follow the start-up procedure. Preheat the grill, with the lid closed, to 375° F.
2. Place leftover brisket in a double layer of foil and warm in grill. Grill: 375 °F
3. Coat the inside of a cast iron skillet with oil and preheat the skillet in the grill for 10 minutes. When skillet is hot, sauté diced peppers, stirring every few minutes until desired doneness.
4. While peppers are cooking, whisk together the eggs, milk, salt and pepper to taste. Add the beaten eggs to the skillet and scramble. Add cheese to the skillet when the eggs are almost done.
5. Remove eggs and heated brisket from grill. Serve eggs in a tortilla topped with brisket. Top with salsa or guacamole if desired. Enjoy!

Crusted Prime Rib With Rosemary

Servings: 4-6
Cooking Time: 180 Minutes

Ingredients:

- 4-6 garlic, cloves
- 1/3 cup olive oil
- chop house steak seasoning
- 7 pound, boned tied and rolled prime rib roast
- 3 tablespoon rosemary, fresh
- 3 tablespoon thyme, fresh sprigs

Directions:

1. In a food processor, blend together the garlic, rosemary, thyme, sage, and oil until a rough paste forms. Place the prime rib on a sheet pan over a wire rack and rub the prime rib generously with the herb paste on all sides.

2. Season the prime rib with Chop House Steak Seasoning generously on all sides, then chill uncovered in the refrigerator overnight, or for 12 hours.

3. Once the prime rib has chilled for 12 hours, supply your smoker with wood pellets and follow the start-up procedure. Preheat the grill, with the lid closed, to 250° F, and grill for 2 hours or until the internal temperature of the roast reaches 110°F, then increase the temperature to 400 and grill for an additional 15-30 minutes, or until the internal temperature reaches 125 - 140°F.

4. Remove the prime rib from the grill, cover tightly in foil and allow to rest for 30 minutes. The final temperature of the prime rib should be 125 - 140°F after resting. Serve and enjoy!

Asian Steak Skewers

Servings: 6

Cooking Time: 80 Minutes

Ingredients:

- 1 1/2 lbs top sirloin steak
- 6 garlic cloves, minced
- 1 red onion
- 1/3 cup sugar
- 3/4 cup soy sauce
- 1 tbsp ground ginger
- 1/4 cup sesame oil
- 3 tbsp sesame seeds
- 1/4 cup vegetable oil
- Bamboo skewers

Directions:

1. Cut sirloin steak into cubes, about 1 inch.

2. Cut red onion into chunks similar in size to the sirloin steak cubes.

3. In a bowl, combine and whisk soy sauce, sesame oil, vegetable oil, minced garlic, sugar, ginger, and sesame seeds.

4. Add steak to sauce bowl and toss to coat until steak is covered in the sauce.

5. Marinate for at least 1 hour in a refrigerator (if you are in a rush it's ok to skip this part, but you'll sacrifice a little bit of flavor).

6. Preheat pellet grill to 350°F.

7. Thread marinated beef and red onion pieces onto bamboo skewers.

8. Grill the skewers, turning after about 4 minutes. Cook for 8 minutes total or until meat reaches your desired doneness.

Smoked Beef Back Ribs

Servings: 6
Cooking Time: 480 Minutes

Ingredients:

- 2 Rack beef back ribs
- 1/2 Cup Beef Rub

Directions:

1. If your butcher has not already done so, remove the thin papery membrane from the bone-side of the ribs by working the tip of a butter knife underneath the membrane over a middle bone. Use paper towels to get a firm grip, then tear the membrane off.

2. Season both sides of ribs with Traeger Beef Rub.

3. Supply your smoker with wood pellets and follow the start-up procedure. Preheat the grill, with the lid closed, to 225° F.

4. Arrange the ribs on the grill grate, bone side down. Cook for 8-10 hours, or until internal temperature reaches 205℉. Grill: 225 ℉ Probe: 205 ℉

5. Remove ribs from grill and let rest, lightly covered for 20 minutes before slicing and serving. Enjoy!

Diva Q's Herb-crusted Prime Rib

Servings: 4
Cooking Time: 300 Minutes

Ingredients:

- 1/4 Cup fresh rosemary leaves
- 1/4 Cup fresh flat-leaf parsley leaves
- 1/4 Cup minced garlic
- 1/4 Cup canola oil
- 3 Tablespoon Dijon mustard
- 2 Tablespoon finely ground black pepper
- 2 Tablespoon kosher salt
- 1 (5-7 lb) bone-in prime rib roast

Directions:

1. Combine rosemary, parsley, garlic, canola oil, mustard, salt and pepper in a food processor. Pulse until the herbs are finely chopped and the ingredients are combined.

2. Coat the entire prime rib with the herb mixture. Refrigerate prime rib uncovered, for 4 hours.

3. Supply your smoker with wood pellets and follow the start-up procedure. Preheat the grill, with the lid closed, to 250° F.

4. Place the prime rib bone side down on the grill. Roast meat (allowing 12 to 15 minutes per pound) until the internal temperature in the thickest part of the prime rib reaches 120℉-130℉ for rare to medium-rare, about 5 hours. Begin taking the internal temperature every 45 minutes after the 2 hour mark. Grill: 250 ℉ Probe: 120 ℉

5. Remove the prime rib from the grill, tent loosely with foil and let rest for 15 minutes before slicing. Enjoy!

Lamb Chopswith Lemon Vinaigrette

Servings: 4
Cooking Time: 16 Minutes

Ingredients:

- 8 lamb rib chops, about 2lb (1kg) total and each about ¾ inch (2cm) thick
- 3 tbsp extra virgin olive oil
- coarse salt
- freshly ground black pepper
- for the vinaigrette
- 4 lemons, halved
- 1 tbsp plus 1 cup extra virgin olive oil, plus more
- 4 large basil leaves, coarsely chopped
- 1 garlic clove, peeled and coarsely chopped
- 1 tsp Dijon mustard
- 1 tsp honey
- 1 tsp coarse salt

- ½ tsp freshly ground black pepper, plus more

Directions:

1. Supply your smoker with wood pellets and follow the start-up procedure. Preheat the grill, with the lid closed, to 450° F.

2. Coat the lamb chops on each side with the olive oil. Season with salt and pepper. (For the best crust, do this 45 minutes before grilling.)

3. Begin making the vinaigrette by brushing the lemon halves with 1 tablespoon of olive oil. Place the halves cut sides down on the grate and grill until they exhibit some charring, about 6 to 8 minutes. Transfer the lemons to a bowl and let cool.

4. Juice 4 lemon halves through a strainer positioned over a blender. (Reserve the remaining lemon halves for garnishing.) Add the basil leaves, garlic, mustard, honey, and salt and pepper to the blender. Add ¼ cup of olive oil and blend until the garlic is minced and everything's well combined. While the machine's running, slowly add the remaining ¾ cup of olive oil. Taste for seasoning, adding more salt. (If the dressing is too tart, add a little more honey or olive oil—the latter 1 tablespoon at a time.) Transfer the vinaigrette to a pitcher or a cruet.

5. Place the lamb chops on the still-hot grate at an angle to the bars. Grill until the chops have grill marks and the internal temperature reaches 125 to 135°F (52 to 57°C), about 3 to 4 minutes per side.

6. Transfer the chops to a platter and let rest for 3 minutes. Drizzle the lemon vinaigrette over the top. Place 1 reserved lemon half on each plate before serving.

Sweet Heat Burnt Ends

Servings: 8-10
Cooking Time: 360 Minutes

Ingredients:

- 1 (6-pound) brisket point
- 2 tablespoons yellow mustard
- 1 batch Sweet Brown Sugar Rub
- 2 tablespoons honey
- 1 cup barbecue sauce
- 2 tablespoons light brown sugar

Directions:

1. Supply your smoker with wood pellets and follow the start-up procedure. Preheat the grill, with the lid closed, to 225°F.

2. Using a boning knife, carefully remove all but about ½ inch of the large layer of fat covering one side of your brisket point.

3. Coat the point all over with mustard and season it with the rub. Using your hands, work the rub into the meat.

4. Place the point directly on the grill grate and smoke until its internal temperature reaches 165°F.

5. Pull the brisket from the grill and wrap it completely in aluminum foil or butcher paper.

6. Increase the grill's temperature to 350°F and return the wrapped brisket to it. Continue to cook until its internal temperature reaches 185°F.

7. Remove the point from the grill, unwrap it, and cut the meat into 1-inch cubes. Place the cubes in an aluminum pan and stir in the honey, barbecue sauce, and brown sugar.

8. Place the pan in the grill and smoke the beef cubes for 1 hour more, uncovered. Remove the burnt ends from the grill and serve immediately.

Smoked Corned Beef Reuben

Servings: 4

Cooking Time: 255 Minutes

Ingredients:

- aluminum foil
- 1 tbsp butter
- 1 cup chicken stock
- 3 lbs corned beef brisket
- 3 tbsp dijon mustard
- 1/2 cup russian dressing
- 1 cup sauerkraut
- 6 slices sourdough bread
- 6 swiss cheese, sliced
- vegetable oil

Directions:

1. Supply your smoker with wood pellets and follow the start-up procedure. Preheat the grill, with the lid closed, to 250° F. If using a gas or charcoal grill, set it up for low, indirect heat.

2. Coat all sides of corned beef brisket flat generously in mustard. Insert a temperature probe into the middle of the brisket flat, then transfer the brisket flat directly on grill grate, fat cap up, and cook for 2 hours.

3. Remove the brisket from the grill and place it in a pan lined with foil, or a disposable aluminum pan. Add chicken stock, then cover with foil and return to the grill.

4. Increase grill temperature to 300°F, and cook an additional 1 ½ to 2 hours, or until brisket is tender and reaches 190°F.

5. Remove from grill and allow brisket to rest for 15 minutes, then slice thin for Reuben sandwiches.

6. Preheat KC Combo griddle to medium-low flame. If using a gas or charcoal grill, preheat a cast iron skillet on medium-low heat.

7. Grease griddle with butter, then set 4 slices of sourdough on griddle, followed by 2 portions of sliced corned beef brisket. Warm brisket 1 to 2 minutes, then flip. Add sauerkraut and 1 ½ slices of Swiss cheese per portion. Close griddle lid for 2 to 3 minutes to melt cheese and crisp up underside of brisket.

8. Spoon dressing on sourdough, then set brisket on every other slice. Set remaining toasted sourdough on top of cheese to complete the Reuben sandwich.

9. Remove from griddle, then repeat with remaining 2 portions. Slice each sandwich on the bias and serve warm with extra dressing for dipping.

Beef Chuck Ribs

Servings: 4

Cooking Time: 300 Minutes

Ingredients:

- ½ cup yellow or Dijon mustard
- 2 tbsp Worcestershire sauce
- 8 bone-in beef chuck ribs, about 2 to 2½lb (1 to 1.2kg) total coarse salt
- fresh coarsely ground black pepper
- steak sauce or Horseradish Sauce
- for the mop sauce
- 1 cup low-carb beer or sugar-free dark-colored soda
- ½ cup cold brewed coffee
- 2 tbsp light soy sauce or liquid aminos
- 2 tbsp unsalted butter, melted

Directions:

1. Supply your smoker with wood pellets and follow the start-up procedure. Preheat the grill, with the lid closed, to 250° F.

2. In a food-safe spray bottle, make the mop sauce by combining the ingredients. Set aside.

3. In a small bowl, combine the mustard and Worcestershire sauce. Lightly brush the mixture on the meaty sides of the short ribs. Season with salt and pepper.

4. Place the ribs bone side down on the grate and smoke until the internal temperature reaches 200°F (93°C), about 4 to 5 hours. Occasionally spritz the meat with the mop sauce after the first hour—about every 30 minutes.

5. Transfer the short ribs to a platter. Serve with steak sauce.

Grilled Balsamic & Blue Steak

Servings: 2
Cooking Time: 12 Minutes

Ingredients:

- 3 Tablespoon olive oil
- 6 Tablespoon balsamic vinegar
- 1 Tablespoon Prime Rib Rub
- 4 Clove garlic, minced
- 1 1/2 Pound top round London broil steak
- 1/4 Cup butter
- 1/4 Cup crumbled blue cheese
- 2 Whole red onion
- 2 Whole Tomatoes, sliced

Directions:

1. Add the olive oil, balsamic vinegar, Prime Rib Rub, thyme, rosemary, and 3 cloves of garlic to a large bowl, whisking to combine. Place the steak in a large, plastic zipper bag. Pour the mixture over the steak, seal the bag, and marinate in the refrigerator for a minimum of 4 hours, or overnight.

2. Remove the steak from the refrigerator 45 minutes before grilling to bring it to room temperature.

3. Combine the butter, blue cheese, and 1 clove of garlic in a small bowl. Mix well. Refrigerate until ready to serve.

4. Supply your smoker with wood pellets and follow the start-up procedure. Preheat the grill, with the lid closed, to 450° F.

5. Place the steak towards the front of the grill grate for 6 minutes on each side to give it a sear, for medium rare (Place in the middle of the grill grate for a few more minutes if you prefer your steak medium or well). Remove from heat and rest for 10-15 minutes.

6. Brush the onion and tomato slices with olive oil, sprinkle with salt and pepper, place towards the front of the grill until they develop slight grill marks, then move them to the middle for 4 more minutes.

7. Slice the steak against the grain, with the grilled onions and tomatoes, a sprinkling of additional rosemary, and a dollop of blue cheese butter. Enjoy!

Baked Ziti With Italian Sausage

Servings: 6
Cooking Time: 20 Minutes

Ingredients:

- 1 Pound Ziti, cooked 1 minute less than directions, and dried
- 1 Jar Spaghetti Sauce
- 1 Teaspoon garlic, minced
- 1 Pinch red pepper flakes
- 1 Pound Italian Sausage, cooked
- salt and pepper
- 2 Cup Mozzarella Cheese, Grated

- 1/4 Cup Parmesan cheese

Directions:

1. Supply your smoker with wood pellets and follow the start-up procedure. Preheat the grill, with the lid closed, to 450° F.

2. In a large bowl, pour your spaghetti sauce over the cooked pasta, add garlic, red pepper flakes, and salt and pepper to taste. Toss. Fold the sausage into the pasta mixture.

3. Coat a 9 x 13 x 2-inch baking dish with nonstick cooking spray.

4. Pour half of the pasta mixture into your prepared baking dish. Sprinkle with half of the mozzarella. Pour remaining pasta into the dish, smooth out the top and add the remaining mozzarella.

5. Bake in Traeger until cheese is golden brown and bubbly, about 20 minutes.

6. Remove and sprinkle with parmesan cheese. Enjoy!

Green Bell Pepper Cheese Steak Burger

Servings: 4
Cooking Time: 30 Minutes

Ingredients:
- 4 Burger Buns
- 1 Green Bell Pepper, Sliced
- 1 Pound Ground Beef
- 1 Tablespoon Olive Oil
- 1 Tablespoon Chop House Steak Seasoning
- 4 Provolone Cheese, Sliced

Directions:

1. In a large bowl, mix the ground beef and Chop House Steal seasoning together until well combined. Form into patties. Supply your smoker with wood pellets and follow the start-up procedure. Preheat the grill, with the lid closed, to 350° F and grill for 5-7 minutes, flipping halfway through. Once you flip the burgers, top with a slice of provolone cheese.

2. Once the burgers have cooked to your desired degree of doneness, remove from the grill and set aside.

3. For the pepper and onion: in a sauté pan over medium heat, heat the olive oil until it shimmers, then add the onion and pepper. Cook until the pepper and onion are soft and start to caramelize and develop a little char, about 15 minutes.

Georgia Smoked Onion Brisket Sandwich

Servings: 4
Cooking Time: 450 Minutes

Ingredients:
- ½ Cup Barbecue Sauce
- ¼ Cup Beef Broth
- 2 Tablespoons Bourbon
- 1, 3 Pound Brisket Flat, Trimmed
- 4 Kaiser Rolls
- ½ Cup Peach Preserves
- Sliced Pickles
- 4 Tablespoons Pulled Pork Rub
- Sliced White Onions

Directions:

1. Supply your smoker with wood pellets and follow the start-up procedure. Preheat the grill, with the lid closed, to 225° F.

2. Generously rub the brisket with the Pulled Pork Rub. Set aside.

3. In a bowl, mix together the barbecue sauce, peach preserves and bourbon. Set aside.

4. Place the brisket in the smoker and smoke for 5 hours, or until the internal temperature reaches 170°F. Once the brisket reaches temperature, remove from the smoker, place the brisket in foil and pour the beef broth over the top. Wrap the brisket tightly in aluminum foil and return to the smoker for another 2 hours, or until the internal temperature reaches 190°F.

5. Remove the brisket from the grill, unwrap the brisket, discard the foil, and brush the brisket generously with the peach glaze mixture. Place the brisket back on the smoker and smoke for 30 minutes, or until the brisket is shiny and glazed. Remove the brisket from the grill and rest for 10 minutes, covered in foil.

6. Once the brisket has rested, slice thickly against the grain and top the Kaiser rolls with the brisket slices, onion slices and pickle slices. Serve immediately.

APPETIZERS AND SNACKS

Chicken Wings With Teriyaki Glaze

Servings: 4
Cooking Time: 50 Minutes

Ingredients:

- 16 large chicken wings, about 3lb (1.4kg) total
- 1 to 1½ tbsp toasted sesame oil
- for the glaze
- ½ cup light soy sauce or tamari
- ¼ cup sake or sugar-free dark-colored soda
- ¼ cup light brown sugar or low-carb substitute
- 2 tbsp mirin or 1 tbsp honey
- 1 garlic clove, peeled, minced or grated
- 2 tsp minced fresh ginger
- 1 tsp cornstarch mixed with 1 tbsp distilled water (optional)
- for serving
- 1 tbsp toasted sesame seeds
- 2 scallions, trimmed, white and green parts sliced sharply diagonally

Directions:

1. Supply your smoker with wood pellets and follow the start-up procedure. Preheat the grill, with the lid closed, to 350° F.
2. Place the chicken wings in a large bowl, add the sesame oil, and turn the wings to coat thoroughly.
3. Place the wings on the grate at an angle to the bars. Grill for 20 minutes and then turn. Continue to cook until the wings are nicely browned and the meat is no longer pink at the bone, about 20 minutes more.
4. To make the glaze, in a saucepan on the stovetop over medium-high heat, combine the ingredients and bring the mixture to a boil. Reduce the glaze by 1/3, about 6 to 8 minutes. If you prefer your glaze to be glossy and thick, add the cornstarch and water mixture to the glaze and cook until it coats the back of a spoon, about 1 to 2 minutes more.
5. Transfer the wings to an aluminum foil roasting pan. Pour the glaze over them, turning to coat thoroughly. Place the pan on the grate and cook the wings until the glaze sets, about 5 to 10 minutes.
6. Transfer the wings to a platter. Scatter the sesame seeds and scallions over the top. Serve with plenty of napkins.

Bacon-wrapped Jalapeño Poppers

Servings: 12
Cooking Time: 30 Minutes

Ingredients:

- 8 ounces cream cheese, softened
- ½ cup shredded Cheddar cheese
- ¼ cup chopped scallions
- 1 teaspoon chipotle chile powder or regular chili powder
- 1 teaspoon garlic powder
- 1 teaspoon salt
- 18 large jalapeño peppers, stemmed, seeded, and halved lengthwise
- 1 pound bacon (precooked works well)

Directions:

1. Supply your smoker with wood pellets and follow the start-up procedure. Preheat, with the

lid closed, to 350°F. Line a baking sheet with aluminum foil.

2. In a small bowl, combine the cream cheese, Cheddar cheese, scallions, chipotle powder, garlic powder, and salt.

3. Stuff the jalapeño halves with the cheese mixture.

4. Cut the bacon into pieces big enough to wrap around the stuffed pepper halves.

5. Wrap the bacon around the peppers and place on the prepared baking sheet.

6. Put the baking sheet on the grill grate, close the lid, and smoke the peppers for 30 minutes, or until the cheese is melted and the bacon is cooked through and crisp.

7. Let the jalapeño poppers cool for 3 to 5 minutes. Serve warm.

Bacon Pork Pinwheels (kansas Lollipops)

Servings: 4-6
Cooking Time: 20 Minutes

Ingredients:
- 1 Whole Pork Loin, boneless
- To Taste salt and pepper
- To Taste Greek Seasoning
- 4 Slices bacon
- To Taste The Ultimate BBQ Sauce

Directions:

1. When ready to cook, start the smoker and set temperature to 500F. Preheat, lid closed, for 10 to 15 minutes.

2. Trim pork loin of any unwanted silver skin or fat. Using a sharp knife, cut pork loin length wise, into 4 long strips.

3. Lay pork flat, then season with salt, pepper and Cavender's Greek Seasoning.

4. Flip the pork strips over and layer bacon on unseasoned side. Begin tightly rolling the pork strips, with bacon being rolled up on the inside.

5. Secure a skewer all the way through each pork roll to secure it in place. Set the pork rolls down on grill and cook for 15 minutes.

6. Brush BBQ Sauce over the pork. Turn each skewer over, then coat the other side. Let pork cook for another 5-10 minutes, depending on thickness of your pork. Enjoy!

Bayou Wings With Cajun Rémoulade

Servings: 8
Cooking Time: 40 Minutes

Ingredients:
- 16 large whole chicken wings or 32 drumettes and flats, about 3lb (1.4kg) total
- for the rub
- 1 tbsp kosher salt
- 1 tsp freshly ground black pepper
- 1 tsp paprika
- ½ tsp ground cayenne, plus more
- ½ tsp garlic powder
- ½ tsp celery salt
- ½ tsp dried thyme
- 2 tbsp vegetable oil
- for the rémoulade
- 1¼ cups reduced-fat mayo
- ¼ cup Creole-style or whole grain mustard
- 2 tbsp horseradish
- 2 tbsp pickle relish
- 1 tbsp freshly squeezed lemon juice
- 1 tsp paprika, plus more
- 1 tsp hot sauce, plus more
- 1 tsp Worcestershire sauce
- coarse salt

- for serving
- lemon wedges
- pickled okra (optional)

Directions:

1. Supply your smoker with wood pellets and follow the start-up procedure. Preheat the grill, with the lid closed, to 350° F.

2. If using whole wings, cut through the two joints, separating them into drumettes, flats, and wing tips. (Discard the wing tips or save them for chicken stock.) Alternatively, leave the wings whole. Place the chicken in a resealable plastic bag.

3. In a small bowl, make the rub by combining the ingredients. Mix well. Pour the rub over the wings and toss them to thoroughly coat. Refrigerate for 2 hours.

4. In a small bowl, make the Cajun rémoulade by whisking together the mayo, mustard, horseradish, pickle relish, lemon juice, paprika, hot sauce, and Worcestershire. Season with salt to taste. The mixture should be highly seasoned. Transfer to a serving bowl and lightly dust with paprika. Cover and refrigerate until ready to serve.

5. Remove the wings from the refrigerator and allow the excess marinade to drip off. Place the wings on the grate at an angle to the bars. Grill for 20 minutes and then turn. (They'll brown more evenly but will also have less of a tendency to stick.) Continue to cook until the wings are nicely browned and the meat is no longer pink at the bone, about 20 minutes more.

6. Remove the wings from the grill and pile them on a platter. Serve with the Cajun rémoulade, lemon wedges, and pickled okra (if using).

Pulled Pork Loaded Nachos

Servings: 4
Cooking Time: 10 Minutes

Ingredients:
- 2 cups leftover smoked pulled pork
- 1 small sweet onion, diced
- 1 medium tomato, diced
- 1 jalapeño pepper, seeded and diced
- 1 garlic clove, minced
- 1 teaspoon salt
- 1 teaspoon freshly ground black pepper
- 1 bag tortilla chips
- 1 cup shredded Cheddar cheese
- ½ cup The Ultimate BBQ Sauce, divided
- ½ cup shredded jalapeño Monterey Jack cheese
- Juice of ½ lime
- 1 avocado, halved, pitted, and sliced
- 2 tablespoons sour cream
- 1 tablespoon chopped fresh cilantro

Directions:

1. Supply your smoker with wood pellets and follow the start-up procedure. Preheat, with the lid closed, to 375°F.

2. Heat the pulled pork in the microwave.

3. In a medium bowl, combine the onion, tomato, jalapeño, garlic, salt, and pepper, and set aside.

4. Arrange half of the tortilla chips in a large cast iron skillet. Spread half of the warmed pork on top and cover with the Cheddar cheese. Top with half of the onion-jalapeño mixture, then drizzle with ¼ cup of barbecue sauce.

5. Layer on the remaining tortilla chips, then the remaining pork and the Monterey Jack cheese. Top with the remaining onion-jalapeño mixture

and drizzle with the remaining ¼ cup of barbecue sauce.

6. Place the skillet on the grill, close the lid, and smoke for about 10 minutes, or until the cheese is melted and bubbly. (Watch to make sure your chips don't burn!)

7. Squeeze the lime juice over the nachos, top with the avocado slices and sour cream, and garnish with the cilantro before serving hot.

Citrus-infused Marinated Olives

Servings: 6
Cooking Time: 30 Minutes

Ingredients:

- 1½ cups mixed brined olives, with pits
- ½ cup extra virgin olive oil
- 1 tbsp freshly squeezed lemon juice
- 1 garlic clove, peeled and thinly sliced
- 1 tsp smoked Spanish paprika
- 2 sprigs of fresh rosemary
- 2 sprigs of fresh thyme
- 2 bay leaves, fresh or dried
- 1 small dried red chili pepper, deseeded and flesh crumbled, or ¼ tsp crushed red pepper flakes
- 3 strips of orange zest
- 3 strips of lemon zest

Directions:

1. Supply your smoker with wood pellets and follow the start-up procedure. Preheat the grill, with the lid closed, to 180° F.

2. Drain the olives, reserving 1 tablespoon of brine. Spread the olives in a single layer in an aluminum foil roasting pan. Place the pan on the grate and cook the olives for 30 minutes, stirring the olives or shaking the pan once or twice.

3. In a small saucepan on the stovetop over low heat, warm the olive oil. Whisk in the lemon juice and the reserved 1 tablespoon of brine. Stir in the garlic and paprika. Add the rosemary, thyme, bay leaves, chili pepper, and orange and lemon zests. Warm over low heat for 10 minutes. Remove the saucepan from the heat.

4. Transfer the olives and olive oil mixture to a pint jar. Tuck the aromatics around the sides of the jar. Let cool and then cover and refrigerate for up to 5 days. Let the olives come to room temperature before serving.

Chorizo Queso Fundido

Servings: 4-6
Cooking Time: 20 Minutes

Ingredients:

- 1 poblano chile
- 1 cup chopped queso quesadilla or queso Oaxaca
- 1 cup shredded Monterey Jack cheese
- ¼ cup milk
- 1 tablespoon all-purpose flour
- 2 (4-ounce) links Mexican chorizo sausage, casings removed
- ⅓ cup beer
- 1 tablespoon unsalted butter
- 1 small red onion, chopped
- ½ cup whole kernel corn
- 2 serrano chiles or jalapeño peppers, stemmed, seeded, and coarsely chopped
- 1 tablespoon minced garlic
- 1 tablespoon freshly squeezed lime juice
- 1 teaspoon ground cumin
- 1 teaspoon salt
- 1 teaspoon freshly ground black pepper
- 1 tablespoon chopped fresh cilantro
- 1 tablespoon chopped scallions
- Tortilla chips, for serving

Directions:

1. Supply your smoker with wood pellets and follow the start-up procedure. Preheat, with the lid closed, to 350°F.

2. On the smoker or over medium-high heat on the stove top, place the poblano directly on the grate (or burner) to char for 1 to 2 minutes, turning as needed. Remove from heat and place in a closed-up lunch-size paper bag for 2 minutes to sweat and further loosen the skin.

3. Remove the skin and coarsely chop the poblano, removing the seeds; set aside.

4. In a bowl, combine the queso quesadilla, Monterey Jack, milk, and flour; set aside.

5. On the stove top, in a cast iron skillet over medium heat, cook and crumble the chorizo for about 2 minutes.

6. Transfer the cooked chorizo to a small, grill-safe pan and place over indirect heat on the smoker.

7. Place the cast iron skillet on the preheated grill grate. Pour in the beer and simmer for a few minutes, loosening and stirring in any remaining sausage bits from the pan.

8. Add the butter to the pan, then add the cheese mixture a little at a time, stirring constantly.

9. When the cheese is smooth, stir in the onion, corn, serrano chiles, garlic, lime juice, cuvmin, salt, and pepper. Stir in the reserved chopped charred poblano.

10. Close the lid and smoke for 15 to 20 minutes to infuse the queso with smoke flavor and further cook the vegetables.

11. When the cheese is bubbly, top with the chorizo mixture and garnish with the cilantro and scallions.

12. Serve the chorizo queso fundido hot with tortilla chips.

Grilled Guacamole

Servings: 6
Cooking Time: 30 Minutes

Ingredients:

- 3 large avocados, halved and pitted
- 1 lime, halved
- ½ jalapeño, deseeded and deveined
- ½ small white or red onion, peeled
- 2 garlic cloves, peeled and skewered on a toothpick
- 1 tsp coarse salt, plus more
- 1½ tbsp reduced-fat mayo
- 2 tbsp chopped fresh cilantro
- 2 tbsp crumbled queso fresco (optional)
- tortilla chips

Directions:

1. Supply your smoker with wood pellets and follow the start-up procedure. Preheat the grill, with the lid closed, to 225° F.

2. Place the avocados, lime, jalapeño, and onion cut sides down on the grate. Use the toothpicks to balance the garlic cloves between the bars. Smoke for 30 minutes. (You want the vegetables to retain most of their rawness.)

3. Transfer everything to a cutting board. Remove the garlic cloves from the toothpick and roughly chop. Sprinkle with the salt and continue to mince the garlic until it begins to form a paste. Scrape the garlic and salt into a large bowl.

4. Scoop the avocado flesh from the peels into the bowl. Squeeze the juice of ½ lime over the avocado. Mash the avocados but leave them somewhat chunky. Finely dice the jalapeño. Dice 2 tablespoons of onion. (Reserve the remaining

onion for another use.) Add the jalapeño, onion, mayo, and cilantro to the bowl. Stir gently to combine. Taste for seasoning, adding more salt, lime juice, and jalapeño as desired.

5. Transfer the guacamole to a serving bowl. Top with the queso fresco (if using). Serve with tortilla chips.

Pigs In A Blanket

Servings: 4-6
Cooking Time: 15 Minutes

Ingredients:
- 2 Tablespoon Poppy Seeds
- 1 Tablespoon Dried Minced Onion
- 2 Teaspoon garlic, minced
- 2 Tablespoon Sesame Seeds
- 1 Teaspoon salt
- 8 Ounce Original Crescent Dough
- 1/4 Cup Dijon mustard
- 1 Large egg, beaten

Directions:
1. When ready to cook, start your smoker at 350 degrees F, and preheat with lid closed, 10 to 15 minutes.
2. Mix together poppy seeds, dried minced onion, dried minced garlic, salt and sesame seeds. Set aside.
3. Cut each triangle of crescent roll dough into thirds lengthwise, making 3 small strips from each roll.
4. Brush the dough strips lightly with Dijon mustard. Put the mini hot dogs on 1 end of the dough and roll up.
5. Arrange them, seam side down, on a greased baking pan. Brush with egg wash and sprinkle with seasoning mixture.

6. Bake in smoker until golden brown, about 12 to 15 minutes.
7. Serve with mustard or dipping sauce of your choice. Enjoy!

Simple Cream Cheese Sausage Balls

Servings: 5
Cooking Time: 30 Minutes

Ingredients:
- 1 pound ground hot sausage, uncooked
- 8 ounces cream cheese, softened
- 1 package mini filo dough shells

Directions:
1. Supply your smoker with wood pellets and follow the start-up procedure. Preheat, with the lid closed, to 350°F.
2. In a large bowl, using your hands, thoroughly mix together the sausage and cream cheese until well blended.
3. Place the filo dough shells on a rimmed perforated pizza pan or into a mini muffin tin.
4. Roll the sausage and cheese mixture into 1-inch balls and place into the filo shells.
5. Place the pizza pan or mini muffin tin on the grill, close the lid, and smoke the sausage balls for 30 minutes, or until cooked through and the sausage is no longer pink.
6. Plate and serve warm.

Deviled Eggs With Smoked Paprika

Servings: 6
Cooking Time: 30 Minutes

Ingredients:
- 6 large eggs

- 3 tbsp reduced-fat mayo, plus more
- 1 tsp Dijon or yellow mustard
- ½ tsp Spanish smoked paprika or regular paprika, plus more
- dash of hot sauce
- coarse salt
- freshly ground black pepper
- for garnishing
- small sprigs of fresh parsley, dill, tarragon, or cilantro
- chopped chives
- minced scallions
- Mustard Caviar
- sliced green or black olives
- celery leaves
- sliced radishes
- diced bell peppers
- sliced cherry tomatoes
- fresh or pickled jalapeños
- sliced or diced pickles
- slivers of sun-dried tomatoes
- bacon crumbles
- smoked salmon
- Hawaiian black salt
- Caviar

Directions:

1. Supply your smoker with wood pellets and follow the start-up procedure. Preheat the grill, with the lid closed, to 180° F.

2. On the stovetop over medium-high heat, bring a saucepan of water to a boil. (Make sure there's enough water in the saucepan to cover the eggs by 1 inch [5cm].) Use a slotted spoon to gently lower the eggs into the water. Lower the heat to maintain a simmer. Set a timer for 13 minutes.

3. Prepare an ice bath by combining ice and cold water in a large bowl. Carefully transfer the eggs to the ice bath when the timer goes off.

4. When the eggs are cool enough to handle, gently tap them all over to crack the shell. Carefully peel the eggs. Rinse under cold running water to remove any clinging bits of shell, but don't dry the eggs. (A damp surface will help the smoke adhere to the egg whites.)

5. Place the eggs on the grate and smoke until the eggs take on a light brown patina from the smoke, about 25 minutes. Transfer the eggs to a cutting board, handling them as little as possible.

6. Slice each egg in half lengthwise with a sharp knife. Wipe any yolk off the blade before slicing the next egg. Gently remove the yolks and place them in a food processor. Pulse to break up the yolks. Add the mayo, mustard, paprika, and hot sauce. Season with salt and pepper to taste. Pulse until the filling is smooth. Add additional mayo 1 teaspoon at a time if the mixture is a little dry. (It shouldn't be too loose either.)

7. Spoon the filling into each egg half or pipe it in using a small resealable plastic bag. You can also use a pastry bag fitted with a fluted tip.

8. Place the eggs on a platter and lightly dust with paprika. Accompany with one or more of the suggested garnishes.

Smoked Cashews

Servings: 6
Cooking Time: 60 Minutes

Ingredients:

- 1 pound roasted, salted cashews

Directions:

1. Supply your smoker with wood pellets and follow the start-up procedure. Preheat the grill, with the lid closed, to 120°F.
2. Pour the cashews onto a rimmed baking sheet and smoke for 1 hour, stirring once about halfway through the smoking time.
3. Remove the cashews from the grill, let cool, and store in an airtight container for as long as you can resist.

Pig Pops (sweet-hot Bacon On A Stick)

Servings: 24
Cooking Time: 30 Minutes

Ingredients:

- Nonstick cooking spray, oil, or butter, for greasing
- 2 pounds thick-cut bacon (24 slices)
- 24 metal skewers
- 1 cup packed light brown sugar
- 2 to 3 teaspoons cayenne pepper
- ½ cup maple syrup, divided

Directions:

1. Supply your smoker with wood pellets and follow the start-up procedure. Preheat, with the lid closed, to 350°F.
2. Coat a disposable aluminum foil baking sheet with cooking spray, oil, or butter.
3. Thread each bacon slice onto a metal skewer and place on the prepared baking sheet.

4. In a medium bowl, stir together the brown sugar and cayenne.
5. Baste the top sides of the bacon with ¼ cup of maple syrup.
6. Sprinkle half of the brown sugar mixture over the bacon.
7. Place the baking sheet on the grill, close the lid, and smoke for 15 to 30 minutes.
8. Using tongs, flip the bacon skewers. Baste with the remaining ¼ cup of maple syrup and top with the remaining brown sugar mixture.
9. Continue smoking with the lid closed for 10 to 15 minutes, or until crispy. You can eyeball the bacon and smoke to your desired doneness, but the actual ideal internal temperature for bacon is 155°F
10. Using tongs, carefully remove the bacon skewers from the grill. Let cool completely before handling.

Chuckwagon Beef Jerky

Servings: 6
Cooking Time: 300 Minutes

Ingredients:

- 2½lb (1.2kg) boneless top or bottom round steak, sirloin tip, flank steak, or venison
- 1 cup sugar-free dark-colored soda
- 1 cup cold brewed coffee
- ½ cup light soy sauce
- ¼ cup Worcestershire sauce
- 2 tbsp whiskey (optional)
- 2 tsp chili powder
- 1½ tsp garlic salt
- 1 tsp onion powder
- 1 tsp pink curing salt

Directions:

1. Slice the meat into ¼-inch-thick (.5cm) strips, trimming off any visible fat or gristle. (Slice against the grain for more tender jerky and with the grain for chewier jerky.) Place the meat in a large resealable plastic bag.

2. In a small bowl, whisk together the soda, coffee, soy sauce, Worcestershire sauce, whiskey (if using), chili powder, garlic salt, onion powder, and curing salt (if using). Whisk until the salt dissolves. Pour the mixture over the meat and reseal the bag. Refrigerate for 24 to 48 hours, turning the bag several times to redistribute the brine.

3. Supply your smoker with wood pellets and follow the start-up procedure. Preheat the grill, with the lid closed, to 150° F.

4. Drain the meat and discard the brine. Place the strips of meat in a single layer on paper towels and blot any excess moisture.

5. Place the meat in a single layer on the grate and smoke for 4 to 5 hours, turning once or twice. (If you're aware of hot spots on your grate, rotate the strips so they smoke evenly.) To test for doneness, bend one or two pieces in the middle. They should be dry but still somewhat pliant. Or simply eat a piece to see if it's done to your liking.

6. For the best texture, when you remove the meat from the grill, place the still-warm jerky in a resealable plastic bag and let rest for 30 minutes. (You might see condensation form on the inside of the bag, but the moisture will be reabsorbed by the meat.) Or let the meat cool completely and then store in a resealable plastic bag or covered container. The jerky will last a few days at room temperature but will last longer (up to 2 weeks) if refrigerated.

Smoked Cheese

Servings: 4
Cooking Time: 150 Minutes

Ingredients:

- 1 (2-pound) block medium Cheddar cheese, or your favorite cheese, quartered lengthwise

Directions:

1. Supply your smoker with wood pellets and follow the start-up procedure. Preheat the grill, with the lid closed, to 90°F.

2. Place the cheese directly on the grill grate and smoke for 2 hours, 30 minutes, checking frequently to be sure it's not melting. If the cheese begins to melt, try flipping it. If that doesn't help, remove it from the grill and refrigerate for about 1 hour and then return it to the cold smoker.

3. Remove the cheese, place it in a zip-top bag, and refrigerate overnight.

4. Slice the cheese and serve with crackers, or grate it and use for making a smoked mac and cheese.

Roasted Red Pepper Dip

Servings: 8
Cooking Time: 45 Minutes

Ingredients:

- 4 red bell peppers, halved, destemmed, and deseeded
- 1 cup English walnuts, divided
- 1 small white onion, peeled and coarsely chopped
- 2 garlic cloves, peeled and smashed with a chef's knife
- ¼ cup extra virgin olive oil, plus more
- 1 tbsp balsamic vinegar or balsamic glaze
- 1 tsp honey (eliminate if using balsamic glaze)

- 1 tsp coarse salt, plus more
- 1 tsp ground cumin
- 1 tsp smoked paprika
- ½ to 1 tsp Aleppo red pepper flakes, plus more
- ¼ cup fresh white breadcrumbs (optional)
- distilled water (optional)
- assorted crudités or wedges of pita bread

Directions:

1. Supply your smoker with wood pellets and follow the start-up procedure. Preheat the grill, with the lid closed, to 400° F.

2. Place the peppers skin side down on the grate and grill until the skins blister and the flesh softens, about 30 minutes. Transfer the peppers to a bowl and cover with plastic wrap. Let cool to room temperature. Remove the skins with a paring knife or your fingers. Coarsely chop or tear the peppers.

3. Place ¾ cup of walnuts in an aluminum foil roasting pan. Place the pan on the grate and toast for 10 to 15 minutes, stirring twice. Remove the pan from the grill and let the walnuts cool.

4. Place the peppers, onion, garlic, and walnuts in a food processor fitted with the chopping blade. Pulse several times. Add the olive oil, balsamic vinegar, honey, salt, cumin, paprika, and red pepper flakes. Process until the mixture is fairly smooth. Taste for seasoning, adding more salt or red pepper flakes (if desired). (If the mixture is too loose, add breadcrumbs until the texture is to your liking. If it's too thick, add olive oil or water 1 tablespoon at a time.)

5. Transfer the dip to a serving bowl. Use the back of a spoon to make a shallow depression in the center. Top with the remaining ¼ cup of walnuts and drizzle olive oil in the depression. Serve with crudités or pita bread.

Delicious Deviled Crab Appetizer

Servings: 30

Cooking Time: 10 Minutes

Ingredients:

- Nonstick cooking spray, oil, or butter, for greasing
- 1 cup panko breadcrumbs, divided
- 1 cup canned corn, drained
- ½ cup chopped scallions, divided
- ½ red bell pepper, finely chopped
- 16 ounces jumbo lump crabmeat
- ¾ cup mayonnaise, divided
- 1 egg, beaten
- 1 teaspoon salt
- 1 teaspoon freshly ground black pepper
- 2 teaspoons cayenne pepper, divided
- Juice of 1 lemon

Directions:

1. Supply your smoker with wood pellets and follow the start-up procedure. Preheat, with the lid closed, to 425°F.

2. Spray three 12-cup mini muffin pans with cooking spray and divide ½ cup of the panko between 30 of the muffin cups, pressing into the bottoms and up the sides. (Work in batches, if necessary, depending on the number of pans you have.)

3. In a medium bowl, combine the corn, ¼ cup of scallions, the bell pepper, crabmeat, half of the mayonnaise, the egg, salt, pepper, and 1 teaspoon of cayenne pepper.

4. Gently fold in the remaining ½ cup of breadcrumbs and divide the mixture between the prepared mini muffin cups.

5. Place the pans on the grill grate, close the lid, and smoke for 10 minutes, or until golden brown.

6. In a small bowl, combine the lemon juice and the remaining mayonnaise, scallions, and cayenne pepper to make a sauce.

7. Brush the tops of the mini crab cakes with the sauce and serve hot.

Smoked Turkey Sandwich

Servings: 1
Cooking Time: 15 Minutes

Ingredients:

- 2 slices sourdough bread
- 2 tablespoons butter, at room temperature
- 2 (1-ounce) slices Swiss cheese
- 4 ounces leftover Smoked Turkey
- 1 teaspoon garlic salt

Directions:

1. Supply your smoker with wood pellets and follow the start-up procedure. Preheat the grill, with the lid closed, to 375°F.

2. Coat one side of each bread slice with 1 tablespoon of butter and sprinkle the buttered sides with garlic salt.

3. Place 1 slice of cheese on each unbuttered side of the bread, and then put the turkey on the cheese.

4. Close the sandwich, buttered sides out, and place it directly on the grill grate. Cook for 5 minutes. Flip the sandwich and cook for 5 minutes more. Remove the sandwich from the grill, cut it in half, and serve.

Sriracha & Maple Cashews

Servings: 10
Cooking Time: 60 Minutes

Ingredients:

- 2 tbsp unsalted butter
- 3 tbsp pure maple syrup
- 1 tbsp sriracha
- 1 tsp coarse salt (use only if nuts are unsalted)
- 2½ cups unsalted cashews

Directions:

1. Supply your smoker with wood pellets and follow the start-up procedure. Preheat the grill, with the lid closed, to 250° F.

2. In a small saucepan on the stovetop over low heat, melt the butter. Add the maple syrup, sriracha, and salt (if using). Stir until combined. Add the nuts and stir gently to coat thoroughly.

3. Spread the nuts in a single layer in an aluminum foil roasting pan coated with cooking spray. Place the pan on the grate and smoke the nuts until they're lightly toasted, about 1 hour, stirring once or twice.

4. Remove the pan from the grill and let the nuts cool for 15 minutes. They'll be sticky at first but will crisp up. Break them up with your fingers and store at room temperature in an airtight container, such as a lidded glass jar.

Jalapeño Poppers With Chipotle Sour Cream

Servings: 8
Cooking Time: 45 Minutes

Ingredients:

- 3 strips of thin-sliced bacon
- 12 large jalapeños, red, green, or a mix
- 8oz (225g) light cream cheese, at room temperature
- 1 cup shredded pepper Jack, Monterey Jack, or Cheddar cheese
- 1 tsp chili powder
- ½ tsp garlic salt

- smoked paprika
- for the sour cream
- 1¼ cups light sour cream
- juice of ½ lime
- ½ to 1 canned chipotle peppers in adobo sauce, finely minced, plus 1 tsp of sauce, plus more
- 1 tbsp minced fresh cilantro leaves
- ½ tsp coarse salt, plus more

Directions:

1. Supply your smoker with wood pellets and follow the start-up procedure. Preheat the grill, with the lid closed, to 375° F.

2. Line a rimmed sheet pan with aluminum foil and place a wire rack on top. Place the bacon in a single layer on the wire rack. Place the pan on the grate and grill until the bacon is crisp and golden brown, about 20 minutes. Transfer the bacon to paper towels to cool and then crumble. Set aside.

3. In a small bowl, make the chipotle sour cream by whisking together the ingredients. Add more salt, chipotle peppers, or adobe sauce to taste. Cover and refrigerate.

4. Slice the jalapeños lengthwise through their stems. Scrape out the veins and seeds with the edge of a small metal spoon.

5. In a small bowl, beat together the cream cheese, shredded cheese, chili powder, and garlic salt. Stir in the crumbled bacon. Mound the cream cheese mixture in the jalapeño halves. Line another rimmed sheet pan with aluminum foil and place a wire rack on top. Place the jalapeños filled side up in a single layer on the wire rack.

6. Place the sheet pan on the grate and roast the jalapeños until the filling has melted and the peppers have softened, about 20 to 25 minutes. (They should no longer look bright in color.)

Remove the pan from the grill and let the peppers rest for 5 minutes.

7. Transfer the poppers to a platter and lightly dust with paprika. Serve with the chipotle sour cream.

Cold-smoked Cheese

Servings: 6
Cooking Time: 180 Minutes

Ingredients:

- 2lb (1kg) well-chilled hard or semi-hard cheese, such as:
- Edam
- Gouda
- Cheddar
- Monterey Jack
- pepper Jack
- goat cheese
- fresh mozzarella
- Muenster
- aged Parmigiano-Reggiano
- Gruyère
- blue cheese

Directions:

1. Unwrap the cheese and remove any protective wax or coating. Cut into 4-ounce (110g) portions to increase the surface area.

2. If possible, move your smoker to a shady area. Place 1 resealable plastic bag filled with ice on top of the drip pan. This is especially important on a warm day because you want to keep the interior temperature of the grill between 70 and 90°F (21 and 32°C) or below.

3. Place a grill mat on one side of the grate. Place the cheese on the mat and allow space between each piece.

4. Fill your smoking tube or pellet maze (see Cast Iron Skillets and Grill Pans) with pellets or sawdust and light according to the manufacturer's instructions. Place the smoking tube on the grate near—but not on—the grill mat. When the tube is smoking consistently, close the grill lid.

5. Smoke the cheese for 1 to 3 hours, replacing the pellets or sawdust and ice if necessary. Monitor the temperature and make sure the cheese isn't beginning to melt. Carefully lift the mat with the cheese to a rimmed baking sheet and let the cheese cool completely before handling.

6. Package the smoked cheese in cheese storage paper or bags or vacuum-seal the cheese, labeling each. (While you can wrap the cheese tightly in plastic wrap, the cheese will spoil faster.) Let the cheese rest for at least 2 to 3 days before eating. It will be even better after 2 weeks.

COCKTAILS RECIPES

Traeger Boulevardier Cocktail

Servings: 2
Cooking Time: 60 Minutes

Ingredients:

- 4 oranges
- 1/2 Cup honey
- 1500 mL rye whiskey
- 1 1/2 Ounce Campari
- 1 1/2 Ounce sweet vermouth
- 2 Tablespoon granulated sugar
- 3 Ounce grilled orange infused rye

Directions:

1. Supply your smoker with wood pellets and follow the start-up procedure. Preheat the grill, with the lid closed, to 350° F.

2. Slice 2 oranges in half and coat cut side with honey. Peel remaining orange and place peels on the grill. Cook 20 to 25 minutes. Grill: 350 °F

3. Remove from grill and let cool. Place orange halves cut side down directly on the grill grate and cook 20 to 30 minutes or until dark grill marks appear. Remove orange halves and allow to cool. Grill: 350 °F

4. Place orange halves into a bottle of rye whiskey and let steep for 10 to 12 hours. The longer they steep, the sweeter and more pronounced the orange flavor will be.

5. Add all ingredients into a mixing glass and stir until diluted. Strain into a fresh coupe glass and serve neat.

6. Garnish with grilled orange peel. Enjoy!

Dublin Delight Cocktail

Servings: 2

Cooking Time: 20 Minutes

Ingredients:

- 2 orange, sliced
- 3 Fluid Ounce Teeling Whiskey
- 1 1/2 Fluid Ounce Smoked Simple Syrup
- 6 Dash aromatic bitters
- 6 Fluid Ounce Guinness beer
- 2 Amarena cherry, for garnish

Directions:

1. Supply your smoker with wood pellets and follow the start-up procedure. Preheat the grill, with the lid closed, to 450° F.

2. Place orange slices directly on the grill grate and cook 20 to 25 minutes. Remove from grill and let cool. Grill: 450 °F

3. In a mixing glass, add whiskey, Traeger Smoked Simple Syrup and bitters. Add ice and shake. Pour over a beer glass filled with ice and top off with cold Guinness.

4. Garnish with a grilled orange slice and Amarena cherry. Enjoy!

In Traeger Fashion Cocktail

Servings: 2
Cooking Time: 20 Minutes

Ingredients:

- 2 Whole orange peel
- 2 Whole lemon peel
- 3 Ounce bourbon
- 1 Ounce Smoked Simple Syrup
- 6 Dash Bitters Lab Charred Cedar & Currant Bitters

Directions:

1. Supply your smoker with wood pellets and follow the start-up procedure. Preheat the grill, with the lid closed, to 350° F.

2. Place the lemon and orange peel directly on the grill grate and cook 20 to 25 minutes or until lightly browned. Grill: 350 °F

3. Add bourbon, Traeger Smoked Simple Syrup and bitters to a mixing glass and stir over ice. Stir until glass is chilled and contents are well diluted.

4. Strain into a new glass over fresh ice and garnish with grilled lemon and orange peel. Enjoy!

Smoked Pumpkin Spice Latte

Servings: 4
Cooking Time: 45 Minutes

Ingredients:

- 1 Small sugar pumpkin
- olive oil
- 1 Can sweetened condensed milk
- 1 Cup whole milk
- 2 Tablespoon Smoked Simple Syrup
- 1 Teaspoon pumpkin pie spice
- pinch of salt
- cinnamon
- whipped cream
- shaved nutmeg
- 8 Ounce smoked cold brew coffee

Directions:

1. Supply your smoker with wood pellets and follow the start-up procedure. Preheat the grill, with the lid closed, to 325° F.

2. Cut the sugar pumpkin in half, scoop out the seeds and discard. Place the pumpkin halves cut side up on a baking sheet and brush lightly with olive oil.

3. Place the sheet tray directly on the grill grate and cook 45 minutes or until the flesh is tender.

Remove from heat and place on the counter to cool. Grill: 325 °F

4. When the pumpkin is cool enough to handle, scoop out the flesh and mash until smooth.

5. Place 3 Tbsp of the pumpkin puree in a separate bowl and reserve the remaining for another use.

6. Add the sweetened condensed milk, whole milk, Traeger Smoked Simple Syrup, pumpkin pie seasoning and salt to the pumpkin puree. Whisk to combine.

7. Pour the cold brew over ice, add desired amount of pumpkin spice creamer and top with whipped cream, cinnamon, and shaved nutmeg if desired. Enjoy!

Smoked Jacobsen Salt Margarita

Servings: 2
Cooking Time: 1 Day

Ingredients:

- kosher sea salt
- 3 Cup Jacobsen Co. Honey
- 6 Ounce tequila
- 4 Ounce fresh squeezed lime juice
- 1/2 Cup Jacobsen Salt Co. Cherrywood Smoked Salt or smoked kosher salt
- 2 Ounce simple syrup
- 2 Teaspoon orange liqueur

Directions:

1. If making your own smoked salt, take kosher sea salt (however much you want to smoke) and spread it out on a tray.

2. Supply your smoker with wood pellets and follow the start-up procedure. Preheat the grill, with the lid closed, to 165° F.

3. Place tray of salt directly on the grill grate and smoke for about 24 hours, stirring the salt every 8

hours. Once it has smoked for 24 hours, take off grill and use in all your favorite dishes. Note: If you want to skip the long smoke session, use Jacobsen Salt Co. Cherrywood Smoked Salt. Grill: 165 °F

4.   Simple Syrup: Put the honey and 1 cup water in a small saucepan. Cook over low heat, stirring, for about 20 min.

5.   Fill a cocktail shaker with ice. Add tequila, lime juice, simple syrup and orange liqueur. Cover and shake until mixed and chilled, about 30 seconds.

6.   Place smoked salt on a plate. Press the rim of a chilled rocks glass into the salt to rim the edge. Strain margarita into the glass. Enjoy!

Grilled Rabbit Tail Cocktail

Servings: 2
Cooking Time: 25 Minutes

Ingredients:

- 1 1/2 Ounce lemon juice
- 4 Ounce Apple Brandy
- 1 Ounce orange juice
- 1 Ounce Smoked Simple Syrup

Directions:

1.   Supply your smoker with wood pellets and follow the start-up procedure. Preheat the grill, with the lid closed, to 350° F.

2.   Place lemon halves directly on the grill grate and cook for 20-25 minutes or until grill marks appear. Remove from grill and let cool. Once cool enough to handle, juice the lemons then chill and reserve the juice. Grill: 350 °F

3.   Using the proportions listed above and considering the size and consumption rate of your tailgate crew or party, mix all the above

ingredients in a large thermos and top with a bit of ice.

4.   Using 6-8 oz glasses or cups, guests can serve themselves from the thermos and garnish each drink with a grilled apple slice. Enjoy!

Smoked Salted Caramel White Russian

Servings: 4
Cooking Time: 20 Minutes

Ingredients:

- 16 Ounce half-and-half
- salted caramel sauce
- 6 Ounce vodka
- 6 Ounce Kahlúa

Directions:

1.   Supply your smoker with wood pellets and follow the start-up procedure. Preheat the grill, with the lid closed, to 180° F.

2.   Pour the half-and-half in a shallow baking dish and place directly on the grill grate. In another shallow baking dish, pour 2 to 3 cups of water and place on the grill next to the half-and-half.

3.   Smoke both the half-and-half and water for 20 minutes. Remove from the grill and let cool. Grill: 180 °F

4.   Place the half-and-half in the fridge until ready to use. Pour the smoked water into ice cube trays and transfer to the freezer until completely frozen.

5.   Separate the smoked ice cubes into four glasses. Drizzle the salted caramel sauce around the inside of the glass.

6.   Pour 1-1/2 ounce vodka and 1-1/2 ounce Kahlúa into each of the glasses and top with the smoked half-and-half. Enjoy!

Grilled Blood Orange Mimosa

Servings: 4

Cooking Time: 15 Minutes

Ingredients:

- 3 blood orange, halved
- 2 Tablespoon granulated sugar
- 1 Bottle sparkling wine
- thyme sprigs, for garnish

Directions:

1. Supply your smoker with wood pellets and follow the start-up procedure. Preheat the grill, with the lid closed, to 375° F.

2. When the grill is hot, dip the cut side of the orange halves in sugar and place cut side down directly on the grill grate. Grill: 375 ˚F

3. Grill the oranges for 10-15 minutes or until grill marks develop. Grill: 375 ˚F

4. Remove from the grill and let cool at room temperature.

5. When cool enough to handle, juice the oranges and strain through a fine strainer removing any pulp.

6. Pour 5 oz of sparkling wine into each glass and top with 1 oz blood orange juice.

7. Garnish with a sprig of thyme. Enjoy!

Traeger Paloma Cocktail

Servings: 2

Cooking Time: 25 Minutes

Ingredients:

- 4 grapefruit, halved
- Smoked Simple Syrup
- 10 Stick cinnamon
- 3 Ounce reposado tequila
- 1 Ounce lime juice
- 1 Ounce Smoked Simple Syrup

- grilled lime, for garnish
- cinnamon stick, for garnish

Directions:

1. Supply your smoker with wood pellets and follow the start-up procedure. Preheat the grill, with the lid closed, to 350° F.

2. Grilled Grapefruit Juice: Cut 2 grapefruits in half. Place a cinnamon stick in each grapefruit half and glaze with Traeger Smoked Simple Syrup. Place on grill grate and cook for 20 minutes or until edges start to burn and it acquires grill marks. Remove from heat and let cool. Grill: 350 ˚F

3. After grapefruits have cooled, squeeze and strain juice. It should yield 10 to 12 ounces of juice.

4. In a mixing glass, add tequila, lime juice, Traeger Smoked Simple Syrup and 2 ounces of the grilled grapefruit juice.

5. Add ice and shake. Strain over ice in an old fashioned glass.

6. Add a grilled lime slice and cinnamon stick to garnish. Enjoy!

Smoky Mountain Bramble Cocktail

Servings: 2

Cooking Time: 15 Minutes

Ingredients:

- 16 Ounce blackberries
- 2 Cup sugar
- 10 smoked blackberries
- 3 Ounce vodka
- 1 1/2 Ounce Alpine Distilling Preserve Liqueur
- 1 1/2 Ounce lemon juice
- 1 Ounce smoked blackberry syrup

Directions:

1. Supply your smoker with wood pellets and follow the start-up procedure. Preheat the grill, with the lid closed, to 180° F.

2. To make Smoked Blackberry Simple Syrup: Place blackberries on a grill mat and smoke for 15 to 20 minutes. Grill: 180 °F

3. Combine 1 cup water and sugar in a small sauce pan and warm over medium heat until sugar dissolves. Remove from heat and place 2/3 of blackberries in the simple syrup and macerate.

4. Strain through a fine mesh strainer and store for up to 14 days.

5. To make the cocktail: Muddle 4 to 5 smoked blackberries in a cocktail shaker. Add vodka, Preserve Liqueur, lemon and smoked blackberry syrup. Add ice and shake vigorously. Double strain into an old fashioned glass.

6. Garnish with a smoked blackberry and lemon twist. Enjoy!

Smoked Pomegranate Lemonade Cocktail

Servings: 2
Cooking Time: 45 Minutes

Ingredients:

- 32 Ounce POM Juice
- 2 Cup pomegranate seeds
- 3 Ounce vodka
- 8 Ounce lemonade
- lemon wheel, for garnish
- fresh mint, for garnish

Directions:

1. Supply your smoker with wood pellets and follow the start-up procedure. Preheat the grill, with the lid closed, to 225° F.

2. For the Smoked Pomegranate Ice Cubes: Pour one small container of POM juice and 1 cup of pomegranate seeds into a shallow sheet pan. Smoke on the Traeger for 45 minutes. Pull off grill and let sit until cooled. Grill: 180 °F

3. Pour smoked POM juice into ice molds of your choice and put into freezer.

4. When ready to serve, place the frozen pomegranate cubes into a mason jar. Pour vodka and lemonade over the ice cubes.

5. Garnish with a lemon wheel and fresh mint. Enjoy!

Grilled Peach Mint Julep

Servings: 2
Cooking Time: 45 Minutes

Ingredients:

- 2 Whole peach
- 4 Ounce whiskey
- 2 Cup sugar
- 4 Tablespoon pink peppercorns
- 20 Whole fresh mint leaves, plus more for garnish
- 2 lime wedge, for garnish
- 4 Ounce bourbon

Directions:

1. For the Grilled Whiskey Peaches: cut peach into slices, then soak peach slices in whiskey in the refrigerator for 4 to 6 hours.

2. For the Pink Peppercorn Simple Syrup: In a shallow pan, combine sugar, 1 cup water and pink peppercorns.

3. Supply your smoker with wood pellets and follow the start-up procedure. Preheat the grill, with the lid closed, to 180° F.

4. Cook syrup down on the grill for 30 minutes, or until desired smoke flavor has been reached. Remove from the grill. Grill: 180 ˚F

5. Increase Traeger temperature to 350˚F and preheat. Place the whiskey peach slices directly on the grill grate and cook 10 to 12 minutes or until peaches soften and get grill marks. Grill: 350 ˚F

6. To make the Julep: Muddle 1/2 ounce Pink Peppercorn Simple Syrup with 10 fresh mint leaves and 4 slices of grilled whiskey peaches.

7. Add crushed ice over the rim of the glass. Pour bourbon over the crushed ice and stir. Garnish with 1 large sprig of mint and fresh lime. Enjoy!

Smoked Texas Ranch Water

Servings: 4
Cooking Time: 60 Minutes

Ingredients:

- 3 Whole limes
- 1 Tablespoon Blackened Saskatchewan Rub
- 12 Ounce blanco tequila
- 24 Ounce Topo Chico or other sparkling mineral water
- 8 Slices jalapeño, optional

Directions:

1. Supply your smoker with wood pellets and follow the start-up procedure. Preheat the grill, with the lid closed, to 225° F.

2. Cut two of the limes in half and sprinkle with Traeger Blackened Saskatchewan Rub. Place the four lime halves on the edge of the grill grate and smoke for 1 hour. Remove from grill and set aside to cool. Grill: 225 ˚F

3. Pour some of the rub onto a small plate. Cut the third lime into 1/4 wedges and use the lime to rub the rim of 4 cocktail glasses, turn the glasses upside down, and into the rub to salt the rim.

4. Place several ice cubes into your rimmed glasses and pour 3 ounces tequila, 6 ounces Topo Chico, squeeze the juice of one smoked lime (discard after squeezing), and add one fresh lime wedge to each. If using the jalapeño, add one or two slices to each glass (muddle if desired).

5. Stir to combine and enjoy!

Smoked Mulled Wine

Servings: 10
Cooking Time: 60 Minutes

Ingredients:

- 2 Bottle red wine
- 1/2 Cup whiskey
- 1/2 Cup white rum
- 1/2 Cup honey
- 1 cinnamon stick
- 2 pods star anise
- 4 whole cloves
- 1 (3 in) orange peel

Directions:

1. Supply your smoker with wood pellets and follow the start-up procedure. Preheat the grill, with the lid closed, to 180° F.

2. In a shallow baking dish, combine wine, whiskey, rum, honey, cinnamon stick, star anise, cloves and orange peel. Stir well until combined.

3. Place the dish directly on the grill grate and smoke for one hour until the mixture is warm. Grill: 180 ˚F

4. Remove from grill and ladle into mugs leaving the mulling spices behind. Garnish with fresh cinnamon sticks, anise, orange zest or a combination. Enjoy!

Smoked Grape Lime Rickey

Servings: 4
Cooking Time: 45 Minutes

Ingredients:

- 1/2 Pound red grapes
- 1/2 Cup plus 1 tablespoon sugar
- 1/2 Cup water
- 1 limes, sliced
- 2 limes, halved
- 1 Tablespoon sugar
- 1 L lemon lime soda

Directions:

1. Supply your smoker with wood pellets and follow the start-up procedure. Preheat the grill, with the lid closed, to 180° F.

2. Rinse grapes well and place in a shallow baking dish. Combine 1/2 cup sugar and water and stir until sugar dissolves. Pour over grapes.

3. Place the baking dish directly on the grill grate and smoke for 30 to 40 minutes until grapes are tender. Grill: 180 ˚F

4. Remove from the grill and pour entire contents of the baking dish in a blender. Puree on high until smooth then pass the mixture through a fine mesh strainer.

5. Increase Traeger temperature to 350˚F. Grill: 350 ˚F

6. Toss the lime slices and lime halves with 1 tablespoon sugar and place directly on the grill grate. Cook for 15 to 20 minutes or until grill marks develop. Remove from grill and set slices aside. When cool enough to handle, juice grilled lime halves. Grill: 350 ˚F

7. To build the drink, fill a pint glass with ice. Pour in 1-1/2 ounce grilled lime juice, 1-1/2 ounce smoked grape syrup and top off with soda. Garnish with grilled lime slice. Enjoy!

Smoked Cold Brew Coffee

Servings: 8
Cooking Time: 120 Minutes

Ingredients:

- 12 Ounce coarse ground coffee
- heavy cream or milk
- sugar

Directions:

1. Place half the coffee grounds in a plastic container and slowly pour 3-1/2 cups water over the top of the grounds. Add remaining grounds and pour another 3-1/2 cups water over the top in a circular motion.

2. Press the grounds down into the water using the back of a spoon. Cover and transfer to the refrigerator and let sit for 18 to 24 hours.

3. Remove from refrigerator and strain into a clean container through a fine mesh strainer or double layer of cheese cloth.

4. Supply your smoker with wood pellets and follow the start-up procedure. Preheat the grill, with the lid closed, to 180° F.

5. Pour cold brew into a shallow baking dish and place directly on the grill grate. Smoke for 1 to 2 hours depending on desired level of smoke. Grill: 180 ˚F

6. Remove from grill and place over an ice bath to cool. Drink as is over ice, with cream or sugar or use in your favorite coffee recipes. Enjoy!

Grilled Hawaiian Sour

Servings: 2
Cooking Time: 15 Minutes

Ingredients:

- 2 Whole pineapple, trimmed and sliced
- 1/2 Cup palm sugar

- 3 Ounce bourbon
- 2 Ounce grilled pineapple juice
- 2 Ounce Smoked Simple Syrup
- 10 Ounce lemon juice
- 2 grilled pineapple chunk, for garnish
- 2 pineapple leaf, for garnish

Directions:

1. Supply your smoker with wood pellets and follow the start-up procedure. Preheat the grill, with the lid closed, to 350° F.

2. For the Grilled Pineapple Juice: Dust pineapple slices with palm sugar. Place directly on the grill grate and cook for 8 minutes per side. Grill: 350 ˚F

3. Remove from grill and let cool. Reserve a few pieces for garnish. Run remaining pineapple pieces through centrifugal juicer to extract juice.

4. To Make the Drink: Add bourbon, grilled pineapple juice, simple syrup and lemon juice to a cocktail strainer with ice. Shake vigorously. Double strain into a chilled coupe glass. Garnish with grilled pineapple chunk and pineapple leaf. Enjoy!

Fig Slider Cocktail

Servings: 2
Cooking Time: 15 Minutes

Ingredients:
- 2 peach, halved
- 4 oranges
- honey
- sugar
- 2 Teaspoon orange fig spread
- 1 Ounce fresh lemon juice
- 4 Ounce bourbon
- 3 Ounce honey glazed grilled orange juice

Directions:

1. Supply your smoker with wood pellets and follow the start-up procedure. Preheat the grill, with the lid closed, to 325° F.

2. Pit the peach and cut in half. Cut one of the oranges in half. Glaze the peach and orange cut sides with honey and set directly on the grill grate until the honey caramelizes and fruit has grill marks. Grill: 325 ˚F

3. Cut the second orange into wheels and coat with granulated sugar on both sides. Place directly on the grill grate and cook 15 minutes each side or until grill marks form. Grill: 325 ˚F

4. In a mixing tin, add grilled peaches, bourbon, orange fig spread, fresh lemon juice and honey glazed orange juice.

5. Shake vigorously to blend the juices and fig spread. Strain over clean ice. Garnish with grilled orange wheel. Enjoy!

Strawberry Mule Cocktail

Servings: 2
Cooking Time: 15 Minutes

Ingredients:
- 8 grilled strawberries, plus more for serving
- 3 Ounce vodka
- 1 Ounce Smoked Simple Syrup
- 1 Ounce lemon juice
- 6 Ounce ginger beer
- fresh mint leaves

Directions:

1. Supply your smoker with wood pellets and follow the start-up procedure. Preheat the grill, with the lid closed, to 400° F.

2. Place strawberries directly on the grill grate and cook 15 minutes or until grill marks appear. Grill: 400 ˚F

3. For the cocktail: Add vodka, grilled strawberries, Traeger Smoked Simple Syrup and lemon juice to a shaker. Shake vigorously.

4. Double strain into a fresh glass or copper mug with crushed ice.

5. Top with ginger beer and garnish with extra grilled strawberries and fresh mint. Enjoy!

Smoke And Bubz Cocktail

Servings: 2
Cooking Time: 45 Minutes

Ingredients:
- 16 Ounce POM Juice
- 2 Cup pomegranate seeds
- 6 Ounce sparkling white wine
- 2 lemon twist, for garnish
- 2 Teaspoon pomegranate seeds

Directions:

1. Supply your smoker with wood pellets and follow the start-up procedure. Preheat the grill, with the lid closed, to 180° F.

2. For the Smoked Pomegranate Juice: Pour POM juice and a cup of pomegranate seeds into a shallow sheet pan. Smoke on the Traeger for 45 minutes. Pull off grill, strain, discard seeds and let sit until chilled. Grill: 180 ˚F

3. Add 1-1/2 ounces of the smoked pomegranate juice to the bottom of a champagne flute.

4. Add sparkling white wine, a few fresh pomegranate seeds and a lemon twist to garnish. Enjoy!

Grilled Peach Smash Cocktail

Servings: 2
Cooking Time: 10 Minutes

Ingredients:
- 2 peach, sliced and grilled
- 10 fresh mint leaves
- 1 1/2 Ounce Smoked Simple Syrup
- 4 Ounce bourbon
- 2 mint sprig, for garnish

Directions:

1. Supply your smoker with wood pellets and follow the start-up procedure. Preheat the grill, with the lid closed, to 375° F.

2. Cut the peach into 6 slices and brush with Traeger Smoked Simple Syrup. Place directly on the grill grate and cook 10 to 12 minutes or until peaches soften and get grill marks. Grill: 375 ˚F

3. In a mixing glass, add 3 slices of grilled peaches, 5 mint leaves and Traeger Smoked Simple Syrup.

4. Muddle ingredients to release oils of the mint and juices from the grilled peaches. Add bourbon and crushed ice.

5. Shake and pour into a stemless wine glass. Top off with more crushed ice. Garnish with a grilled peach and mint sprig. Enjoy!

Smoked Pineapple Hotel Nacional Cocktail

Servings: 2
Cooking Time: 20 Minutes

Ingredients:
- 2 pineapple
- 1/2 Cup water
- 1/2 Cup sugar
- 3 Fluid Ounce white rum
- 1 1/2 Fluid Ounce lime juice
- 1 1/2 Fluid Ounce Pineapple Syrup
- 1 Fluid Ounce apricot brandy
- 2 Dash Angostura bitters

Directions:

1. For the Syrup: Supply your smoker with wood pellets and follow the start-up procedure. Preheat the grill, with the lid closed, to 180° F.

2. Trim both ends of the pineapple, discard the ends. Cut the pineapple into slices about 3/4" thick. Don't worry about the skin, it doesn't hurt to leave it on. Place the pineapple slices on the grill and smoke for about 15 minutes on each sideTrim both ends of the pineapple and discard the ends. Cut the pineapple into slices about 3/4 inch thick. Don't worry about the skin, it doesn't hurt to leave it on. Place the pineapple slices on the grill and smoke for about 15 minutes per side. Grill: 180 °F

3. While the pineapple is smoking, combine 1/4 cup water and sugar in a saucepan over low heat, stirring constantly, until sugar is dissolved. Pour syrup into a large bowl and set aside.

4. When the pineapple is done cooking, cut each slice into eight or so wedges and add the wedges to the bowl with the simple syrup, tossing to coat and cover.

5. Leave the mixture to macerate for at least 4 hours (or up to 24) in the refrigerator, stirring from time to time.

6. Strain the syrup into a clean bowl through a fine-mesh strainer and press on the pineapple with a ladle to extract as much liquid as possible. You can bottle and refrigerate the syrup for up to 4 days.

7. To make the cocktail: Combine the rum, lime juice, pineapple syrup, apricot brandy, and bitters in a cocktail shaker or mixing glass. Fill with ice cubes and shake until cold.

8. Strain into a chilled cocktail glass. Garnish with a lime wheel and serve. Enjoy!

Grilled Frozen Strawberry Lemonade

Servings: 4
Cooking Time: 15 Minutes

Ingredients:
- 1 Pound fresh strawberries
- 1/2 Cup turbinado sugar
- 8 lemon, halved
- 1/4 Cup Cointreau
- 1/4 Cup simple syrup
- 2 Cup ice
- 1 Cup Titos Vodka

Directions:

1. Supply your smoker with wood pellets and follow the start-up procedure. Preheat the grill, with the lid closed, to High heat.

2. Dip the lemon halves in turbinado sugar and place directly on the grill grate. Toss the strawberries with remaining sugar and place next to the lemons.

3. Cook until grill marks develop on both, about 15 min for lemons and 10 min for strawberries.

4. Remove from heat and let cool.

5. Juice grilled lemons straining out any seeds or pulp. Pour into a blender pitcher.

6. Remove stems from grilled strawberries and place in blender pitcher with lemon juice. Add simple syrup, vodka, cointreau, and 2 cups of ice.

7. Puree until smooth and transfer to 4-6 glasses. Garnish with grilled strawberries and grilled lemon slices if desired. Enjoy!

Bacon Old-fashioned Cocktail

Servings: 2

Cooking Time: 20 Minutes

Ingredients:

- 16 Slices bacon
- 1/2 Cup warm water (110°F to 115°F)
- 1500 mL bourbon
- 1/2 Fluid Ounce maple syrup
- 4 Dash Angostura bitters
- 2 fresh orange peel

Directions:

1. Smoke bacon prior to making Old Fashioned using this recipe for Applewood Smoked Bacon.

2. To Make Bacon: Supply your smoker with wood pellets and follow the start-up procedure. Preheat the grill, with the lid closed, to 325° F.

3. Place bacon in a single layer on a cooling rack that fits inside a baking sheet pan. Cook in Traeger for 15-20 minutes or until bacon is browned and crispy. Reserve bacon for later. Let the fat cool slightly; you'll use the fat to infuse the bourbon. Grill: 325 °F

4. Combine 1/4 cup of warm (not hot) liquid bacon fat with the entire contents of a 750ml bottle of bourbon in a glass or heavy plastic container.

5. Use a fork to stir well. Let it sit on the counter for a few hours, stirring every so often.

6. After about four hours, put bourbon fat mixture into the freezer. After about an hour, the fat will congeal and you can simply scoop it out with a spoon. You can fine-strain the mixture through a sieve to remove all fat if desired.

7. Combine ingredients with ice and stir until cold. Strain over fresh ice in an Old Fashioned glass and garnish with reserved bacon and orange peel. Enjoy!

Smoky Scotch & Ginger Cocktail

Servings: 2

Cooking Time: 60 Minutes

Ingredients:

- 1 Ounce ginger syrup
- 1/2 Ounce brandied cherry juice
- 1/2 Ounce agave nectar
- 4 Ounce scotch
- 1 1/2 Ounce lemon juice
- 2 Slices grilled lemon, for garnish
- 2 cherry, for garnish

Directions:

1. Supply your smoker with wood pellets and follow the start-up procedure. Preheat the grill, with the lid closed, to 180° F.

2. For the smoked ginger cherry syrup: Place ginger syrup, cherry juice and agave nectar in a shallow dish and place the dish directly on the grill grate.

3. Smoke for 60 minutes, or until the mixture has picked up the smoke flavor. Remove from grill and allow to cool for 30 minutes. Grill: 180 °F

4. Place smoked ginger cherry syrup, scotch and lemon juice into a shaker tin and shake with ice. Strain into a glass over fresh ice and garnish with a grilled lemon wheel and cherry. Enjoy!

Cran-apple Tequila Punch With Smoked Oranges

Servings: 2

Cooking Time: 15 Minutes

Ingredients:

- 6 Cup apple juice, chilled
- 6 Cup light cranberry cocktail
- 1 Cup cranberries, fresh or thawed

- 3 Large oranges, halved
- 1 Cup sugar, for rimming glasses
- 2 Tablespoon lemon juice
- 2 Cup reposado tequila
- 1 Cup orange-flavored liqueur, such as Grand Marnier or Cointreau
- 2 Bottle sparkling wine (such as prosecco) or sparkling water

Directions:

1. Combine 1 cup each of the apple and cranberry juices, then pour into ice cube trays. If the cube molds are big enough, place a few cranberries into each cube. Freeze for 6 hours to overnight.

2. Supply your smoker with wood pellets and follow the start-up procedure. Preheat the grill, with the lid closed, to 180° F.

3. Place the orange halves cut-side down on the grill and smoke for 15 minutes. Remove from the grill and juice oranges. Reserve smoked orange juice. Grill: 180 ˚F

4. When ready to serve, place the sugar on a flat plate. Pour the lemon juice into a bowl that will fit the rim of each glass.

5. Carefully dip the rim of each glass in the lemon juice, then dip in the sugar to create a 1/8" sugar rim. Turn the glass right-side up and allow to dry for a few minutes before using.

6. Just before serving, mix the remaining apple juice, cranberry cocktail and smoked orange juice with the tequila, orange liqueur, and sparkling wine in a large bowl or pitcher. Taste, adding more of any ingredient to meet your preference.

7. When ready to serve, place a few ice cubes in each glass, then pour a cup of the punch over the top. Alternatively, place all of the ice cubes in the punch bowl and allow guests to help themselves. Enjoy!

Honey Glazed Grapefruit Shandy Cocktail

Servings: 2
Cooking Time: 20 Minutes

Ingredients:
- 4 grapefruits
- 4 Tablespoon honey
- granulated sugar
- 2 Ounce bourbon
- 1 Ounce Smoked Simple Syrup
- 4 Ounce honey glazed grilled grapefruit, juiced
- 2 Bottle Ballast Point Grapefruit Sculpin

Directions:

1. Supply your smoker with wood pellets and follow the start-up procedure. Preheat the grill, with the lid closed, to 375° F.

2. For the honey glazed grapefruit: Slice one grapefruit in half and coat with 2 tablespoons honey.

3. Take the other grapefruit and slice into wheels. Toss the wheels in granulated sugar until well coated.

4. Place the grapefruit halves and wheels directly on the grill grate, cut side down, and cook for 20 to 30 minutes. Remove from grill and set the wheels aside. Grill: 375 ˚F

5. Squeeze the grapefruit halves into a measuring cup. It should yield about 2 oz juice.

6. Pour the grapefruit juice into a shaker and add bourbon and Traeger Smoked Simple Syrup then top with ice. Shake for 10-15 seconds.

7. Strain into glass, add ice and fill with beer. Garnish with the grilled grapefruit wheel. Enjoy!

Smoked Eggnog

Servings: 4
Cooking Time: 60 Minutes

Ingredients:

- 2 Cup whole milk
- 1 Cup heavy cream
- 4 egg yolk
- Cup sugar
- 3 Ounce bourbon
- 1 Teaspoon vanilla extract
- 1 Teaspoon nutmeg
- 4 egg white
- whipped cream

Directions:

1. Plan ahead, this recipe requires chill time.

2. Supply your smoker with wood pellets and follow the start-up procedure. Preheat the grill, with the lid closed, to 180° F.

3. Pour the milk and the cream into a baking pan and smoke on the Traeger for 60 minutes. Grill: 180 ˚F

4. Meanwhile, in the bowl of a stand mixer, beat the egg yolks until they lighten in color. Gradually add 1/3 cup sugar and continue to beat until sugar completely dissolves.

5. After the milk and cream have smoked, add them along with the bourbon, vanilla and nutmeg into the egg mixture and stir to combine.

6. Place the egg whites in the bowl of a stand mixer and beat to soft peaks. When you lift the beaters the whites will make a peak that slightly curls down.

7. With the mixer still running, gradually add 1 tablespoon of sugar and beat until stiff peaks form.

8. Gently fold the egg whites into the cream mixture and then whisk to thoroughly combine.

9. Chill eggnog for a couple hours to let the flavors meld. Garnish with a dash of nutmeg and whipped cream on top. Enjoy!

Traeger Smoked Daiquiri

Servings: 2
Cooking Time: 25 Minutes

Ingredients:

- 2 limes, sliced
- 2 Tablespoon granulated sugar
- 3 Ounce Rum
- 1 Ounce Smoked Simple Syrup
- 1 1/2 Ounce lime juice

Directions:

1. Supply your smoker with wood pellets and follow the start-up procedure. Preheat the grill, with the lid closed, to 350° F.

2. Toss the lime slices with granulated sugar and place directly on the grill grate. Cook 20-25 minutes or until grill marks form. Remove from grill and cool. Grill: 350 ˚F

3. In a mixing glass add rum, Traeger Simple Syrup, and fresh lime juice. Add ice to the mixing glass and shake. Strain contents into a chilled glass.

4. Garnish with a grilled lime wheel. Enjoy!

Smoked Barnburner Cocktail

Servings: 2
Cooking Time: 45 Minutes

Ingredients:

- 16 Ounce fresh raspberries
- 1/2 Cup Smoked Simple Syrup
- 1 1/2 Ounce smoked raspberry syrup
- 3 Ounce reposado tequila
- 1 Ounce lime juice
- 1 Ounce lemon juice

- 2 grilled lime wheel, for garnish

Directions:

1. Supply your smoker with wood pellets and follow the start-up procedure. Preheat the grill, with the lid closed, to 180° F.

2. For Smoked Raspberry Syrup: Place fresh raspberries on a grill mat and smoke for 30 minutes. After the raspberries have been smoked, reserve a few for garnish and place the remainder into a shallow sheet pan with Traeger Smoked Simple Syrup. Grill: 180 ˚F

3. Place sheet pan on the grill grate and smoke for 45 minutes. Remove from grill and let cool. Strain through a fine mesh sieve discarding solids. Transfer the syrup to the refrigerator until ready to use. Makes about 1/2 cup of smoked raspberry syrup. Grill: 180 ˚F

4. For cocktail: Add 3/4 ounce smoked raspberry syrup, tequila, lime juice and lemon juice with ice into a mixing glass. Shake and pour over clean ice. Garnish with smoked raspberries and a grilled lime wheel. Enjoy!

Ryes And Shine Cocktail

Servings: 2
Cooking Time: 30 Minutes

Ingredients:

- 2 lemon, cut into wheels for garnish
- 6 Tablespoon granulated sugar
- 2 Ounce rye
- 1 Ounce bourbon
- 3 Ounce lemon juice
- 1 Ounce Smoked Simple Syrup
- 6 Dash Fernet-Branca

Directions:

1. Supply your smoker with wood pellets and follow the start-up procedure. Preheat the grill, with the lid closed, to 325° F.

2. Toss lemon wheels with granulated sugar to coat on both sides. Place wheels directly on the grill grate and cook for 15 minutes on each side or until grill marks form. Grill: 325 ˚F

3. Add rye, bourbon, lemon juice, Traeger Smoked Simple Syrup and Fernet-Branca to a shaker and shake until slightly diluted (about 10 to 15 seconds).

4. Pour into a fresh glass, serve neat and garnish with a grilled lemon wheel. Enjoy!

Smoked Hibiscus Sparkler

Servings: 4
Cooking Time: 30 Minutes

Ingredients:

- 1/2 Cup sugar
- 2 Tablespoon dried hibiscus flowers
- 1 Bottle sparkling wine
- crystallized ginger, for garnish

Directions:

1. Supply your smoker with wood pellets and follow the start-up procedure. Preheat the grill, with the lid closed, to 180° F.

2. Place water in a shallow baking dish and place directly on the grill grate. Smoke the water for 30 minutes or until desired smoke flavor is achieved. Grill: 180 ˚F

3. Pour water into a small saucepan and add sugar and hibiscus flowers. Bring to a simmer over medium heat and cook until sugar is dissolved.

4. Strain out the hibiscus flowers and transfer your simple syrup to a small container and refrigerate until chilled.

5. Pour 1/2 ounce smoked hibiscus simple syrup in the bottom of a champagne glass and top with sparkling wine.

6. Drop in a few pieces of crystallized ginger to garnish. Enjoy!

Smoked Hot Buttered Rum

Servings: 4
Cooking Time: 30 Minutes

Ingredients:
- 2 Cup water
- 1/4 Cup brown sugar
- 1/2 Stick butter, melted
- 1 Teaspoon ground cinnamon
- 1/4 Teaspoon ground nutmeg
- ground cloves
- salt
- 6 Ounce Rum

Directions:

1. Supply your smoker with wood pellets and follow the start-up procedure. Preheat the grill, with the lid closed, to 180° F.

2. In a shallow baking dish, combine 2 cups water with all ingredients except for the rum and place directly on the grill grate. Smoke for 30 minutes. Grill: 180 ˚F

3. Remove from the grill and pour into the pitcher of a blender. Process until somewhat frothy.

4. Pour 1.5 ounces of rum each into 4 glasses. Split hot butter mixture evenly between the four glasses.

5. Garnish with a cinnamon stick and freshly grated nutmeg. Enjoy!

Smoked Berry Cocktail

Servings: 2

Cooking Time: 15 Minutes

Ingredients:
- 1/2 Cup strawberries, stemmed
- 1/2 Cup blackberries
- 1/2 Cup blueberries
- 8 Ounce bourbon or iced tea
- 2 Ounce lime juice
- 3 Ounce simple syrup
- soda water
- fresh mint, for garnish

Directions:

1. Supply your smoker with wood pellets and follow the start-up procedure. Preheat the grill, with the lid closed, to 180° F.

2. Wash berries well, spread them on a clean cookie sheet and place on the grill. Smoke berries for 15 minutes. Grill: 180 ˚F

3. Remove berries from grill and transfer to a blender. Puree berries until smooth then pass through a fine mesh strainer to remove seeds.

4. To create a layered cocktail, pour 2 ounces of berry puree in the bottom of a glass. Next, pour 2 ounces of bourbon or iced tea over the back of a spoon into the glass, then 1/2 ounce lime juice and 1/2 ounce simple syrup, top with soda water and ice. Finish with mint or extra berries for garnish.

5. Repeat the same process for 3 more servings. Enjoy!

Smoked Irish Coffee

Servings: 2
Cooking Time: 15 Minutes

Ingredients:
- 10 Ounce hot coffee
- 1/2 Cup heavy cream
- 1 Tablespoon sugar

- 2 Ounce Irish whiskey
- freshly grated nutmeg, for garnish (optional)

Directions:

1. Supply your smoker with wood pellets and follow the start-up procedure. Preheat the grill, with the lid closed, to 180° F.

2. Place the coffee and cream in separate shallow baking dishes and place both directly on the grill grate. Smoke for 10 to 15 minutes until the liquids pick up a slight smoke flavor. Grill: 180 °F

3. Remove from the grill and cool the cream. When the cream is cool, add sugar and whip in a stand mixer or by hand to soft peaks.

4. Pour the hot coffee into two mugs then add 2 ounces of whiskey to each.

5. Top with smoked whipped cream and finish with freshly grated nutmeg, if desired. Enjoy!

Smoked Sangria

Servings: 6
Cooking Time: 45 Minutes

Ingredients:

- 1 (750 ml) medium-bodied red wine
- 1/4 Cup Grand Marnier
- 1/4 Cup Smoked Simple Syrup
- 1 Cup fresh cranberries
- 1 Whole apple, sliced
- 2 Whole limes, sliced
- 4 cinnamon stick
- soda water

Directions:

1. Supply your smoker with wood pellets and follow the start-up procedure. Preheat the grill, with the lid closed, to 180° F.

2. In a shallow dish, combine red wine, Grand Marnier, Traeger Smoked Simple Syrup and cranberries, and place directly on the grill grate.

3. Smoke for 30 to 45 minutes or until the liquid picks up desired amount of smoke. Remove from grill and place in the fridge to cool. Grill: 180 °F

4. When the mixture has cooled, place in a large pitcher. Add sliced apples, limes, cinnamon sticks and ice to pitcher.

5. Top with soda water, if desired. Enjoy!

Batter Up Cocktail

Servings: 2
Cooking Time: 60 Minutes

Ingredients:

- 2 whole nutmeg
- 4 Ounce Michter's Bourbon
- 3 Teaspoon pumpkin puree
- 1 Ounce Smoked Simple Syrup
- 2 Large egg

Directions:

1. Supply your smoker with wood pellets and follow the start-up procedure. Preheat the grill, with the lid closed, to 180° F.

2. Place whole nutmeg on a sheet tray and place in the grill. Smoke 1 hour. Remove from grill and let cool. Grill: 180 °F

3. Add everything to a shaker and shake without ice. Add ice, then shake and strain into a chilled highball glass.

4. Garnish with grated, smoked nutmeg. Enjoy!

Sunset Margarita

Servings: 2
Cooking Time: 55 Minutes

Ingredients:

- 4 oranges
- 2 Cup plus 1 teaspoon agave
- 1/2 Cup water
- 1 Ounce burnt orange agave

- 3 Ounce reposado tequila
- 1 1/2 Ounce fresh squeezed lime juice
- Jacobsen Salt Co. Cherrywood Smoked Salt

Directions:

1. Supply your smoker with wood pellets and follow the start-up procedure. Preheat the grill, with the lid closed, to 350° F.

2. For the Burnt Orange Agave Syrup: Cut one orange in half and brush cut side with agave. Place cut side down directly on the grill grate and grill for 15 minutes or until grill marks develop. Grill: 350 °F

3. While the orange halves are grilling, slice the other orange and brush both sides of the slices with agave. Place slices directly on the grill grate next to the halves and cook for 15 minutes or until grill marks develop. Grill: 350 °F

4. Remove orange halves from grill grate and let cool. After they have cooled, juice halves and strain. Set aside.

5. Combine 1/4 cup water and agave in a shallow dish and mix well. Remove orange slices from the grill and place in the agave mixture, reserving a few for garnish.

6. Reduce the grill temperature to 180 degrees F and place the shallow dish with agave and oranges directly on the grill grate. Smoke for 40 minutes. Remove from heat and strain. Set aside. Grill: 180 °F

7. To Mix Drink: Rim glass with Jacobsen Smoked Salt. Combine tequila, fresh lime juice, grilled orange juice and burnt orange agave syrup in a glass. Add ice and shake well.

8. Strain into a rimmed glass over clean ice. Garnish with a grilled orange slice. Enjoy!

Grilled Peach Sour Cocktail

Servings: 2
Cooking Time: 15 Minutes

Ingredients:

- 2 peach, sliced
- 2 Tablespoon sugar
- 1 1/2 Ounce Smoked Simple Syrup
- 4 Ounce bourbon
- 6 Dash Bitters Lab Apricot Vanilla Bitters
- 2 Sprig fresh thyme, for garnish

Directions:

1. Supply your smoker with wood pellets and follow the start-up procedure. Preheat the grill, with the lid closed, to 325° F.

2. Toss peach slices with granulated sugar and place directly on grill grate. Cook for 20 minutes or until grill marks form. Remove from grill and let cool. Grill: 325 °F

3. Place peaches and Traeger Smoked Simple Syrup into tin and muddle. Peaches should form about an ounce of juice during the muddling. Once completed, add remaining ingredients and shake.

4. Pour contents into glass over fresh ice and garnish with fresh thyme. Enjoy!

Smoked Ice Mojito Slurpee

Servings: 2
Cooking Time: 30 Minutes

Ingredients:

- water
- 1 Cup white rum
- 1/2 Cup lime juice
- 1/4 Cup Smoked Simple Syrup
- 12 Whole fresh mint leaves
- 4 Sprig mint

- 4 Whole lime wedge, for garnish

Directions:

1. Supply your smoker with wood pellets and follow the start-up procedure. Preheat the grill, with the lid closed, to 180° F.

2. For optimal flavor, use Super Smoke if available. Grill: 180 ˚F

3. Remove water from grill and pour smoked water into ice cube trays. Place in freezer until frozen.

4. Add rum, lime juice, Traeger Smoked Simple Syrup, mint and smoked ice to a blender.

5. Blend until a slushy consistency and pour into glasses.

6. Garnish with a mint sprig and lime wedge. Enjoy!

Traeger Gin & Tonic

Servings: 2

Cooking Time: 45 Minutes

Ingredients:

- 1/2 Cup berries
- 2 orange, sliced
- 4 Tablespoon granulated sugar
- 3 Ounce gin
- 1 Cup tonic water
- 2 Sprig fresh mint, for garnish

Directions:

1. Supply your smoker with wood pellets and follow the start-up procedure. Preheat the grill, with the lid closed, to 180° F.

2. For the Smoked Berries: Spread mixed fresh berries on a sheet pan and place directly on the grill grate. Smoke for 30 minutes then remove from grill. Grill: 180 ˚F

3. For the Orange Slices: Increase the grill temperature to 450˚F and preheat, lid closed for 15 minutes. Grill: 450 ˚F

4. Toss the orange slices with granulated sugar and place directly on grill grate. Cook for about 5 minutes, turning once or until the slices have developed grill marks. Grill: 450 ˚F

5. Pour gin into a glass, add ice and berries, then top with tonic water. Garnish with a fresh mint sprig and grilled orange wheel. Enjoy!

Traeger Old Fashioned

Servings: 2

Cooking Time: 60 Minutes

Ingredients:

- 2 orange
- 2 Cup cherries
- 3 Ounce bourbon
- 1 Ounce Smoked Simple Syrup
- 8 Dash Bitters Lab Apricot Vanilla Bitters

Directions:

1. Supply your smoker with wood pellets and follow the start-up procedure. Preheat the grill, with the lid closed, to 180° F.

2. While Traeger preheats, slice whole orange into wheels.

3. Place cherries on a small sheet pan and place in the Traeger. Place orange slices directly on the grill grate.

4. Smoke cherries for 1 hour and oranges for 25 minutes, depending on taste, before removing from the grill. Let oranges and cherries cool. Grill: 180 ˚F

5. Pour bourbon into glass, followed by Traeger Smoked Simple Syrup and bitters. Add ice and stir for 45 seconds or until drink is well-diluted.

6. Strain contents into new glass over fresh ice. Skewer orange wheel and add cherry for garnish. Enjoy!

A Smoking Classic Cocktail

Servings: 2

Cooking Time: 60 Minutes

Ingredients:

- 2 Bottle Angostura orange bitters
- 10 sugar cubes
- 8 Ounce Champagne
- lemon twist

Directions:

1. Supply your smoker with wood pellets and follow the start-up procedure. Preheat the grill, with the lid closed, to 180° F.

2. For the Smoked Orange Bitters: In a small skillet, combine 1 bottle of Angostura orange bitters with a splash of water and 4 sugar cubes.

3. Place skillet on the grill grate and smoke for 60 minutes. Cool the smoked bitters and put back into the bottle. Grill: 180 ˚F

4. Add a sugar cube to each Champagne flute and soak the sugar cubes with the smoked bitters.

5. Add champagne and a lemon twist in a flute glass. Enjoy!

Smoked Apple Cider

Servings: 2

Cooking Time: 30 Minutes

Ingredients:

- 32 Ounce apple cider
- 2 cinnamon sticks
- 4 whole cloves
- 3 star anise
- 2 Pieces orange peel
- 2 Pieces lemon peel

Directions:

1. Supply your smoker with wood pellets and follow the start-up procedure. Preheat the grill, with the lid closed, to 225° F.

2. Combine the cider, cinnamon stick, star anise, clove, lemon and orange peel in a shallow baking dish.

3. Place directly on the grill grate and smoke for 30 minutes. Remove from grill, strain and transfer to four mugs. Grill: 225 ˚F

4. Finish with a slice of apple and a cinnamon stick to serve. Enjoy!

Zombie Cocktail Recipe

Servings: 2

Cooking Time: 45 Minutes

Ingredients:

- fresh squeezed orange juice
- pineapple juice
- 2 Ounce light rum
- 2 Ounce dark rum
- 2 Ounce lime juice
- 1 Ounce Smoked Simple Syrup
- 6 Ounce smoked orange and pineapple juice
- 2 grilled orange peel, for garnish
- 2 grilled pineapple chunks, for garnish

Directions:

1. Supply your smoker with wood pellets and follow the start-up procedure. Preheat the grill, with the lid closed, to 180° F.

2. Smoked Orange and Pineapple Juice: Pour equal parts fresh squeezed orange juice and pineapple juice into a shallow sheet pan and smoke for 45 minutes. Remove and let cool. Measure out 3 ounces of juice and reserve any remaining juice in the refrigerator for future use. Grill: 180 ˚F

3. Add dark and light rums, 3 ounces smoked orange and pineapple juice, lime juice and Traeger Smoked Simple Syrup to a mixing glass.

4. Add ice, shake and strain over clean ice into a Tiki glass.

5. Garnish with a grilled orange peel and grilled pineapple. Enjoy!

Smoked Raspberry Bubbler Cocktail

Servings: 2

Cooking Time: 45 Minutes

Ingredients:

- 2 Cup fresh raspberries
- Smoked Simple Syrup
- 8 Ounce sparkling wine

Directions:

1. Supply your smoker with wood pellets and follow the start-up procedure. Preheat the grill, with the lid closed, to 180° F.

2. Smoked Raspberry Syrup: Place 1 cup fresh raspberries on a grill mat and smoke for 30 minutes. Grill: 180 ˚F

3. After the raspberries have been smoked, set a few aside for garnish. Place the remainder into a shallow sheet pan with Traeger Smoked Simple Syrup. Place back on the grill grate and let smoke for 45 minutes. Remove from heat and allow to cool. Strain and refrigerate until ready to use. Grill: 180 ˚F

4. Place 1 ounce of the smoked raspberry syrup in the bottom of a champagne flute and top off with sparkling white wine or champagne.

5. Garnish with smoked raspberries. Enjoy!

RECIPE INDEX

Roasted Sweet Potato Steak Fries 84
Roasted Tomatoes With Hot Pepper Sauce 82
Roasted Vegetable Napoleon 85
Rub-injected Pork Shoulder 75
Ryes And Shine Cocktail 161

S
Salt Crusted Baked Potatoes 88
Savory Smoked Beef Short Ribs 114
Savory Teriyaki Smoked Steak Bites 115
Seared Bluefin Tuna Steaks 54
Simple Cream Cheese Sausage Balls 140
Smoke And Bubz Cocktail 156
Smoked Apple Cider 166
Smoked Asparagus Soup 89
Smoked Bacon Brisket Flat 115
Smoked Barnburner Cocktail 160
Smoked Bbq Onion Brussels Sprout 90
Smoked Beef Back Ribs 128
Smoked Beet-pickled Eggs 84
Smoked Berry Cocktail 162
Smoked Blackberry Pie 24
Smoked Cashews 142
Smoked Cheese 143
Smoked Chicken Legs 105
Smoked Chicken Vermicelli Noodles 97
Smoked Cold Brew Coffee 154
Smoked Corned Beef & Cabbage 120
Smoked Corned Beef Reuben 131
Smoked Crab Legs 48
Smoked Drumsticks 112
Smoked Eggnog 160
Smoked Grape Lime Rickey 154
Smoked Hibiscus Sparkler 161
Smoked Hot Buttered Rum 162
Smoked Ice Mojito Slurpee 164
Smoked Irish Coffee 162
Smoked Jacobsen Salt Margarita 149

Smoked Lemon Cheesecake 27
Smoked Macaroni Salad 84
Smoked Mango Shrimp 55
Smoked Mulled Wine 153
Smoked Mushrooms 86
Smoked Pico De Gallo 81
Smoked Pig Shots 59
Smoked Pineapple Hotel Nacional Cocktail 156
Smoked Pomegranate Lemonade Cocktail 152
Smoked Porchetta With Italian Salsa Verde 63
Smoked Pork Tomato Tamales 66
Smoked Pumpkin Spice Latte 149
Smoked Raspberry Bubbler Cocktail 167
Smoked Salted Caramel White Russian 150
Smoked Sangria 163
Smoked Sausage & Potatoes 72
Smoked Spare Ribs 65
Smoked Sugar Halibut 47
Smoked Sweet Beer Bread 31
Smoked Teriyaki Jerky 125
Smoked Texas Bbq Brisket 121
Smoked Texas Ranch Water 153
Smoked Turkey Breast 102
Smoked Turkey Jerky 107
Smoked Turkey Legs 97
Smoked Turkey Sandwich 145
Smoked Vanilla Apple Pie 23
Smoked Wings 101
Smoked, Salted Caramel Apple Pie 26
Smoker Wheat Bread 33
Smoke-roasted Beer-braised Brats 61
Smoke-roasted Chicken Thighs 109
Smoke-roasted Halibut With Mixed Herb
Vinaigrette 51
Smoky Mountain Bramble Cocktail 151
Smoky Scotch & Ginger Cocktail 158
Sourdough Pizza 35

9 781803 202020